Nicolas Vandeput

Data Science for Supply Chain Forecasting

Nicolas Vandeput

Data Science for Supply Chain Forecasting

2nd edition

DE GRUYTER

ISBN 978-3-11-067110-0
e-ISBN (PDF) 978-3-11-067112-4
e-ISBN (EPUB) 978-3-11-067120-9

Library of Congress Control Number: 2020951955

Bibliographic information published by the Deutsche Nationalbibliothek
The Deutsche Nationalbibliothek lists this publication in the Deutsche Nationalbibliografie;
detailed bibliographic data are available on the Internet at http://dnb.dnb.de.

© 2021 Walter de Gruyter GmbH, Berlin/Boston
Cover image: Raphael - Stitched together from vatican.va, Public Domain,
https://commons.wikimedia.org/w/index.php?curid=4406048
Typesetting: VTeX UAB, Lithuania
Printing and binding: CPI books GmbH, Leck

www.degruyter.com

Thinking must never submit itself, neither to a dogma, nor to a party, nor to a passion, nor to an interest, nor to a preconceived idea, nor to whatever it may be, if not to facts themselves, because, for it, to submit would be to cease to be.

Henri Poincare

Acknowledgments

Second Edition

We can see in Raphael's fresco *The School of Athens*, philosophers—practitioners and theorists alike—debating and discussing science. I like to use the same approach when working on projects: discussing ideas, insights, and models with other supply chain data scientists worldwide. It is always a pleasure for me.

For the second edition of *Data Science for Supply Chain Forecasting*, I surrounded myself with a varied team of supply chain practitioners who helped me to review chapter after chapter, model after model. I would like to thank each of them for their time, dedication, and support.

I would like to thank my dear friend Gwendoline Dandoy for her work on this book. She helped me to make every single chapter as clear and as simple as possible. She worked tirelessly on this book, as she did on my previous book *Inventory Optimization: Models and Simulations*. Along with her help in reviewing this book, I could always count on her support, iced tea, and kindness. Thank you, Gwendoline.

Thanks to Mike Arbuzov for his help with the advanced machine learning models. It is always a pleasure to discuss with such a data science expert.

I had the chance this year to be surrounded by two inspiring, brilliant entrepreneurs: João Paulo Oliveira, co-founder of BiLD analytic (a data science consultancy company) and Edouard Thieuleux, founder of AbcSupplyChain (do not hesitate to visit his website abcsupplychain.com for supply chain training material and coaching). I would like to thank them both for their help reviewing the book. It is always a pleasure to discuss models and entrepreneurship with them.

I would like to thank Michael Gilliland (author of *The Business Forecasting Deal*— the book that popularized the forecast value added framework) for his help and numerous points of advice on Part III of the book.

I was also helped by a group of talented supply chain practitioners, both consultants and in-house experts. I would like to thank Léo Ducrot for his help on the third part of the book. Léo is an expert in supply chain planning and inventory optimization—discussing supply chain best practices with him is a rewarding pleasure. I would also like to thank Karl-Eric Devaux, who helped me to review the first chapters of the book; thanks to his amazing consultancy experience as demand planner. I am blessed by the help and advice that Karl-Eric shared with me over the last years. Thanks, also, to Steven Pauly (who earlier helped me for my inventory book) for his advice and ideas for the third part of the book.

I could also count on the incredible online community of supply chain and data science practitioners. Many thanks to Evangelos Spiliotis (PhD and research fellow at the National Technical University of Athens), who reviewed the statistical models in detail. His strong academic background and wide experience with statistical models was of great help. Thank you to Suraj Vissa (who also kindly helped me with my

https://doi.org/10.1515/9783110671124-201

previous book) for his review of multiple chapters. And Vincent Isoz, for his careful review of the neural network chapter. You can read his book about applied mathematics, *Opera Magistris*, here: www.sciences.ch/Opera_Magistris_v4_en.pdf. Thank you to Eric Wilson for his review of Part III (do not hesitate to check his demand planning YouTube channel: www.youtube.com/user/DemandPlanning). Thanks, also, to Mohammed Hichame Benbitour for his review of Part I.

As for the first edition of this book—and my second book!—I could count on the help of an all-star team of friends: François Grisay and his experience with supply chains, as well as Romain Faurès, Nathan Furnal, and Charles Hoffreumon with their experience with data science.

I would also like to mention a few friends for their support and help. Thank you to my friend Emmeline Everaert for the various illustrations she drew for this second edition. Thanks, also, to my sister Caroline Vandeput, who drew the timelines you can see through the book. Thank you to My-Xuan Huynh, Laura Garcia Marian, and Sébastien Van Campenhoudt for their reviews of the first chapters.

Finally, thank you to my (previous) master's students Alan Hermans, Lynda Dhaeyer, and Vincent Van Loo for their reviews.

Nicolas Vandeput
September 2020
nicolas.vandeput@supchains.com

First Edition

Discussing problems, models, and potential solutions has always been one of my favorite ways to find new ideas—and test them. As with any other big project, when I started to write *Data Science for Supply Chain Forecasting*, I knew discussions with various people would be needed to receive feedback. Thankfully, I have always been able to count on many friends, mentors, and experts to share and exchange these thoughts.

First and foremost, I want to express my thanks to Professor Alassane Ndiaye, who has been a true source of inspiration for me ever since we met in 2011. Not only does Alassane have the ability to maintain the big picture and stay on course in any situation—especially when it comes to supply chain—but he also has a sense of leadership that encourages each and everyone to shine and come face to face with their true potential. Thank you for your trust, your advice, and for inspiring me, Alassane.

Furthermore, I would like to thank Henri-Xavier Benoist and Jon San Andres from Bridgestone for their support, confidence, and the many opportunities they have given me. Together, we have achieved many fruitful endeavors, knowing that many more are to come in the future.

Of course, I also need to mention Lokad's team for their support, vision, and their incredible ability to create edge models. Special thanks to Johannes Vermorel (CEO and founder) for his support and inspiration—he is a real visionary for quantitative supply chain models. I would also like to thank the all-star team, Simon Schalit, Alexandre Magny, and Rafael de Rezende for the incredible inventory model we have created for Bridgestone.

There are few passionate professionals in the field of supply chains who can deal with the business reality and the advanced quantitative models. Professor Bram De Smet is one of those. He has inspired me, as well as many other supply chain professionals around the globe. In February 2018, when we finally got the chance to meet in person, I shared my idea of writing a book about supply chain and data science. He simply said, "Just go for it and enjoy it to the fullest." Thank you, Bram, for believing in me and pushing me to take that first step.

Just like forests are stronger than a single tree by itself, I like to surround myself with supportive and bright friends. I especially would like to thank each and every one of the following amazing people for their feedback and support: Gil Vander Marcken, Charles Hoffremont, Bruno Deremince, and Emmeline Everaert, Romain Faurès, Alexis Nsamzinshuti, François Grisay, Fabio Periera, Nicolas Pary, Flore Dargent, and Gilles Belleflamme. And of course, a special thanks goes to Camille Pichot. They have all helped me to make this book more comprehensive and more complete. I have always appreciated feedback from others to improve my work, and I would never have been able to write this book alone without the help of this fine team of supportive friends.

On another note, I would also like to mention Daniel Stanton for the time he took to share his experience with business book publishing with me.

Last but not least, I would like to thank Jonathan Vardakis truly. Without his dedicated reviews and corrections, this book would simply not have come to its full completion. Throughout this collaboration, I have realized that we are a perfect fit together to write a book. Many thanks to you, Jon.

Nicolas Vandeput
November 2017
nicolas.vandeput@supchains.com

About the Author

Nicolas Vandeput is a supply chain data scientist specializing in demand forecasting and inventory optimization. He founded his consultancy company SupChains in 2016 and co-founded SKU Science—a smart online platform for supply chain management—in 2018. He enjoys discussing new quantitative models and how to apply them to business reality. Passionate about education, Nicolas is both an avid learner and enjoys teaching at universities; he has taught forecasting and inventory optimization to master's students since 2014 in Brussels, Belgium. He published *Data Science for Supply Chain Forecasting* in 2018 and *Inventory Optimization: Models and Simulations* in 2020.

Foreword – Second Edition

In a recent interview, I was asked what the two most promising areas in the field of forecasting were. My answer was "Data Science" and "Supply Chain" that combined, were going to fundamentally shape the theory and practice of forecasting in the future, providing unique benefits to business firms able to exploit their value. The second edition of *Data Science for Supply Chain Forecasting* is essential reading for practitioners in search of information on the newest developments in these two fields and ways of harnessing their advantages in a pragmatic and useful way.

Nicolas Vandeput, a supply chain data scientist, is an academic practitioner perfectly knowledgeable in the theoretical aspects of the two fields, having authored two successful books, but who is also a consultant, having founded a successful company, and well connected with some of the best known practitioners in the supply chain field as referenced in his acknowledgments. The third part of this book has benefited from advice from another prominent practitioner, Michael Gilliland, author of the *Business Forecasting Deal* (2nd ed.) while Evangelos Spiliotis, my major collaborator in the M4 and M5 competitions, has reviewed in detail the statistical models included in the book.

Nicolas' deep academic knowledge combined with his consulting experience and frequent interactions with experienced experts in their respected fields are the unique ingredients of this well-balanced book covering equally well both the theory and practice of forecasting. This second edition expands on his successful book, published in 2018, with more than 50% new content and a large, second part of over 150 pages, describing machine learning (ML) methods, including gradient boosting ones similar to the lightGBM that won the M5 accuracy competition and was used by the great majority of the 50 top contestants. In addition, there are two new chapters in the third part of the book, covering the critical areas of judgmental forecasting and forecast value added aimed at guiding the effective supply chain implementation process within organizations.

The objective of *Data Science for Supply Chain Forecasting* is to show practitioners how to apply the statistical and ML models described in the book in simple and actionable "do-it-yourself" ways by showing, first, how powerful the ML methods are, and second, how to implement them with minimal outside help, beyond the "do-it-yourself" descriptions provided in the book.

Prof. Spyros Makridakis
Founder of the Makridakis Open Forecasting Center (MOFC)
and organizer of the M competitions
Institute For the Future (IFF), University of Nicosia

https://doi.org/10.1515/9783110671124-202

Foreword – First Edition

Tomorrow's supply chain is expected to provide many improved benefits for all stakeholders, and across much more complex and interconnected networks than the current supply chain.

Today, the practice of supply chain science is striving for excellence: innovative and integrated solutions are based on new ideas, new perspectives and new collaborations, thus enhancing the power offered by data science.

This opens up tremendous opportunities to design new strategies, tactics and operations to achieve greater anticipation, a better final customer experience and an overall enhanced supply chain.

As supply chains generally account for between 60% and 90% of all company costs (excluding financial services), any drive toward excellence will undoubtedly be equally impactful on a company's performance as well as on its final consumer satisfaction.

This book, written by Nicolas Vandeput, is a carefully developed work emphasizing how and where data science can effectively lift the supply chain process higher up the excellence ladder.

This is a gap-bridging book from both the research and the practitioner's perspective, it is a great source of information and value.

Firmly grounded in scientific research principles, this book deploys a comprehensive set of approaches particularly useful in tackling the critical challenges that practitioners and researchers face in today and tomorrow's (supply chain) business environment.

Prof. Dr. Ir. Alassane B. Ndiaye
Professor of Logistics & Transport Systems
Universite Libre de Bruxelles, Belgium

https://doi.org/10.1515/9783110671124-203

Contents

Part I: Statistical Forecasting

Part III: Data-Driven Forecasting Process Management

Introduction

Artificial intelligence is the new electricity.

Andrew Ng[1]

In the same way electricity revolutionized the second half of the 19th century, allowing industries to produce more with less, artificial intelligence (AI) will drastically impact the decades to come. While some companies already use this new electricity to cast new light upon their business, others are still using old oil lamps or even candles, using manpower to manually change these candles every hour of the day to keep the business running.

As you will discover in this book, AI and machine learning (ML) are not just a question of coding skills. Using data science to solve a problem will require more a scientific mindset than coding skills. We will discuss many different models and algorithms in the later chapters. But as you will see, you do not need to be an IT wizard to apply these models. There is another more important story behind these: a story of experimentation, observation, and questioning everything—a truly scientific method applied to supply chain. In the field of data science as well as supply chain, simple questions do not come with simple answers. To answer these questions, you need to think like a scientist and use the right tools. In this book, we will discuss how to do both.

Supply Chain Forecasting

Within all supply chains lies the question of planning. The better we evaluate the future, the better we can prepare ourselves. The question of future uncertainty, how to reduce it, and how to protect yourself against this unknown has always been crucial for every supply chain. From negotiating contract volumes with suppliers to setting safety stock targets, everything relates to the ultimate question:

What Is Tomorrow Going to Be Like?

Yesterday, big companies provided forecasting software that allowed businesses to use a statistical forecast as the backbone of their S&OP[2] process. These statistical forecast models were proposed sixty years ago by Holt and Winters[3] and haven't changed much since: at the core of any statistical forecast tool, you still find exponential smoothing. Software companies sell the idea that they can add a bit of extra

---

1 Andrew Ng is the co-founder of Coursera, the leading online-classes platform.
2 The sales and operations planning (S&OP) process focuses on aligning mid- and long-term demand and supply.
3 See Section 3.3 for more information about Holt-Winters models.

https://doi.org/10.1515/9783110671124-204

intelligence into it, or some less-known statistical model, but in the end, it all goes back to exponential smoothing, which we will discuss in the first part of this book. In the past, one demand planner on her/his own personal computer couldn't compete with these models.

Today, things have changed. Thanks to the increase in computing power, the inflow of data, better models, and the availability of free tools, one can make a difference. **You** can make a difference. With a few coding skills and an appetite for experimentation, powered by machine learning models, you will be able to bring to any business more value than any off-the-shelf forecasting software can deliver. We will discuss machine learning models in Part II.

We often hear that the recent rise of artificial intelligence (or machine learning) is due to an increasing amount of data available, as well as cheaper computing power. This is not entirely true. Two other effects explain the recent interest in machine learning. In previous years, many machine learning models were improved, giving better results. As these models became better and faster, the tools to use them have become more user-friendly. It is much easier today to use powerful machine learning models than it was ten years ago.

Tomorrow, demand planners will have to learn to work hand-in-hand with advanced ML-driven forecast models. Demand planners will be able to add value to those models as they understand the ML shortcomings. We will discuss this in Part III.

How to Read This Book

Data Science for Supply Chain Forecasting is written the way I wish someone explained to me how to forecast supply chain products when I started my career. It is divided into three parts: we will first discuss statistical models, then move to machine learning models, and, finally, discuss how to manage an *efficient* forecasting process.

Old-school Statistics and Machine Learning

One could think that these statistical models are already outdated and useless as machine learning models will take over. But this is wrong. These old-school models will allow us to *understand* and *see* the demand patterns in our supply chain. Machine learning models, unfortunately, won't provide us any explanation nor understanding of the different patterns. Machine learning is only focused on one thing: getting the right answer. The *how* does not matter. This is why both the statistical models and the machine learning models will be helpful for you.

Concepts and Models

The first two parts of this book are divided into many chapters: each of them is either a new model or a new concept. We will start by discussing statistical models in Part I, then machine learning models in Part II. Both parts will start with simple models and end with more powerful (and complex) ones. This will allow you to build your understanding of the field of data science and forecasting step by step. Each new model or concept will allow us to overcome a limitation or to go one step further in terms of forecast accuracy.

On the other hand, not every single existing forecast model is explained here. We will only focus on the models that have proven their value in the world of supply chain forecasting.

Do It Yourself

We also make the decision not to use any black-box forecasting function from Python or Excel. The objective of this book is not to teach you how to use software. It is twofold. Its first purpose is to teach you how to experiment with different models on your own datasets. This means that you will have to tweak the models and experiment with different variations. You will only be able to do this if you take the time to implement these models yourself. Its second purpose is to allow you to acquire in-depth knowledge on how the different models work as well as their strengths and limitations. Implementing the different models yourself will allow you to learn by doing as you test them along the way.

At the end of each chapter, you will find a *Do It Yourself* (DIY) section that will show you a step-by-step implementation of the different models. I can only advise you to start testing these models on your own datasets ASAP.

Can I Do This? Is This Book for Me?

Data Science for Supply Chain Forecasting has been written for supply chain practitioners, demand planners, and analysts who are interested in understanding the inner workings of the forecasting science.[4] By the end of the book, you will be able to create, fine-tune, and use **your own models** to populate a demand forecast for your supply chain. Demand planners often ask me what the best model is for demand forecasting. I always explain that there is no such thing as a *perfect* forecasting model that could beat any other model for any business. As you will see, tailoring models to your demand dataset will allow you to achieve a better level of accuracy than by using black-box tools. This will be especially appreciable for machine learning, where there is definitely no one-size-fits-all model or silver bullet: machine learning models need to be tailor-fit to the demand patterns at hand.

---

4 Even though we will focus on supply chain demand forecasting, the principles and models explained in this book can be applied to any forecasting problem.

You do not need technical IT skills to start using the models in this book today. You do not need a dedicated server or expensive software licenses—only your own computer. You do not need a PhD in Mathematics: we will only use mathematics when it is directly useful to tweak and understand the models. Often—especially for machine learning—a deep understanding of the mathematical inner workings of a model will not be necessary to optimize it and understand its limitations.

The Data Scientist's Mindset

As the business world discovers data science, many supply chain practitioners still rely on rules of thumb and simple approximations to run their businesses. Most often, the work is done directly in Excel. A paradigm shift will be needed to go from manual approximations done in Excel toward automated powerful models in Python. We need to leave oil lamps behind and move to electricity. This is what we will do—step by step—in this book. Before discussing our supply chain data-scientist tools, let's discuss what our data scientist mindset should be.

Data is gold. If artificial intelligence is the new electricity—allowing us to achieve more in a smarter way—data is the modern gold. Gold, unfortunately, does not grow on trees; it comes from gold ore that needs to be extracted and cleaned. Data is the same: it needs to be mined, extracted, and cleaned. We even have to think about where to mine to get the data. As supply chain data scientists, we are both goldsmiths and miners. Even though this book does not cover the specific topic of data cleaning nor the question of data governance, it will show you how to make the best use out of data.

> *Data cleaning: it takes time, it is not sexy, it is required.*

Start small, and iterate. It is easy to lose yourself in details as you try to model the real business world. To avoid this, we will always start tackling broad supply chain questions with simple models. And then we will iterate on these models, adding complexity layers one by one. It is an illusion to think that one could grasp all the complexity of a supply chain at once in one model. As your understanding of a supply chain grows, so does the complexity of your model.

Experiment! There is no definitive answer nor model to each supply chain question. We are not in a world of one-size-fits-all. A model that worked for one company might not work for you. This book will propose many models and ideas and will give you the tools to play with them and to experiment. Which one to choose in the end is up to you! I can only encourage you to experiment with small variations on them—and then bigger ones—until you find the one that suits your business. Unfortunately, many people forget that experimenting means trial and error. Which means that you will face the risk of failing. Experimenting with new ideas and models is not a linear task: days or weeks can be invested in dead-ends. On the other hand, a single stroke of genius can drastically improve a model. What is important is to fail fast and start a new cycle rapidly. Don't get discouraged by a couple of trials without improvement.

Automation is the key to fast experimentation. As you will see, we will need to run tens, hundreds, or even thousands of experiments on some datasets to find the best model. In order to do so, only automation can help us out. It is tremendously important to keep our data workflow fully automated to be able to run these experiments without any hurdle. Only automation will allow you to scale your work.

Automation is the key to reliability. As your model grows in complexity and your datasets grow in size, you will need to be able to reliably populate results (and act upon them). Only an automated data workflow coupled to an automated model will give you reliable results over and over again. Manual work will slow you down and create random mistakes, which will result in frustration.

Don't get misled by overfitting and luck. As we will see in Chapter 8, overfitting (i. e., your model will work extremely well on your current dataset, but fail to perform well on new data) is the number one curse for data scientists. Do not get fooled by luck or overfitting. You should always treat astonishing results with suspicion and ask yourself the question: *Can I replicate these results on new (unseen) data?*

Sharing is caring. Science needs openness. You will be able to create better models if you take the time to share their inner workings with your team. Openly sharing results (good and bad) will also create trust among the team. Many people are afraid to share bad results, but it is worth doing so. Sharing bad results will allow you to trigger a debate among your team to build a new and better model. Maybe someone external will bring a brand-new idea that will allow you to improve your model.

Simplicity over complexity. As a model grows bigger, there is always a temptation to add more and more specific rules and exceptions. Do not go down this road. As more special rules add up in a model, the model will lose its ability to perform reliably well on new data. And soon you will lose the understanding of all the different interdependencies. You should always prefer a structural fix to a specific new rule (also known as *quick fix*). As the pile of quick fixes grows bigger, the potential amount of interdependences will exponentially increase and you will not be able to identify why your model works in a specific way.

Communicate your results. Communication skills are important for data scientists. Communicating results in the best way is also part of the data science process: clarity comes from simplicity. When communicating your results, always ask yourself the following questions:
- Who am I communicating to?
- What are they interested in?
- Do I show them everything they are interested in?
- Do I show them only what they are interested in?

In a world of big data, it is easy to drown someone in numbers and graphs. Just keep your communication simple and straight to the point. Remember that our brain easily analyzes and extrapolates graphs and curves. So prefer a simple graph to a table of data when communicating your results.

Perfection is achieved not when there is nothing more to add, but when there is nothing left to take away.

Antoine de Saint-Exupéry

The Data Scientist's Toolkit

We will use two tools to build our models, experiment, and share our results: Excel and Python.

Excel

Excel is the data analyst's Swiss knife. It will allow you to easily perform simple calculations and to plot data. The big advantage of Excel compared to any programming language is that we can *see* the data. It is much easier to debug a model or to test a new one if you see how the data is transformed at each step of the process. Therefore, Excel can be the first go-to in order to experiment with new models or data.

Excel also has many limitations. It won't perform well on big datasets and will hardly allow you to automate difficult tasks.

Python

Python is a programming language initially published in 1991 by Guido van Rossum, a Dutch computer scientist. If Excel is a Swiss knife, Python is a full army of construction machines awaiting instructions from any data scientist. Python will allow you to perform computations on huge datasets in a fast, automated way. Python also comes with many libraries dedicated to data analysis (pandas), scientific computations (NumPy and SciPy), or machine learning (scikit-learn).[5] These will soon be your best friends.

Why Python?
We chose to use Python over other programming languages as it is both user-friendly (it is easy to read and understand) and one of the most used programming languages in the world.

---

5 See Pedregosa et al. (2011), Virtanen et al. (2020), Oliphant (2006), Hunter (2007), McKinney (2010).

Should You Start Learning Python?

Yes, you should.

Excel will be perfect to visualize results and the different data transformation steps you perform, but it won't allow you to scale your models to bigger datasets nor to easily automate any data cleaning. Excel is also unable to run any machine learning algorithm.

Many practitioners are afraid to learn a coding language. Everyone knows a colleague who uses some macros/VBA in Excel—maybe you are this colleague—and the complexity of these macros might be frightening. **Python is much simpler than Excel macros.** It is also **much more powerful.** As you will see for yourself in the following chapters, even the most advanced machine learning models won't require so many lines of code or complex functions. It means that you do not have to be an IT genius to use machine learning on your own computer. You can do it yourself, today. Python will definitely give you an edge compared to anyone using Excel.

Today is a great day to start learning Python. Many resources are available, such as videos, blogs, articles, and books. You can, for example, look for Python courses on the following online platforms:

www.edx.org

www.coursera.org

www.udemy.com

www.datacamp.com

I personally recommend the MIT class *"Introduction to Computer Science and Programming Using Python,"* available on EdX.[6] This will teach you everything you need to know about Python to start using the models presented in this book.

If you want a short introduction to Python and want to learn along the way, I introduce the most useful concepts in Appendix A. This will be enough for you to understand the first code extracts.

Python Code Extracts

Simplicity vs. Efficiency

The various Python code extracts throughout the book are made with the objectives of simplicity and clarity. Simple code is much easier to understand, maintain, share, and improve than complex code. This simplification was sometimes done at the expense of efficiency or speed. This means that the codes are not as fast as an experienced Python user could produce, but the implementations are easy to understand—which is the primary goal here.

---

6 See MITx (2019).

Python Libraries

We will use throughout the book some of Python's very well-known libraries. As you can see here, we will use the usual import conventions. For the sake of clarity, we won't show the import lines over and over again in each code extract.

```python
1  import numpy as np
2  import pandas as pd
3  import scipy.stats as stats
4  from scipy.stats import norm
5  import matplotlib.pyplot as plt
```

Other Resources

You can download the Python code shown in this book as well as the Excel templates on supchains.com/resources-2nd (password: SupChains-2nd). There is also a Glossary (and an Index) at the end of the book, where you can find a short description of all the specific terms we will use. Do not hesitate to consult it if you are unsure about a term or an acronym.

Part I: **Statistical Forecasting**

1 Moving Average

The first forecast model that we will develop is the simplest. As supply chain data scientists, we love to start experimenting quickly. First, with a simple model, then with more complex ones. Henceforth, this chapter is more of a pretext to set up our first forecast function in Python and our Excel template—we will use both in all of the following chapters.

1.1 Moving Average Model

The moving average model is based on the idea that **future demand is similar to the recent demand we observed**. With this model, we simply assume that the forecast is the average demand during the last n periods. If you look at monthly demand, this could translate as: *"We predict the demand in June to be the average of March, April, and May."*

If we formalize this idea, we obtain this formula:

$$f_t = \frac{1}{n} \sum_{i=1}^{n} d_{t-i}$$

Where,
    f_t is the forecast for period t
    n is the number of periods we take the average of
    d_t is the demand during period t

Initialization
As you will see for further models, we always need to discuss how to initialize the forecast for the first periods. For the moving average method, we won't have a forecast until we have enough historical demand observations. So the first forecast will be done for $t = n + 1$.

Future Forecast
Once we are out of the historical period, we simply define any future forecast as the last forecast that was computed based on historical demand. This means that, with this model, the future forecast is flat. This will be one of the major restrictions of this model: its inability to extrapolate any trend.

https://doi.org/10.1515/9783110671124-001

Notation

In the scientific literature, you will often see the output you want to predict noted as y. This is due to the mathematical convention where we want to estimate y based on x. A prediction (a forecast in our case) would then be noted $\hat{y}$. This hat represents the idea that we do an estimation of y. To make our models and equations as simple to read and understand as possible, we will avoid this usual convention and use something more practical:

Demand will be noted as **d**

Forecast will be noted as **f**

When we want to point to a specific occurrence of the forecast (or the demand) at time t, we will note it f_t (or d_t). Typically:

d_0 is the demand at period 0 (e. g., first month, first day, etc.)

f_0 is the forecast for the demand of period 0

We will call the demand of each period a **demand observation**. For example, if we measure our demand on monthly buckets, it means that we will have 12 demand observations per year.

1.2 Insights

In Figure 1.1, we have plotted two different moving average forecasts.

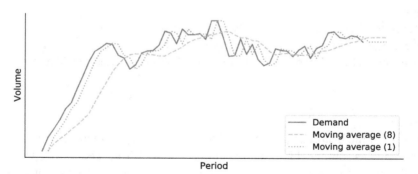

Figure 1.1: Moving averages.

As you can see, the moving average forecast where $n = 1$ is a rather specific case: the forecast is the demand with a one-period lag. This is what we call a naïve forecast: "Tomorrow will be just as today."

> **Naïve Forecast**
>
> A naïve forecast is the simplest forecast model: it always predicts the last available observation.

A naïve forecast is interesting as it will instantly react to any variation in the demand, but on the other hand, it will also be sensitive to **noise** and outliers.

> **Noise**
>
> In statistics, the noise is an unexplained variation in the data. It is often due to the randomness of the different processes at hand.

To decrease this sensitivity, we can go for a moving average based on more previous demand observations ($n > 1$). Unfortunately, the model will also take more time to react to a change in the demand level. In Figure 1.1, you can observe that the moving average with $n = 8$ takes more time to *react* to the changing demand level during the first phase. But during the second phase, the forecast is more stable than the naïve one. **We have to make a trade-off between reactivity and smoothness.** As you will see, we will have to make this trade-off repeatedly in all the exponential smoothing models that we will see later.

Limitations

There are three main limitations at the core of a moving average.
1. **No Trend**   The model does not see any trend (and therefore won't project any). We will learn how to include those in Chapters 5 and 7.
2. **No Seasonality**   The model will not properly react to seasonality. We will include seasonality in Chapters 9 and 11.
3. **Flat Historical Weighting**   A moving average will allocate an *equal* weight to all the historical periods that are taken into account. For example, if you use a moving average with $n = 4$, you allocate a weight (importance) of 25 % to the last four periods. But, the latest observation should somehow be more important than the one four periods ago. For example, if you want to forecast June based on the demand of the latest months, you should give more importance to the demand observed in May compared to any other month.
   Although, you might also want to give a small importance to the demand observed five periods ago: May might be the *most* interesting month, but there may be *some* interest to look at last December as well.
   We will solve this in Chapter 3 by using an *exponential*—rather than a *flat* — weighting of the historical periods.

1.3 Do It Yourself

Excel

Let's build an example with a moving average model based on the last three demand occurrences ($n = 3$), as shown in Figure 1.2, by following these steps:

1. We start our data table by creating three columns:

   Date in column A

   Demand in column B

   Forecast in column C

   You can define the first line as Date = 1 (cell A2=1) and increase the date by one on each line.

2. For the sake of the example, we will always use the same dummy demand in Excel. You can type these numbers (starting on date 1 until date 10): 37, 60, 85, 112, 132, 145, 179, 198, 150, 132.

3. We can now define the first forecast on date 4. You can simply use the formula C5=AVERAGE(B2:B4) and copy and paste it until the end of the table. You can continue until row 12 (date 11), which will be the last forecast based on historical demand.

4. The future forecasts will all be equivalent to this last point. You can use C13=C12 and copy and paste this formula until as far as you want to have a forecast. In the example, we go until date 13.

5. You should now have a table that looks like Figure 1.2.

	A	B	C
1	Date	Demand	Forecast
2	1	37	
3	2	60	
4	3	85	
5	4	112	61
6	5	132	86
7	6	145	110
8	7	179	130
9	8	198	152
10	9	150	174
11	10	132	176
12	11		160
13	12		160
14	13		160
15			

Historical periods (rows 2–10), Future (rows 12–14)

Figure 1.2: Final table for moving average.

Python

If you are new to Python and you want to get a short introduction, I introduce the most useful concepts in Appendix A. This will be enough to understand the first code extracts and learn along the way.

Moving Average Function

Throughout the book, we will implement multiple models in separate functions. These functions will be convenient as they will all use the same kind of inputs and return similar outputs. These functions will be the backbone of your statistical forecast toolbox, as by keeping them consistent you will be able to use them in an optimization engine, as shown in Chapter 6.

We will define a function `moving_average(d, extra_periods=1, n=3)` that takes three inputs:

d A time series that contains the historical demand (can be a list or a NumPy array)

extra_periods The number of periods we want to forecast in the future

n The number of periods we will average

```python
def moving_average(d, extra_periods=1, n=3):

    # Historical period length
    cols = len(d)
    # Append np.nan into the demand array to cover future periods
    d = np.append(d,[np.nan]*extra_periods)
    # Define the forecast array
    f = np.full(cols+extra_periods,np.nan)

    # Create all the t+1 forecast until end of historical period
    for t in range(n,cols):
        f[t] = np.mean(d[t-n:t])

    # Forecast for all extra periods
    f[t+1:] = np.mean(d[t-n+1:t+1])

    # Return a DataFrame with the demand, forecast & error
    df = pd.DataFrame.from_dict({'Demand':d,'Forecast':f,'Error':d-f})

    return df
```

> **Python Mastery – NumPy**
>
> If you are new to Python, you will notice that we have introduced two special elements in our code:
>
> `np.nan` is a way to represent something that is not a number (nan stands for **n**ot **a n**umber).
>
> In our function, we used `np.nan` to store dummy values in our array f, until they get replaced by actual values. If we had initialized f with actual digits (e. g., ones or zeros), this could have been misleading as we wouldn't know if these ones or zeros were actual forecast values or just the dummy initial ones.
>
> `np.full(shape,value)` this function will return an array of a certain shape, filled in with the given `value`.
>
> In our function, we used `np.full()` to create our forecast array f.

Our function `moving_average(d,extra_periods,n)` will return a DataFrame. We can save it to use it later, as shown here with a simple demand time series:

```
1  d = [28,19,18,13,19,16,19,18,13,16,16,11,18,15,13,15,13,11,13,10,12]
2  df = moving_average(d, extra_periods=4, n=3)
```

Visualization with Pandas

You can easily plot any DataFrame simply by calling the method `.plot()` on it. Typically, if you want to plot the demand and the forecast that we just populated, you can simply type:

```
1  df[['Demand','Forecast']].plot()
```

You will get a figure similar to Figure 1.3.

You can also customize `.plot()` by specifying some parameters.

`figsize(width,height)` Defines the size of the figure. Dimensions are given in inches.

`title` Displays a title if given.

`ylim=(min,max)` Determines the range of the y axis of our plot.

`style=[]` Defines the style of each of the lines that are plotted. `'-'` will be a continuous line whereas `'--'` will be a discontinous line.

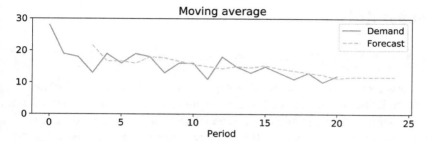

Figure 1.3: .plot() output.

Here's an example:

```
1  df[['Demand','Forecast']].plot(figsize=(8,3), title='Moving average',
   ↪   ylim=(0,30), style=['-','--'])
```

By default, .plot() will use the DataFrame index as the x axis. Therefore, if you want to display a legend on the x axis, you simply can name the DataFrame index.

```
1  df.index.name = 'Period'
```

As you can see in Figure 1.3, the future forecast (as of period 20) is flat. As discussed, this is due to the fact that this moving average model does not *see* a trend and, therefore, can't project any.

2 Forecast KPI

Note to the Reader

This chapter focuses on the *quantitative* aspects of forecast accuracy. For the sake of simplicity, we will look at the error on the very next period (lag 1) and at a single item at a time. In Chapter 27, we will discuss which lags are the most important as well as how to deal with forecast error across a product portfolio.

2.1 Forecast Error

Now that we have created our first forecast model, we need to quantify its accuracy. As you will see, measuring forecast accuracy (or error) is not an easy task, as **there is no one-size-fits-all indicator**. Only experimentation will show you which **Key Performance Indicator** (**KPI**) is best for you. As you will see, each indicator will avoid some pitfalls but will be prone to others.

The first distinction we have to make is the difference between the **accuracy** of a forecast and its **bias**.

Accuracy

The accuracy of your forecast measures how much spread you had between your forecasts and the actual values. The accuracy gives an idea of the magnitude of the errors, but not their overall direction.

Bias

The bias represents the overall direction of the historical average error. It measures if your forecasts were on average too high (i. e., you *overshot* the demand) or too low (i. e., you *undershot* the demand).

Of course, as you can see in Figure 2.1, what we want to have is a forecast that is both accurate and unbiased.

Computing the Forecast Error

Let's start by defining the error during one period (e_t) as the difference between the forecast (f_t) and the demand (d_t).

$$e_t = f_t - d_t$$

https://doi.org/10.1515/9783110671124-002

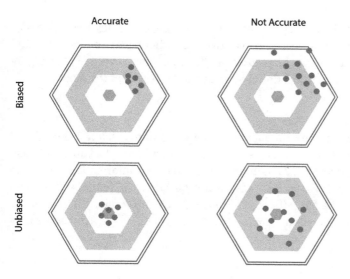

Figure 2.1: Accuracy and bias.

Note that with this definition, if the forecast overshoots the demand, the error will be positive; if the forecast undershoots the demand, the error will be negative.

DIY

Excel

You can easily compute the error as the forecast minus the demand.

Starting from our example from Section 1.3, you can do this by inputting =C5-B5 in cell D5. This formula can then be dragged onto the range C5:D11.

Python

You can access the error directly via df['Error'] as it is included in the DataFrame returned by our function moving_average(d).

2.2 Bias

The (average) bias of a forecast is defined as its average error.

$$\text{bias} = \frac{1}{n}\sum_n e_t$$

Where n is the number of historical periods where you have both a forecast and a demand (i. e., periods where an error can be computed).

The bias alone won't be enough to evaluate your forecast accuracy. Because a positive error in one period can offset a negative error in another period, a forecast model can achieve very low bias and not be accurate at the same time. Nevertheless, a highly biased forecast is already an indication that something is wrong in the model.

Scaling the Bias

The bias computed as in the formula above will give you an *absolute* value like 43 or –1400. As a demand planner investigating your product forecasts, you should ask yourself the following question: *Is 43 a good bias?* Without information about the product's average demand, you cannot answer this question. Therefore, a more relevant KPI would be the *scaled* bias (or *normalized* bias). We can compute it by dividing the total error by the total demand (which is the same as dividing the average error by the average demand).

$$\text{bias\%} = \frac{\frac{1}{n}\sum e_t}{\frac{1}{n}\sum d_t} = \frac{\sum e_t}{\sum d_t}$$

Attention Point

A common mistake (especially in Excel) is to divide the average error observed in a specific time period by the average demand observed in another (wider) time range. As you will see in the DIY sections, be sure to divide the average error by the average demand during the **corresponding** period.

Pro-Tip

It usually brings no insights to compute the bias of *one* item during *one* period. You should either compute it for many products at once (during one period) or compute it for a single item over many periods (best to perform its computation over a full season cycle).

DIY – Bias in Excel

You can compute the average bias by simply averaging the forecast error in Excel.

In our example, as shown in Figure 2.2, you can compute it as G2=AVERAGE(D5:D11). You can also compute the scaled bias by dividing the absolute bias by the average demand with H2=G2/AVERAGE(B5:B11). Note that we use the corresponding cell range in both columns B and D: we do **not** include the demand observed in periods 1 to 3 in our demand average, as there is no forecast error computed in those periods.

	A	B	C	D	E	F	G	H
1	Date	Demand	Forecast	Error			Absolute	Scaled
2	1	37				Bias	- 23	-15%
3	2	60						
4	3	85						
5	4	112	61	- 51				
6	5	132	86	- 46				
7	6	145	110	- 35				
8	7	179	130	- 49				
9	8	198	152	- 46				
10	9	150	174	24				
11	10	132	176	44				
12	11		160					

Figure 2.2: Bias computation in Excel.

DIY – Bias in Python

In Python, we will create a function kpi(df) that will take a forecast DataFrame as an input and print the bias.

```
1  def kpi(df):
2      dem_ave = df.loc[df['Error'].notnull(),'Demand'].mean()
3      bias_abs = df['Error'].mean()
4      bias_rel = bias_abs / dem_ave
5      print('Bias: {:0.2f}, {:.2%}'.format(bias_abs,bias_rel))
```

Python Mastery – String Formatting

We use here specific formatting instructions in the print() function in order to print the absolute and scaled bias as (rounded) absolute value and percentage, respectively. Python provides many string formatting options. See pyformat.info for detailed explanations.

When computing the scaled bias, it is important to divide the bias by the average demand during the periods where we could measure forecast error. We define the relevant demand average in line 2, where we select only the rows where an error is defined.
  Finally, you should obtain these results:

```
1  d = [37, 60, 85, 112, 132, 145, 179, 198, 150, 132]
2  df = moving_average(d, extra_periods=4, n=3)
3  kpi(df)
4  >> Bias: 22.95, 15.33%
```

2.3 MAPE

The **Mean Absolute Percentage Error** (or MAPE) is one of the most commonly used KPIs to measure forecast accuracy. MAPE is computed as the average of the **individual** absolute errors divided by the demand (each period is divided separately). To put it simply, it is the average of the percentage absolute errors.

$$\text{MAPE} = \frac{1}{n}\sum_{n}\frac{|e_t|}{d_t}$$

MAPE is a strange forecast KPI. It is quite well-known among business managers, despite being a really poor accuracy indicator. As you can see in the formula, MAPE divides each error individually by the demand, so it is skewed: high errors during low-demand periods will have a major impact on MAPE. You can see this from another point of view: if you choose MAPE as an error KPI, an extremely low forecast (such as 0) can only result in a maximum error of 100%, whereas any too-high forecast will not be capped to a specific percentage error. Due to this, optimizing MAPE will result in a strange forecast that will most likely undershoot the demand. Just avoid it. If MAPE is mentioned in this book, it is not to promote its use, but as a plea *not* to use it.

DIY – MAPE in Excel

Computing the MAPE will require the following modifications in our previous Excel data table:
1. Add two new columns between columns D and E.
2. Compute the absolute error ($|Error|$) in column E. Cell E5 should be defined as =ABS(D5). You can then drag out this formula until cell E11.
3. You can then compute the scaled error in column F. Start by typing F5=E5/B5 and drag out this formula until F11.
4. You can now compute the MAPE in cell J3 as =AVERAGE(F5:F11).

You should obtain a table similar to Figure 2.3

	A	B	C	D	E	F	G	H	I	J
1	Date	Demand	Forecast	Error	|Error|	Error %			Absolute	Scaled
2	1	37						Bias	- 23	-15%
3	2	60						MAPE		29%
4	3	85								
5	4	112	61	- 51	51	46%				
6	5	132	86	- 46	46	35%				
7	6	145	110	- 35	35	24%				
8	7	179	130	- 49	49	28%				
9	8	198	152	- 46	46	23%				
10	9	150	174	24	24	16%				
11	10	132	176	44	44	33%				
12	11		160							

Figure 2.3: MAPE computation in Excel.

Going Further

You can use an array formula to compute the MAPE without the two extra error columns. You can define cell J3 as:

$$J3 = AVERAGE(ABS(D5:D11)/B5:B11)$$

If you are not familiar with Excel array formulas, these are formulas that can perform operations over multiple cells (hence the term *array*). In order to use one, simply type your formula (for example, the one above), then validate the cell by pressing CTRL+SHIFT+ENTER (and not simply ENTER). If the formula is properly validated, you should see it being surrounded by { }. Array formulas are powerful tools in Excel, but can be confusing for the users. Use them with care.

DIY – MAPE in Python

Let's update our kpi(df) function to print the MAPE as well.

```
def kpi(df):
    dem_ave = df.loc[df['Error'].notnull(),'Demand'].mean()
    bias_abs = df['Error'].mean()
    bias_rel = bias_abs / dem_ave
    print('Bias: {:0.2f}, {:.2%}'.format(bias_abs,bias_rel))
    MAPE = (df['Error'].abs()/df['Demand']).mean()
    print('MAPE: {:.2%}'.format(MAPE))
```

Note that, unlike for the bias, here we don't need to worry about selecting the proper demand range to compute the MAPE. As we divide df['Error'] directly by df['Demand'] **before** computing the mean, pandas by default is removing the rows where the demand is not defined.

You should obtain the following results:

```
kpi(df)
>> Bias: 22.95, 15.33%
>> MAPE: 29.31%
```

2.4 MAE

The **Mean Absolute Error** (MAE) is a very good KPI to measure forecast accuracy. As the name implies, it is the mean of the absolute error.

$$\text{MAE} = \frac{1}{n}\sum_n |e_t|$$

As for the bias, the MAE is an absolute number. If you are told that MAE is 10 for a particular item, you cannot know if this is good or bad. If your average demand is 1,000, it is, of course, astonishing, but if the average demand is 1, an MAE of 10 is a very poor accuracy. To solve this, it is common to divide MAE by the average demand to get a scaled percentage:

$$\text{MAE\%} = \frac{\frac{1}{n}\sum |e_t|}{\frac{1}{n}\sum d_t} = \frac{\sum |e_t|}{\sum d_t}$$

Attention Point

Many practitioners use the MAE formula and call it MAPE. This can cause a lot of confusion. When discussing forecast error with someone, I advise you to explicitly specify how you compute the forecast error to be sure to compare apples with apples.

DIY – MAE in Excel

As we already have a column with the absolute error (column E), we can easily compute the mean absolute error with these two simple formulas:

MAE (absolute): I4 = AVERAGE(E5:E11)

MAE (scaled): J4 = I4/AVERAGE(B5:B11)

You should obtain results as shown in Figure 2.4.

	A	B	C	D	E	F	G	H	I	J
1	Date	Demand	Forecast	Error	|Error|	Error %			Absolute	Scaled
2	1	37						Bias	- 23	-15%
3	2	60						MAPE		29%
4	3	85						MAE	42	28%
5	4	112	61	- 51	51	46%				
6	5	132	86	- 46	46	35%				
7	6	- 145	110	- 35	35	24%				
8	7	179	130	- 49	49	28%				
9	8	198	152	- 46	46	23%				
10	9	150	174	24	24	16%				
11	10	132	176	44	44	33%				
12	11		160							

Figure 2.4: MAE computation in Excel.

DIY – MAE in Python

We can add a few lines to compute the MAE in our kpi(df) function.

```
1  def kpi(df):
2      dem_ave = df.loc[df['Error'].notnull(),'Demand'].mean()
3      bias_abs = df['Error'].mean()
4      bias_rel = bias_abs / dem_ave
5      print('Bias: {:0.2f}, {:.2%}'.format(bias_abs,bias_rel))
6      MAPE = (df['Error'].abs()/df['Demand']).mean()
7      print('MAPE: {:.2%}'.format(MAPE))
8      MAE_abs = df['Error'].abs().mean()
9      MAE_rel = MAE_abs / dem_ave
10     print('MAE: {:0.2f}, {:.2%}'.format(MAE_abs,MAE_rel))
```

You should now obtain these results:

```
1  kpi(df)
2  >> Bias: 22.95, 15.33%
3  >> MAPE: 29.31%
4  >> MAE: 42.29, 28.24%
```

2.5 RMSE

The **Root Mean Square Error** (RMSE) is a difficult KPI to interpret, as it is defined as the square root of the average squared forecast error. Nevertheless, it can be very helpful, as we will see later.

$$\text{RMSE} = \sqrt{\frac{1}{n} \sum_n e_t^2}$$

Just as for MAE, RMSE is not scaled to the demand, so it needs to be put in percentages to be understandable. We can then define RMSE% as:

$$\text{RMSE\%} = \frac{\sqrt{\frac{1}{n} \sum_n e_t^2}}{\frac{1}{n} \sum d_t}$$

Actually, many algorithms—especially for machine learning—are based on the **Mean Square Error** (MSE), which is directly related to RMSE.

$$\text{MSE} = \frac{1}{n} \sum_n e_t^2$$

Many algorithms use MSE instead of RMSE since MSE is faster to compute and easier to manipulate. But it is not scaled to the original error (as the error is squared), resulting in a KPI that we cannot relate to the original demand scale. Therefore, we won't use it to evaluate our statistical forecast models.

DIY – RMSE in Excel

As shown in Figure 2.5, let's add a new column Error² in column G. You can type =D5^2 in cell G5 and then drag out the formula until cell G11.

	A	B	C	D	E	F	G	H	I	J	K
1	Date	Demand	Forecast	Error	|Error|	Error %	Error²			Absolute	Scaled
2	1	37							Bias	- 23	-15%
3	2	60							MAPE		29%
4	3	85							MAE	42	28%
5	4	112	61	- 51	51	46%	2.635		RMSE	43	29%
6	5	132	86	- 46	46	35%	2.147				
7	6	145	110	- 35	35	24%	1.248				
8	7	179	130	- 49	49	28%	2.434				
9	8	198	152	- 46	46	23%	2.116				
10	9	150	174	24	24	16%	576				
11	10	132	176	44	44	33%	1.907				
12	11		160								

Figure 2.5: RMSE computation in Excel.

Afterward, you can compute the RMSE in cell J5 by using the following formula:

$$J5 = SQRT(AVERAGE(G5:G11))$$

The RMSE% can be computed in cell K5 by dividing the RMSE by the average demand:

$$K5 = J5/AVERAGE(B5:B11)$$

DIY – RMSE in Python

As usual, we can simply extend our kpi(df) function to include our new KPI.

```python
def kpi(df):
    dem_ave = df.loc[df['Error'].notnull(),'Demand'].mean()
    bias_abs = df['Error'].mean()
    bias_rel = bias_abs / dem_ave
    print('Bias: {:0.2f}, {:.2%}'.format(bias_abs,bias_rel))
    MAPE = (df['Error'].abs()/df['Demand']).mean()
    print('MAPE: {:.2%}'.format(MAPE))
```

```
8    MAE_abs = df['Error'].abs().mean()
9    MAE_rel = MAE_abs / dem_ave
10   print('MAE: {:0.2f}, {:.2%}'.format(MAE_abs,MAE_rel))
11   RMSE_abs = np.sqrt((df['Error']**2).mean())
12   RMSE_rel = RMSE_abs / dem_ave
13   print('RMSE: {:0.2f}, {:.2%}'.format(RMSE_abs,RMSE_rel))
```

You should obtain these results:

```
1  kpi(df)
2  >> Bias: 22.95, 15.33%
3  >> MAPE: 29.31%
4  >> MAE: 42.29, 28.24%
5  >> RMSE: 43.20, 28.85%
```

A Question of Error Weighting

Compared to MAE, RMSE does not treat each error the same. It gives more importance to the biggest errors. That means that one big error is enough to get a very bad RMSE. Let's use an example with a dummy demand time series.

Period	1	2	3	4	5	6	7	8	9	10	11	12
Demand	10	12	14	8	9	5	8	10	12	11	10	15

Let's imagine we want to compare two slightly different forecasts.

Period	1	2	3	4	5	6	7	8	9	10	11	12
Demand	10	12	14	8	9	5	8	10	12	11	10	15
Forecast #1	12	14	15	10	7	4	5	8	12	14	13	8
Error #1	2	2	1	2	-2	-1	-3	-2	0	3	3	-7
Forecast #2	12	14	15	10	7	4	5	8	12	14	13	9
Error #2	2	2	1	2	-2	-1	-3	-2	0	3	3	-6

The only difference in the two datasets is the forecast on the latest demand observation: forecast #1 undershot it by 7 units and forecast #2 undershot it by *only* 6 units. Note that for both forecasts, period 12 is the worst period in terms of accuracy. If we look at the KPI of these two forecasts, this is what we obtain:

KPI	MAE	RMSE
Forecast #1	2.33	2.86
Forecast #2	2.25	2.66

What is interesting here is that by just changing the error of this last period (the one with the *worst* accuracy) by a single unit, we decrease the total RMSE by 6.9% (2.86 to 2.66), but MAE is only reduced by 3.6% (2.33 to 2.25), so the impact on MAE is nearly twice as low. Clearly, RMSE puts much more importance on the largest errors, whereas MAE gives the same importance to each error. You can try this for yourself and reduce the error of one of the *most* accurate periods to observe the impact on MAE and RMSE.

Spoiler: There is nearly no impact on RMSE.[1]

As we will see later, RMSE has some other very interesting properties.

2.6 Which Forecast KPI to Choose?

We went through the definitions of these KPIs (bias, MAPE, MAE, RMSE), but it is still unclear what difference it can make for our model to use one instead of another. You might think that using RMSE instead of MAE or MAE instead of MAPE doesn't change anything. But nothing is further from the truth.

Let's do a quick example to show this. Imagine a product with a low and rather flat weekly demand that occasionally has a big order (maybe due to promotions, or to clients ordering in batches). Here is the weekly demand observed so far:

	W1	W2	W3	W4	W5
Mon	3	3	4	1	5
Tue	1	4	1	2	2
Wed	5	5	1	1	12
Thu	20	4	3	2	1
Fri	13	16	14	5	20

Now let's imagine we propose three different forecasts for this product. The first one predicts 2 pieces/day, the second one 4 and the last one 6. Let's plot the actual demand and the forecasts in Figure 2.6.

---

1 Remember, RMSE is not so much impacted by low forecast error. So reducing the error of the period that has already the lowest forecast error won't significantly impact RMSE.

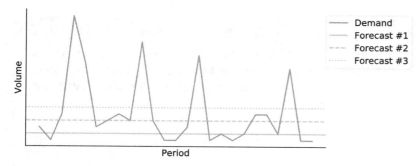

Figure 2.6: Demand and forecasts.

Table 2.1: KPI comparison.

	Forecast #1	Forecast #2	Forecast #3
Bias	−3.9	−1.9	0.1
MAPE	**64%**	109%	180%
MAE	4.4	**4.1**	4.8
RMSE	7.1	6.2	**5.9**

You can see in Table 2.1 how each of these forecasts performed in terms of bias, MAPE, MAE, and RMSE on the historical period. Forecast #1 was the best during the historical periods in terms of MAPE, forecast #2 was the best in terms of MAE, and forecast #3 was the best in terms of RMSE and bias (but the worst on MAE and MAPE).

Let's now reveal how these forecasts were made:

Forecast #1 is just a very low amount. It resulted in the best MAPE (but the worst RMSE).

Forecast #2 is the demand *median*.[2] It resulted in the best MAE.

Forecast #3 is the average demand. It resulted in the best RMSE and bias (but the worst MAPE).

Median vs. Average – Mathematical Optimization

Before discussing the different forecast KPIs further, let's take some time to understand why a forecast of the median will get a good MAE while a forecast of the mean will get a good RMSE.

---

2 The median is the value for which half the dataset is higher and half of the dataset is lower.

> **Note to the Reader**
>
> The math ahead is not required for you to use the KPIs or the further models in this book. If these equations are unclear to you, this is not an issue—don't get discouraged. Just skip them and jump to the conclusion of the **RMSE** and **MAE** paragraphs.

RMSE

Let's start with RMSE:

$$RMSE = \sqrt{\frac{1}{n} \sum e_t^2}$$

Actually, to simplify the algebra, let's use a simplified version, the Mean Squared Error (MSE):

$$MSE = \frac{1}{n} \sum e_t^2 = \frac{1}{n} \sum (f_t - d_t)^2$$

If you set MSE as a target for your forecast model, it will *minimize* it. You can minimize a mathematical function by setting its derivative to zero. Let's try this.

$$\frac{\partial\, MSE}{\partial f} = \frac{\partial \frac{1}{n} \sum (f_t - d_t)^2}{\partial f}$$

$$\frac{2}{n} \sum (f_t - d_t) = 0$$

$$\sum f_t = \sum d_t$$

Conclusion

To optimize a forecast's (R)MSE, the model will have to aim for the total forecast to be equal to the total demand. That is to say that optimizing (R)MSE aims to produce a prediction that is correct *on average* and, therefore, unbiased.

MAE

Now let's do the same for MAE.

$$\frac{\partial\, MAE}{\partial f} = \frac{\partial \frac{1}{n} \sum |f_t - d_t|}{\partial f}$$

Or,

$$|f_t - d_t| = \begin{cases} f_t - d_t & d_t < f_t \\ \text{indefinite} & d_t = f_t \\ d_t - f_t & d_t > f_t \end{cases}$$

and

$$\frac{\partial |f_t - d_t|}{\partial f} = \begin{cases} 1 & d_t < f_t \\ \text{indefinite} & d_t = f_t \\ -1 & d_t > f_t \end{cases}$$

Which means that

$$\frac{\partial \, \text{MAE}}{\partial f} = \frac{1}{n} \sum \begin{cases} 1 & d_t < f_t \\ -1 & d_t > f_t \end{cases}$$

Conclusion

To optimize MAE (i. e., set its derivative to 0), the forecast needs to be as many times higher than the demand as it is lower than the demand. In other words, we are looking for a value that splits our dataset into two equal parts. This is the exact definition of the *median*.

MAPE

Unfortunately, the derivative of MAPE won't show some elegant and straightforward property. We can simply say that MAPE is promoting a very low forecast as it allocates a high weight to forecast errors when the demand is low.

Conclusion

As we saw in the previous section, we have to understand that a big difference lies in the mathematical roots of RMSE, MAE, and MAPE. The optimization of RMSE will seek to be correct on average. The optimization of MAE will try to overshoot the demand as often as undershoot it, which means targeting the demand median. Finally, the optimization of MAPE will result in a biased forecast that will undershoot the demand. In short, **MAE is aiming at demand median, and RMSE is aiming at demand average.**

MAE or RMSE – Which One to Choose?

Is it best to aim for the median or the average of the demand? Well, the answer is not black and white. As we will discuss in the next pages, each technique has some benefits and some risks. Only experimentation will reveal which technique works best for a specific dataset. You can even choose to use both RMSE and MAE.

Let's take some time to discuss the impact of choosing either RMSE or MAE on forecast bias, outliers sensitivity, and intermittent demand.

Bias

For many products, you will observe that the median demand is not the same as the average demand. The demand will most likely have some peaks here and there that will result in a skewed distribution. These skewed demand distributions are widespread in supply chain, as the peaks can be due to periodic promotions or clients ordering in bulk. This will cause the demand median to be below the average demand, as shown in Figure 2.7.

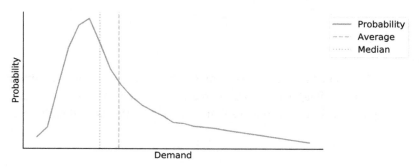

Figure 2.7: Median vs. Average.

This means that a forecast that is **minimizing MAE will result in a bias,** most often resulting in an undershoot of the demand. A forecast that is minimizing RMSE will not result in bias (as it aims for the average). This is definitely MAE's main weakness.

Sensitivity to Outliers

As we discussed, RMSE gives a bigger importance to the highest errors. This comes at a cost: a sensitivity to outliers. Let's imagine an item with a smooth demand pattern as shown in Table 2.2.

Table 2.2: Demand without outliers (median: 8.5, average: 9.5).

Period	1	2	3	4	5	6	7	8	9	10
Demand	16	8	12	9	6	12	5	7	6	14

The median is 8.5 and the average is 9.5. We already observed that if we make a forecast that minimizes MAE, we will forecast the median (8.5) and we would be on average undershooting the demand by 1 unit (bias = −1). You might then prefer to minimize RMSE and to forecast the average (9.5) to avoid this situation. Nevertheless, let's now imagine that we have one new demand observation of 100, as shown in Table 2.3.

Table 2.3: Demand with outliers (median: 8.5, average: 18.1).

Period	1	2	3	4	5	6	7	8	9	10
Demand	16	8	12	9	6	12	5	7	6	100

The median is still 8.5—it hasn't changed!—but the average is now 18.1. In this case, you might not want to forecast the average and might revert back to a forecast of the median.

Generally speaking, the median is more robust to outliers than the average. In a supply chain environment, this is important because we can face many outliers due to demand peaks (marketing, promotions, spot deals) or encoding mistakes. We will discuss outliers further in Chapter 10.

Intermittent Demand

Is robustness to outliers always a good thing? No.

Unfortunately, as we will see, the median's robustness to outliers can result in a very annoying effect for items with intermittent demand.

Let's imagine that we sell a product to a single client. It is a highly profitable product and our unique client seems to make an order one week out of three, but without any recognizable pattern. The client always orders the product in batches of 100. We then have an average weekly demand of 33 pieces and a demand median of... 0.

We have to populate a weekly forecast for this product. Let's imagine we do a first forecast that aims for the average demand (33 pieces). Over the long-term, we will obtain a total squared error of 6 667 (RMSE of 81.6), and a total absolute error of 133.

Week	Demand	Forecast	Error	|Error|	Error^2
1	100	33	67	67	4 445
2	0	33	−33	33	1 111
3	0	33	−33	33	1 111
Total	100	100	0	133	6 667

Now, if we forecast the demand median (0), we obtain a total absolute error of 100 (MAE of 33) and a total squared error of 10.000 (RMSE of 58).

Week	Demand	Forecast	Error	|Error|	Error^2
1	100	0	−100	100	10 000
2	0	0	0	0	0
3	0	0	0	0	0
Total	100	0	−100	100	10 000

As we can see, MAE is a bad KPI to use for intermittent demand. As soon as you have more than half of the periods without demand, the optimal forecast is... 0!

> **Going Further**
>
> A trick to use against intermittent demand items is to aggregate the demand to a higher time horizon. For example, if the demand is intermittent at a weekly level, you could test a monthly forecast or even a quarterly forecast. You can always disaggregate the forecast back into the original time bucket by simply dividing it. This technique can allow you to use MAE as a KPI and smooth demand peaks at the same time.

Conclusion

MAE provides protection against outliers, whereas RMSE provides the assurance to get an unbiased forecast. Which indicator should you use? There is, unfortunately, no definitive answer. As a supply chain data scientist, you should experiment: if using MAE as a KPI results in a high bias, you might want to use RMSE. If the dataset contains many outliers, resulting in a skewed forecast, you might want to use MAE.

> **Pro-Tip – KPI and Reporting**
>
> Note as well that you can choose to report forecast accuracy to management using one or more KPIs (typically MAE and bias), but use another one (RMSE?) to optimize your models. We will further discuss how to manage the forecasting process in Part III.

3 Exponential Smoothing

3.1 The Idea Behind Exponential Smoothing

Simple exponential smoothing is one of the simplest ways to forecast a time series; we will use it in later chapters as a building block in many more powerful models. Just as for a moving average, the basic idea of this model is to assume that the future will be more or less the same as the (recent) past. The only pattern that this model will be able to learn from demand history is its **level**.

> **Level**
>
> The level is the average value around which the demand varies over time. As you can observe in Figure 3.1, the level is a smoothed version of the demand.

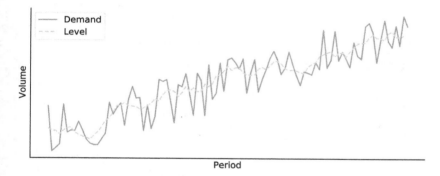

Figure 3.1: Demand level estimation.

The exponential smoothing model will then forecast the future demand as its last estimation of the level. It is important to understand that there is no definitive mathematical definition of the level—instead it is up to our model to **estimate** it.

The simple exponential smoothing model will have some advantages compared to a naïve[1] or a moving average model (see Chapter 1):

- The weight that is put on each observation decreases **exponentially**[2] over time. In other words, in order to determine the forecast, the historical, most recent period has the highest importance; then each subsequent (older) period has less and less importance. This is often better than moving average models, where the same importance (weight) is given to a handful of historical periods.
- Outliers and noise have less impact than with a naïve forecast.

---

1 Remember, a naïve forecast simply projects the latest available observation in the future.
2 We'll discuss this in more detail in the paragraph "Why Is It Called *Exponential* Smoothing?"

https://doi.org/10.1515/9783110671124-003

3.2 Model

The underlying idea of any exponential smoothing model is that, at each period, the model will **learn** a bit from the **most recent demand observation** and **remember** a bit of **the last forecast** it did. The smoothing parameter (or learning rate) **alpha (α)** will determine how much importance is given to the most recent demand observation (see Figure 3.2). Let's represent this mathematically:

$$f_t = \alpha d_{t-1} + (1 - \alpha)f_{t-1}$$
$$0 < \alpha \leq 1$$

The magic about this formula is that the last forecast made by the model was already including a part of the previous demand observation and a part of the previous forecast. **This means that the previous forecast includes everything the model learned so far based on demand history.**

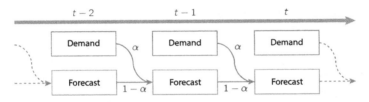

Figure 3.2: Simple exponential smoothing algorithm.

What Is the Intuition Behind This Formula?
α is a ratio (or a percentage) of how much importance the model will allocate to the most recent observation compared to the importance of demand history.
αd_{t-1} represents the learning rate times the previous demand observation. You could say that the model attaches certain importance (alpha) to the last demand occurrence.
$(1 - \alpha)f_{t-1}$ represents how much the model remembers from its previous forecast. Note that this is where the recursive magic happens, as f_{t-1} was itself defined as partially d_{t-2} and f_{t-2}.

There is an important trade-off to be made here between *learning* and *remembering*, between being reactive and being stable. If alpha is high, the model will allocate more importance to the most recent demand observation (i. e., the model will learn fast), and it will be reactive to a change in the demand level. But it will also be sensitive to outliers and noise. On the other hand, if alpha is low, the model won't rapidly notice a change in level, but will also not overreact to noise and outliers.

Future Forecast

Once we are out of the historical period, we need to populate a forecast for future periods. This is simple: the last forecast—the one based on the most recent demand observation—is simply extrapolated into the future, as shown in Figure 3.3. If we define f_{t^*} as the last forecast that we could make based on demand history, we simply have:

$$f_{t>t^*} = f_{t^*}$$

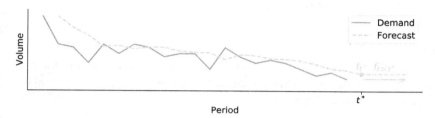

Figure 3.3: Future forecast with simple exponential smoothing.

Model Initialization

Take a method and try it. If it fails, admit it frankly and try another. But by all means, try something.

Franklin Roosevelt

As with every model, an important question is to decide how we initialize the forecast. Unfortunately, this simple question does not have a simple, straightforward answer. Actually, this will often be the case in this book: the simplest questions won't always have definitive and absolute answers. Only experimentation will allow you to understand which technique works best for your dataset. Let's discuss some ideas; we are supply chain data scientists—we experiment.

Simple Initialization
We initialize the first forecast (period 0) as the first demand observation. We then have

$$f_0 = d_0$$

This is a simple and fair way to initialize the forecast.

Average

We initialize the forecast as the average of the first n demand occurrences.

$$f_0 = \frac{1}{n} \sum_{t=0}^{n} d_t$$

In such a case, I would advise that you test different values of n. It could either be set as a fixed small value (3 to 5) or as the inverse of the learning rate ($\frac{1}{\alpha}$). If n is set as the inverse of the learning rate, this allows a smoother estimation of f_0 as the learning rate decreases. This makes sense, as a low value for α means that we want our model to react smoothly to variations.

Data Leakage

If you choose an initialization method that includes information about multiple periods ahead—for example, if you define the initial forecast as the average of the first five periods—you face a **data leakage**.

> **Data Leakage**
>
> In the case of forecast models, a data leakage describes a situation where a model is given pieces of information about future demand.

Basically, you ask your model: Can you provide me a forecast of the next period, knowing that the average of the demand for the next five periods is 10? This is a typical example of overfitting (as we will discuss in detail in Chapter 8): the model will give you a good forecast accuracy for the initial periods (that's easy—you gave it the average demand of these periods!), but won't be able to replicate such accuracy in the future.

When you initialize the different parameters of a model, always be cautious not to give it too much information about the future.

> **A Brief History of Holt-Winters Models**
>
> The exponential smoothing models are often called "Holt-Winters," based on the names of the researchers who proposed them. An early form of exponential smoothing forecasting was initially proposed by R. G. Brown in 1956.[a] His equations were refined in 1957 by Charles C. Holt—a US engineer from MIT and the University of Chicago—in his paper "Forecasting Trends and Seasonals by Exponentially Weighted Averages."[b] The exponential smoothing models were again improved three years later by Peter Winters.[c] Their two names were remembered and given to the different exponential smoothing techniques that we sometimes call "Holt-Winters."

Holt and Winters proposed different exponential smoothing models (simple, double, and triple) that can also understand and project a trend or a seasonality. This ensemble of models is then quite robust to forecast any time series. And, as Holt and Winters already explained in 1960, these forecasts only require a modest use of computation power.

a See Brown (1956).

b See Holt (2004).

c See Winters (1960).

3.3 Insights

Impact of α

In Figure 3.4, we see that a forecast made with a low alpha value (here, 0.1) will take more time to react to changing demand, whereas a forecast with a high alpha value (here, 0.8) will (too) closely follow demand fluctuations. The edge case, $\alpha = 1$, will transform the simple exponential smoothing model into a naïve forecast. We will see how to optimize alpha in Chapter 6.

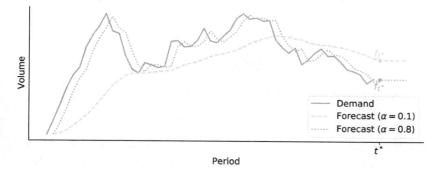

Figure 3.4: Simple exponential smoothing model.

> **Pro-Tip – Acceptable Range for α**
>
> Usually, a reasonable range for α is between 0.05 and 0.5. If α is higher than 0.5, it means that the model is allocating nearly no importance to demand history. The forecast will almost solely be based on the latest observations. That would be a hint that something is wrong with the model.

Why Is It Called *Exponential* Smoothing?

This model is called exponential smoothing because the weight given to each demand observation is exponentially reduced, as shown in Table 3.1.

Table 3.1: Weight allocated to each historical period.

Period	Moving Average n					Exponential Smoothing α					
	5	4	3	2	1	.2	.4	.6	.8	1	
$t-1$	.2	.25	.33	.5	1	.20	.40	.60	.80	1	$= \alpha$
$t-2$	.2	.25	.33	.5		.16	.24	.24	.16		$= \alpha(1-\alpha)$
$t-3$	.2	.25	.33			.13	.14	.10	.03		$= \alpha(1-\alpha)^2$
$t-4$	.2	.25				.10	.09	.04	.01		$= \alpha(1-\alpha)^3$
$t-5$	.2					.08	.05	.02			$= \alpha(1-\alpha)^4$

If you are interested in the mathematical foundations of this model—if not, feel free to jump to the paragraph "Limitations of Exponential Smoothing"—we can show how it results in exponential weighting. We will start from the forecast equation:

$$f_t = \alpha d_{t-1} + (1-\alpha)f_{t-1}$$

As you can see, the weight given to the most recent demand observation d_{t-1} is α. Now let's replace f_{t-1} by its formula.

$$f_t = \alpha d_{t-1} + (1-\alpha)f_{t-1}$$
$$= \alpha d_{t-1} + (1-\alpha)\left(\alpha d_{t-2} + (1-\alpha)f_{t-2}\right)$$

If we do a bit of algebra, we obtain the following formula:

$$f_t = \alpha d_{t-1} + \alpha(1-\alpha)d_{t-2} + (1-\alpha)^2 f_{t-2}$$

We see that the weight given to the second most recent demand observation d_{t-2} is $\alpha(1-\alpha)$, which is lower than the weight given to d_{t-1}. Let's go further and replace f_{t-2} by its formula.

$$f_t = \alpha d_{t-1} + \alpha(1-\alpha)d_{t-2} + (1-\alpha)^2 f_{t-2}$$
$$= \alpha d_{t-1} + \alpha(1-\alpha)d_{t-2} + (1-\alpha)^2\left(\alpha d_{t-3} + (1-\alpha)f_{t-3}\right)$$
$$= \alpha d_{t-1} + \alpha(1-\alpha)d_{t-2} + \alpha(1-\alpha)^2 d_{t-3} + (1-\alpha)^3 f_{t-3}$$

We see that the weight given to d_{t-3} is $\alpha(1-\alpha)^2$; which is the weight given to d_{t-2} multiplied by $(1-\alpha)$. From here, we deduce that the weight given to each further demand observation is reduced by a factor $(1-\alpha)$. This is why we call this method **exponential** smoothing.

Limitations of Exponential Smoothing

This simple exponential smoothing model is slightly smarter than the moving average model, thanks to its clever weighting of the historical demand observations. But it still has many limitations:

- It does not project trends. We will solve this with our next model: the exponential smoothing with trend, otherwise known as **double exponential smoothing**.
- It does not recognize any seasonal pattern. We will solve this with the **triple exponential smoothing** model.
- It cannot (natively) use any external explanatory variables (such as pricing or marketing expenses).

Conclusion

This first exponential smoothing model will be most likely too simple to achieve good results, but it is a foundation stone on top of which we will create more complex models later.

3.4 Do It Yourself

Let's see how you can implement your own exponential smoothing model in Excel and in Python.

Excel

1. We start our data table by creating three columns:
   Date in column A
   Demand in column B
   Forecast in column C
2. Next, let's add a cell with alpha (F1 in our example). Don't forget to clearly indicate that this cell is alpha.
3. Once this is done, you can simply initialize the first forecast (cell C2) as the first demand (cell B2), as shown in Figure 3.5.
4. You can now populate your forecast; as of cell C3, you can use this formula (as shown in Figure 3.6):

$$C3 = \$F\$1*B2+(1-\$F\$1)*C2$$
$$f_t = \alpha d_{t-1} + (1 - \alpha)f_{t-1}$$

	A	B	C	D	E	F
1	Date	Demand	Forecast		Alpha:	10%
2	1	37	37			
3	2	60				
4	3	85				
5	4	112				
6	5	132				
7	6	145				
8	7	179				
9	8	198				
10	9	150				
11	10	132				
12	11					
13	12					
14	13					

Figure 3.5: Table setup.

	A	B	C	D	E	F
1	Date	Demand	Forecast		Alpha:	10%
2	1	37	37			
3	2	60	=$F$1*B2+(1-$F$1)*C2			
4	3	85	39			

Figure 3.6: Simple exponential smoothing formula.

5. To continue your forecast until the end of the historical period, you can simply drag this formula to the end of the table.
6. As for all the future forecasts (i. e., the forecasts out of the historical period), they will simply be equivalent to the very last forecast based on historical demand (as shown in Figure 3.7).

	A	B	C	D	E	F
1	Date	Demand	Forecast		Alpha:	10%
8	7	179	67			
9	8	198	79			
10	9	150	91			
11	10	132	96			
12	11		=C11			
13	12		96			
14	13		96			

Figure 3.7: Future forecast.

Python

Simple Smoothing Function

We will define a function `simple_exp_smooth()` that takes three parameters:

d The time series to forecast

extra_periods=1 The number of periods that need to be forecast into the future

alpha=0.4 The smoothing alpha parameter

```python
1   def simple_exp_smooth(d, extra_periods=1, alpha=0.4):
2
3       # Historical period length
4       cols = len(d)
5       # Append np.nan into the demand array to cover future periods
6       d = np.append(d,[np.nan]*extra_periods)
7
8       # Forecast array
9       f = np.full(cols+extra_periods,np.nan)
10      # initialization of first forecast
11      f[1] = d[0]
12
13      # Create all the t+1 forecast until end of historical period
14      for t in range(2,cols+1):
15          f[t] = alpha*d[t-1]+(1-alpha)*f[t-1]
16
17      # Forecast for all extra periods
18      for t in range(cols+1,cols+extra_periods):
19          # Update the forecast as the previous forecast
20          f[t] = f[t-1]
21
22      df = pd.DataFrame.from_dict({'Demand':d,'Forecast':f,'Error':d-f})
23
24      return df
```

Playing with Your Function

You can then simply call the function (here with a dummy demand time series):

```python
1   d = [28,19,18,13,19,16,19,18,13,16,16,11,18,15,13,15,13,11,13,10,12]
2   df = simple_exp_smooth(d, extra_periods=4)
```

You can also get the various accuracy KPI thanks to the function kpi(df) from Section 2.5.

```
1  kpi(df)
2  >> Bias: -2.02, -13.56%
3  >> MAPE: 19.25%
4  >> MAE: 2.74, 18.39%
5  >> RMSE: 3.89, 26.11%
```

Another very interesting step is to plot the results in order to analyze how the model behaves. You can see the results in Figure 3.8.

```
1  df.index.name = 'Period'
2  df[['Demand','Forecast']].plot(figsize=(8,3), title='Simple Smoothing',
   ↪  ylim=(0,30), style=['-','--'])
```

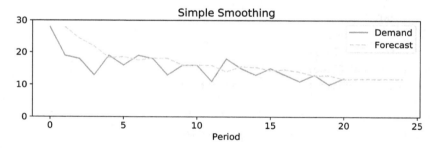

Figure 3.8: Example of simple smoothing forecast.

4 Underfitting

All models are wrong, but some are helpful.

George Box

A model aims to describe reality. As reality can be rather complex, a model will be built on some assumptions (i. e., simplifications), as summarized by statistician George Box. Unfortunately, due to these assumptions or some limitations, some forecast models will not be able to predict or properly explain the reality they are built upon.

We say that a model is **underfitted** if it does not explain reality accurately enough.

To analyze our model's abilities, we will divide our dataset (i. e., the historical demand in the case of a forecast) into two different parts: the training set and the test set.

> ### Training Set
>
> The training set is used to train (*fit*) our model (i. e., optimize its parameters).

> ### Test Set
>
> The test set is the dataset that will assess the accuracy of our model against **unseen** data. This dataset is kept aside from the model during its training phase, so that the model is not aware of this data and can thus be tested against unseen—and right away available—data.

Typically, in the case of statistical forecast models, we use historical demand as the training set to optimize the different parameters (α for the simple exponential smoothing model). To test our forecast, we can keep the latest periods out of the training set to see how our models behave during these periods.

We need to be very careful with our test set. We can never use it to optimize our model. Keep in mind that this dataset is here to show us how our model would perform against new data. If we optimize our model on the test set, we will never know what accuracy we can expect against new demand.

One could say that an underfitted model lacks a good understanding of the training dataset. As the model does not perform properly on the training dataset, it will not perform well on the test set either. In the case of demand forecasting, a model that does not achieve good accuracy on historical demand will not perform properly on future demand either.

We will now look into two possible causes of underfitting and how to solve them.

https://doi.org/10.1515/9783110671124-004

4.1 Causes of Underfitting

Model Complexity

The first possible reason for underfitting (i. e., the model does not achieve satisfying results on the training dataset) is that its inner complexity is too low. In other words, the
model cannot learn (understand) the appropriate patterns from the historical dataset.

In Figure 4.1, you can see a dummy dataset of demand points that follows a noisy
quadratic curve ($y = -x^2$). On top of this, you see two models that we fit into this
dataset. The first one is a linear regression, and the second one is an exponential
smoothing.

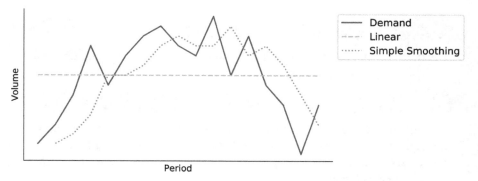

Figure 4.1: Linear regression vs. simple smoothing.

As you can see, the linear model fits this historical demand poorly (with an RMSE of
34%). Most likely, if we used this model to predict the demand over the next periods—
which is likely to be close to zero—the model would fail and continue to predict the
average historical demand.

The forecast made with a simple exponential smoothing model achieves a much
better fit on the historical dataset: it has an RMSE of 30%. We observe that this model
understands that the demand level changes over time and, therefore, we can then
expect this model to behave better on future demand. The linear model was simply
not complex enough to understand the relationship behind the data.

Lack of Explanatory Variables

Let's imagine another case where you sell ice cream near a school. The sales are rather
high during the week and are much lower during the weekend. Let's plot this situation
and a simple exponential smoothing forecast, as shown in Figure 4.2.

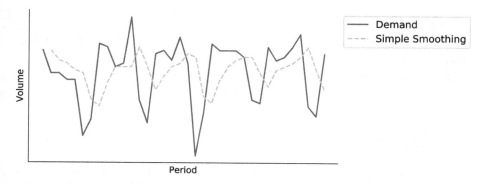

Figure 4.2: Example of simple smoothing applied to ice cream sales.

We see that our simple exponential smoothing is absolutely not adapted to this demand pattern. The model over-forecasts the weekends and then under-forecasts the first weekdays. We will see later (in Chapter 9) a perfect model for this situation: a seasonal exponential smoothing model. But for now, let's just imagine a model that understands the difference between a weekday and the weekend. To do this, we will use two different models: one will forecast weekdays and the other one weekends. Both of these will be simple exponential smoothing models.

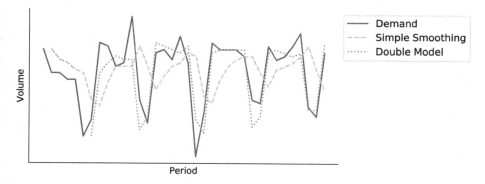

Figure 4.3: Double model vs. simple smoothing.

With our new model duo, we fit the demand much better (as shown in Figure 4.3), as our model understands that weekdays and weekends are not the same. In other words, our model has a new **explanatory variable**: *Is it a weekday?* The initial model (the simple exponential smoothing) simply didn't get the information about weekends/weekdays difference, so it could not understand the underlying relationship.

In many industries, we could have similar stories with pricing and marketing: high demand during periods with promotions or advertisement and otherwise lower demand. In such cases, a model that does not take these factors into account will fail to properly predict the demand. It would underfit the demand patterns. Unfortunately, **exponential smoothing models are not able to take these explanatory variables into account.**

We will discuss how to use these exogenous variables in Chapter 20, once we have powerful machine learning models in our toolbox.

4.2 Solutions

We have identified a typical problem with (predictive) models: **underfitting**. That is to say that a model is not smart enough to understand the relationships present in the training data. Two solutions can be used to increase the predictive abilities of an underfitted model:

- Use more explanatory variables (such as weekdays/weekends, marketing expenses, pricing).
- Change the model to a more complex one (add a trend, a seasonality).

> **Pro-Tip**
>
> As a final piece of advice, don't use your model to predict future demand if it does not perform well on the historical dataset.

5 Double Exponential Smoothing

When the facts change, I change my mind. What do you do, sir?

John Maynard Keynes

5.1 The Idea Behind Double Exponential Smoothing

We saw with the simple exponential smoothing algorithm how we could create a simple forecast, assuming that the future of the demand would be similar to its (recent) past. A major issue of this simple smoothing is that it can only see a level, and is unable to identify and project a **trend**.

> **Trend**
>
> We define the trend as the average variation of the time series level between two consecutive periods. Remember that the level is the average value around which the demand varies over time.

If you assume that your time series follows a trend, you will most likely not know its magnitude in advance—especially as this magnitude could vary over time. This is fine, because we will create a model that will learn *by itself* the trend over time. Just as for the level, this new model will estimate the trend based on an exponential weight **beta (β)**, giving more (or less) importance to the most recent observations.

5.2 Double Exponential Smoothing Model

Remember that for the simple exponential smoothing model, we updated the forecast at each period partially based on
1. the **most recent observation** of the demand.
2. the **previous estimation** of the demand (that is the previous forecast).

Similarly, the general idea behind exponential smoothing models is that each demand component (currently, the level and the trend, later the seasonality, as well) will be updated after each period based on two same pieces of information: the last observation and the previous estimation of this component. Let's apply this principle to estimate the demand level (a_t and trend b_t).

Level Estimation
Let's see how the model will estimate the level:

$$a_t = \alpha d_t + (1 - \alpha)(a_{t-1} + b_{t-1})$$

https://doi.org/10.1515/9783110671124-005

This should look familiar: it is the same logic as the forecast for the simple exponential smoothing. The model will update its estimation of the level a_t at each period, thanks to two pieces of information: the last demand observation d_t, and the previous level estimation increased by the trend $a_{t-1}+b_{t-1}$ (remember, we assume the level to change by the trend at each period). Alpha is the level learning rate: α represents how much weight is given to the most recent level observation (d_t), and $(1 - \alpha)$ is the importance given to the previous level estimation $(a_{t-1} + b_{t-1})$.

Trend Estimation

The model will also have to estimate the trend. In order to do so, we will apply similar logic:

$$b_t = \beta(a_t - a_{t-1}) + (1 - \beta)b_{t-1}$$

β is the learning parameter for the trend (just as α is for level).

Forecast

Finally, we simply set the forecast for period $t + 1$ as

$$\text{Forecast} = \text{Level} + \text{Trend}$$

$$f_{t+1} = a_t \quad + b_t$$

We have now a full model that we can generalize for a forecast of period $t + \lambda$

$$a_t = \alpha d_t + (1 - \alpha)(a_{t-1} + b_{t-1})$$
$$b_t = \beta(a_t - a_{t-1}) + (1 - \beta)b_{t-1}$$
$$f_{t+\lambda} = a_t + \lambda b_t$$

Future Forecast

As soon as we are out of the historical period:
- the trend stays constant.
- the level and the forecast are now equivalent: they are both computed as the previous level plus the (ongoing) trend.

We then have this system:[1]

$$a_t = a_{t-1} + b_{t^*}$$
$$b_t = b_{t^*}$$
$$f_{t+1} = a_t + b_t$$

Remember, t^* is the latest period for which we know the demand observation.

---

1 We compute here the level and the trend for the sake of being complete. You could simply compute any future forecast with $f_{t^*+\lambda} = a_{t^*} + \lambda b_{t^*}$

This basically means that the model will extrapolate the latest trend it could observe. Forever. As we will see later, this might become a problem.

> **Going Further**
>
> Instead of an additive trend, you can also use a **multiplicative** trend with the following set of equations:
>
> $$a_t = \alpha d_t + (1 - \alpha)(a_{t-1}\, b_{t-1})$$
> $$b_t = \beta \frac{a_t}{a_{t-1}} + (1 - \beta)b_{t-1}$$
> $$f_{t+\lambda} = a_t b_t^{\lambda}$$
>
> Nevertheless, pay close attention to such models, as they can quickly end up with a massive (and wrong) forecast in the case of high trends. This is especially the case for low-volumes items where this model could overreact to any small variation.

Model Initialization

Just as for the simple exponential smoothing model, we have to discuss how to initialize the first estimations of our level and trend (a_0 and b_0). As it is often the case, simple questions don't have simple absolute answers. Only experimentation will tell you which initialization works best in your case.

Simple Initialization

We can initialize the level and the trend simply based on:

$$a_0 = d_0$$
$$b_0 = d_1 - d_0$$

This is a simple and fair initialization method. You have limited data leakage (see the paragraph "Data Leakage" in Section 3.2), but the initial forecast is entirely dependent on the first two demand observations.

Note that if we do this, the first forecast f_1 will be perfect, as:

$$\begin{aligned} f_1 &= a_0 + b_0 \\ &= d_0 + (d_1 - d_0) \\ &= d_1 \end{aligned}$$

Since the first forecast (f_1) will be perfect, you will give an unfair advantage in terms of accuracy to this initialization method compared to any other method.[2] On big datasets, this is fine—as you only improve one prediction over many—but on smaller sets, this advantage might result in overfitting (as we will discuss later, in Chapter 8). A simple solution is to remove the first forecast from the forecast error computation.

Linear Regression

Another way to initialize a_0 and b_0 would be to use a linear regression of the first n demand observations. Again, n could be defined as an arbitrarily rather low number (e. g., 3 or 5) or as something proportional to the average of $\frac{1}{\beta}$ and $\frac{1}{\alpha}$. Pay attention that as n grows, the data leakage becomes more important.

How to make linear regressions is out of the scope of this book. Nevertheless, you can take a look at the function np.polyfit(x,y,deg=1) in Python or LINEST() in Excel. You can also do a linear regression analysis in Excel if you activate the add-on Data Analysis.[3] Once it is activated, you can launch it by going to the ribbon to Data/Analysis/Data Analysis and then selecting Regression in the menu.

5.3 Insights

Let's plot a first example in Figure 5.1 with a rather low α (0.2) and β (0.4).

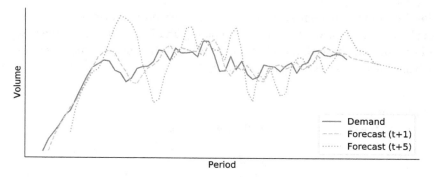

Figure 5.1: Forecast with $\alpha = 0.2$ and $\beta = 0.4$.

We made two forecasts: one for period $t+1$ and another one for $t+5$. The forecast at $t+1$ is rather good (as expected), but we observe that the forecast at $t+5$ can be wrong due to the trend *extrapolation*. As we noted already, the model is assuming that the trend is ever ongoing. For a forecast at $t+1$, this is fine as the trend is regularly updated, but if you look five periods ahead, this might become an issue.

---

2 The initialization of the forecast can be interpreted as: *Can you forecast tomorrow, knowing that we are going to sell 5 today and 10 units more tomorrow?*
3 The procedure is similar to the one for Excel Solver (see Section 6.3).

Trend and Error

There is an interesting relationship between the forecast error and the trend. As you can observe in Figure 5.2, the trend decreases when the error is positive, and the trend increases when the error is negative. The intuition is that our model learns from its mistakes—something not everyone can do. If the model undershot the last demand, it will increase the trend. If it overshot the last demand, it will decrease the trend.

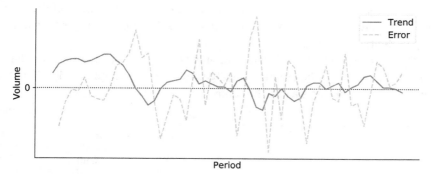

Figure 5.2: Trend and error.

There is now a real temptation: shouldn't we increase the trend learning rate, so that the model would learn faster from its previous mistakes? As supply chain data scientists, let's experiment and try a model powered by high learning rates (α and β set to 0.8).

We get Figure 5.3.

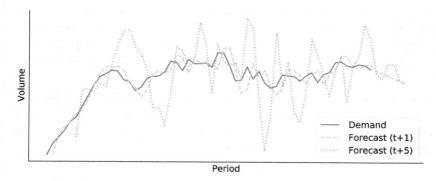

Figure 5.3: Forecast with $\alpha = 0.8$ and $\beta = 0.8$.

We now see that the forecast at $t + 5$ starts to oscillate around the demand. This is very bad—even dangerous!—for a supply chain, as it will most likely result in a bullwhip effect.[4] We will discuss how to set the learning parameters properly in the next chapters.

How the Model Sees the Demand

Exponential smoothing models are handy, as they allow us to **understand** a forecast or a time series, thanks to the decomposition they do between the level and the trend (and, as we will see later, the seasonality). You can check the state of any of the demand sub-components at any point in time, exactly as if you could inspect what is happening under the hood of the model.

Do not hesitate to plot these different components to understand how your model *sees* (or *understands*) a specific product (see Figure 5.4 for an example). This will explain why your model forecasts a specific value.

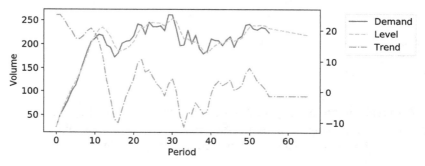

Figure 5.4: Level and trend components.

The value of the different smoothing parameters (α and β for now, ϕ and y later) will also tell you something about the variability or smoothness of your product. High values will denote products where each variation should impact any future forecast; low values will denote products with more consistent behaviors that shouldn't be impacted by short-term fluctuations.

As we will discuss in the second part of the book, it is unfortunate that machine learning models won't provide us this kind of understanding or interpretation of a time series' sub-components. This is one of the reasons why exponential smoothing models are complementary to machine learning.

---

4 The bullwhip effect is observed in supply chains when small variations in the downstream demand result in massive fluctuations in the upstream supply chain. See my book *Inventory Optimization: Models and Simulations* for a detailed discussion.

Limitations

Our double exponential smoothing model is now able to recognize a trend and extrapolate it into the future. This is a major improvement compared to simple exponential smoothing (or moving average). But, unfortunately, this comes with a risk...

> *In 50 years, every street in London will be buried under nine feet of manure.*
>
> The Times (1894)

As this prediction from the famous newspaper, our model will assume that the trend will go on forever.[5] This might result in some issues for mid- and long-term forecasts. We will solve this thanks to the damped trend model (see Chapter 7)—a model that was only published 25 years later than Holt-Winters, in 1985!
　　Next to this risk of infinite trend, we still have:
- The lack of seasonality. This will be solved via the triple exponential smoothing model.
- The impossibility to take external information into account (like marketing budget or price variations).

5.4 Do It Yourself

Let's implement this model in Excel and Python.

Excel

1. Let's define a table with 5 columns: Date (column A), Demand (column B), Forecast (column C), Level (column D), and Trend (column E).
2. We will also indicate the learning rates: alpha and beta (cells H1 and H2).
3. We can initialize the first level as the first demand observation. The trend can be initialized as the difference between the first two demand observations.

$$a_0 = d_0$$
$$D2 = B2$$
$$b_0 = d_1 - d_0$$
$$E2 = B3-B2$$

4. We can now work on the forecast. We will start working on it from the second row (as a forecast for $t = 1$ makes little sense). Populating the forecast is rather easy.

---

5 In the end, London wasn't buried under manure—it was saved, twenty years later, by motor vehicles.

Cell C3 should be defined as:

$$f_{t+1} = a_t + b_t$$

$$C3 = D2{+}E2$$

You can then copy and paste this formula until the end of the table. ·
You should now have a table similar to Figure 5.5.

	A	B	C	D	E	F	G	H
1	Date	Demand	Forecast	Level (a)	Trend (b)		Alpha:	30%
2	1	37		37	23		Beta:	40%
3	2	60	60					
4	3	85						
5	4	112						
6	5	132						
7	6	145						
8	7	179						
9	8	198						
10	9	150						
11	10	132						
12	11							
13	12							
14	13							

Figure 5.5: Double exponential smoothing (initial) template in Excel.

5. We will now create the level formula, and we have to define D3 such as:

$$a_t = \alpha d_t + (1 - \alpha)(a_{t-1} + b_{t-1})$$

$$D3 = \$H\$1{*}B3{+}(1{-}\$H\$1){*}(D2{+}E2)$$

You can then copy and paste this formula until the end of the table.
6. We can now do the trend by defining E3, such as:

$$b_t = \beta(a_t - a_{t-1}) + (1 - \beta)b_{t-1}$$

$$E3 = \$H\$2{*}(D3{-}D2){+}(1{-}\$H\$2){*}E2$$

You can also copy and paste this formula until the end of the Demand column (until
cell C11, in our case). You should have now a result similar to Figure 5.6.
7. Let's now extrapolate the forecast into the future. This is rather simple: in the cell
C13, just type =C12+$E$11. You can then copy and paste this formula further to see
how the model predicts the demand.

	A	B	C	D	E	F	G	H
1	Date	Demand	Forecast	Level (a)	Trend (b)		Alpha:	30%
2	1	37		37	23		Beta:	40%
3	2	60	60	60	23			
4	3	85	83	84	23			
5	4	112	107	108	24			
6	5	132	132	132	24			
7	6	145	156	153	23			
8	7	179	175	176	23			
9	8	198	199	199	23			
10	9	150	222	200	14			
11	10	132	214	190	4			
12	11		194					
13	12		198					
14	13		203					

Figure 5.6: Double exponential smoothing (complete) template in Excel.

Python

Double Smoothing Function

Just like for the simple model, we will define a function double_exp_smooth() that takes a time series d as an input (it can be either a NumPy array or a simple list) and returns a DataFrame that contains the historical demand, the forecast, the error, the level, and the trend. The function can also take extra_periods as an optional input, which is the number of periods we want to forecast in the future. The last two optional inputs are the alpha and beta parameters.

```
1   def double_exp_smooth(d, extra_periods=1, alpha=0.4, beta=0.4):
2
3       # Historical period length
4       cols = len(d)
5       # Append np.nan into the demand array to cover future periods
6       d = np.append(d,[np.nan]*extra_periods)
7
8       # Creation of the level, trend and forecast arrays
9       f,a,b = np.full((3,cols+extra_periods),np.nan)
10
11      # Level & Trend initialization
12      a[0] = d[0]
13      b[0] = d[1] - d[0]
14
15      # Create all the t+1 forecast
16      for t in range(1,cols):
17          f[t] = a[t-1] + b[t-1]
```

```
18    a[t] = alpha*d[t] + (1-alpha)*(a[t-1]+b[t-1])
19    b[t] = beta*(a[t]-a[t-1]) + (1-beta)*b[t-1]
20
21    # Forecast for all extra periods
22    for t in range(cols,cols+extra_periods):
23        f[t] = a[t-1] + b[t-1]
24        a[t] = f[t]
25        b[t] = b[t-1]
26
27    df = pd.DataFrame.from_dict({'Demand':d,'Forecast':f,'Level':a, ⏎
      ↩  'Trend':b, 'Error':d-f})
28
29    return df
```

Note that we create the arrays for a, b, and f in one instruction via:

```
1  f,a,b = np.full((3,cols+extra_periods),np.nan)
```

The array generated by np.full((3,cols+extra_periods),np.nan) is actually un-packed by Python along its first axis and allocated to 3 variables (f,a,b, in our case).

Playing with Our Function

Let's use the same dummy demand time series as in Chapter 3 and call our new func-tion to forecast it.

```
1  d = [28,19,18,13,19,16,19,18,13,16,16,11,18,15,13,15,13,11,13,10,12]
2  df = double_exp_smooth(d, extra_periods=4)
```

If we compute the accuracy KPIs, we'll see that we get much *worse* results than what we obtained with our simple smoothing model (see the paragraph "Playing with Your Function", in Section 3.4).

```
1  kpi(df)
2  >> Bias: 2.64, 17.71%
3  >> MAPE: 28.14%
4  >> MAE: 4.38, 29.40%
5  >> RMSE: 6.26, 42.02%
```

In order to understand what is happening, let's visualize our forecast.

```
1  df.index.name = 'Period'
2  df[['Demand','Forecast']].plot(figsize=(8,3), title='Double Smoothing',
   ↵  ylim=(0,30), style=['-','--'])
```

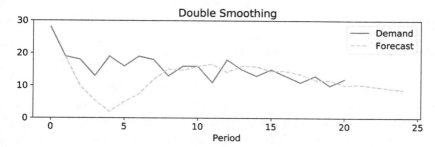

Figure 5.7: Example of double smoothing forecast.

As you can see in Figure 5.7, the model overreacts to the initial trend.

Here are some ways to improve it:

– Test other smoothing parameters for the trend and the level (we'll discuss this in Chapter 6).
– Change the initialization method for the trend (see the paragraph "Model Initialization" in Section 5.2).
– Dampen the trend (we will discuss this in Chapter 7).

6 Model Optimization

It is difficult to make predictions, especially about the future.

Author unknown

Now that we have seen a couple of forecast models, we can discuss parameter optimization. Let's recap the models we have seen so far and their different parameters,

Moving Average n (Chapter 1)
Simple Exponential Smoothing alpha (Chapter 3)
Double Exponential Smoothing alpha, beta (Chapter 5)

As we have seen in the double exponential smoothing case, a wrong parameter optimization will lead to catastrophic results. To optimize our models, we could manually search for the best parameter values. But remember, that would be against our supply chain data science best practices: we need to automate our experiments in order to scale them. Thanks to our favorite tools—Excel and Python—we will be able to automatically look for the best parameter values. The idea is to set an objective (either RMSE or MAE),[1] automatically run through different parameter values, and then select the one that gave the best results.

6.1 Excel

To optimize the parameters in Excel, we will use Excel Solver. If you have never used Excel Solver before, do not worry. It is rather easy.

Solver Activation

The first step is to activate Solver in Excel. If you have a Windows machine with Excel 2010 or a more recent version, you can activate it via the following steps,
1. Open Excel, go to `File/Options/Add-ins`.
2. Click on the `Manage` drop-down menu, select `Excel Add-ins` and click on the `Go...` button just to the right of it.
3. On the add-ins box, click on the `Solver Add-in` check box and then click the `OK` button to confirm your choice.
4. Let's now confirm that Solver is activated. In the Excel ribbon, go to the `Data` tab, there on the sub-menu `Analyze` (normally on the far right), you should see the `Solver` button.

---

1 We discussed their strengths and limitations in Chapter 2.

https://doi.org/10.1515/9783110671124-006

If you have another version of Excel or if you use a Mac, do not hesitate to Google "How to activate Excel Solver" for help.

Forecast KPI

Let's go back to the Excel sheet that we made for our double exponential smoothing implementation. We had a table that looked like Figure 6.1.

	A	B	C	D	E	F	G	H
1	Date	Demand	Forecast	Level (a)	Trend (b)		Alpha:	30%
2	1	37		37	23		Beta:	40%
3	2	60	60	60	23			
4	3	85	83	84	23			
5	4	112	107	108	24			
6	5	132	132	132	24			
7	6	145	156	153	23			
8	7	179	175	176	23			
9	8	198	199	199	23			
10	9	150	222	200	14			
11	10	132	214	190	4			
12	11		194					
13	12		198					
14	13		203					

Figure 6.1: Double exponential smoothing template in Excel.

Let's add some columns to calculate RMSE and MAE. In order to do so, we will follow a similar procedure as in Chapter 2.
1. Create two new columns between columns E and F. One named |error| (column F), and the other named Error^2 (column G).
2. Calculate the absolute error in cell F4 as =abs(C4-B4), then the squared error in cell G4 as =F4^2. We won't compute the forecast error for the first two demand observations (on row 2:3) as it simply doesn't make sense.[2]
3. Copy and paste the formula in cells F4 and G4 until the end of the table. Don't go beyond the historical period; it makes no sense to calculate the error for future forecasts, as there is no demand to compare it to!

---

[2] As discussed in the paragraph "Simple Initialization" from Section 5.2, the first forecast is always equal to the demand. Henceforth the error of the first period will be zero and should be left out of any KPI computation.

4. Finally, add two new cells for RMSE and MAE (cells J3 and J4, respectively), and
    define them as follows:

$$RMSE = \sqrt{\overline{e^2}}$$

$$J3 = SQRT(AVERAGE(G:G))$$

$$MAE = \overline{|e|}$$

$$J4 = AVERAGE(F:F)$$

with $\overline{e}$ being the average error.

You should now have a table like Figure 6.2.

	A	B	C	D	E	F	G	H	I	J
1	Date	Demand	Forecast	Level (a)	Trend (b)	|Error|	Error²		Alpha:	30,0%
2	1	37		37	23				Beta:	40,0%
3	2	60	60	60	23				RMSE	38,9
4	3	85	83	84	23	2	4		MAE	22,2
5	4	112	107	108	24	5	27			
6	5	132	132	132	24	0	0			
7	6	145	156	153	23	11	121			
8	7	179	175	176	23	4	14			
9	8	198	199	199	23	1	2			
10	9	150	222	200	14	72	5.144			
11	10	132	214	190	4	82	6.791			
12	11		219							

Figure 6.2: Double exponential smoothing template in Excel (with error).

Attention Point – Safety First

Before going further with Excel Solver, I would advise you to save your documents and close any other Excel document. Excel Solver will perform a lot
of computations and it can take some time to run—especially on big files. Do
not worry—our example will just take a couple of seconds to run, but we don't
want Excel to crash with unsaved documents in case of an error.

Solver Optimization

We can now use the solver to find the best parameters. To do so, you need to access
the Data menu in the Excel ribbon and then click on the Solver button in the Analyze
submenu (normally on the far right of the screen). You will then have a menu such as
the one shown in Figure 6.3 (except yours will be empty).

Figure 6.3: Excel Solver in Excel 2016.

You need to change four parameters:

I. Objective – In the Set Objective cell, you will need to indicate the cell you want to optimize. Typically, you want to optimize the model for the lowest MAE (cell J4) or RMSE (cell J3). Then, to tell Excel that you want to minimize the MAE/RMSE, you need to change the To: field to Min.

II. Variables – Now, we need to tell Solver what parameters it can play with. For this model, Excel can only play with alpha and beta. So we need to indicate cells $J$1 : $J$2. Do not worry about the $ signs—you can input the cell range without them, and Excel will add them automatically.

III. Constraints – We now have to give some constraints to Solver. Typically for this model, we don't want alpha and beta to be above 1 or below 0. To add these constraints, click on the Add button on the right. You will then have a dialog box, as shown in Figure 6.4. In the Cell Reference box, you will need to input the cell you want to put a constraint on. For our example, these will be the alpha and beta cells (J1 and J2). Then you indicate the constraint type ($\leq$ or $\geq$) and the constraint.

You will have to do this twice: once to indicate that alpha and beta should be below 1, and a second time to indicate that they should be above 0.

	I	J	K	L	M
1	Alpha:	30,0%			
2	Beta:	40,0%			
3	RMSE	38,9			
4	MAE	22,2			

Figure 6.4: Add a constraint.

IV. Method – You have to select the Evolutionary method in the list. The other methods won't work on this type of optimization problem (the explanation of these methods goes beyond the scope of this book).

Once this is done, click on the solve button and wait for Excel to optimize the parameter values. If everything goes fine, you will get values similar to Figure 6.5. For an optimization of MAE, Excel will choose alpha = 99.3% and beta = 58.4% (the exact values might change, as Excel Solver is using a random initialization).

	A	B	C	D	E	F	G	H	I	J
1	Date	Demand	Forecast	Level (a)	Trend (b)	|Error|	Error²		Alpha:	99,9%
2	1	37		37	23				Beta:	57,5%
3	2	60	60	60	23				RMSE	26,0
4	3	85	83	85	24				MAE	14,4
5	4	112	109	112	26					
6	5	132	138	132	22					
7	6	145	154	145	17					
8	7	179	162	179	27					
9	8	198	206	198	22					
10	9	150	220	150	18					
11	10	132	132	132	18					
12	11		114							
13										
14										

Figure 6.5: Optimization results.

6.2 Python

Creating Your Own Forecast Engine

We will implement an optimization function exp_smooth_opti(d, extra_periods= 6) that will test multiple models and return the best one. This function will be pretty handy, as it will be able to select the best model for any demand time series based on your KPI of preference and the model library we will compose throughout Part I.

We will use a simple method: we will test multiple values of alpha and beta for each model and select the one with the best outcome (based on any KPI we want). More specifically, we will loop through different alpha and beta values and save, for each model (simple smoothing and double smoothing, in this example), the parameter values, the model output, and the KPI achieved (here, MAE). At the end of all the trials, we will select the model which achieved the best KPI. In order to return the model that achieved the lowest error, we will have to use a new function: np.argmin().

Python Mastery – New Function: np.argmin()

np.argmin() returns the location of the minimum value in an array. Remember that, in Python, the index (location) of the first element in an array is 0, so that the 5th element has an index of 4.

```
1  np.argmin([1,2,3,4,-20])
2  >> 4
```

The function np.argmax() also exists. It returns the position of the highest element in an array.

```python
def exp_smooth_opti(d, extra_periods=6):

    params = []   # contains all the different parameter sets
    KPIs = []     # contains the results of each model
    dfs = []   # contains all the DataFrames returned by the
    ↪    different models

    for alpha in [0.05,0.1,0.2,0.3,0.4,0.5,0.6]:

        df = simple_exp_smooth(d,extra_periods=extra_periods,
        ↪    alpha=alpha)
        params.append(f'Simple Smoothing, alpha: {alpha}')
        dfs.append(df)
        MAE = df['Error'].abs().mean()
        KPIs.append(MAE)

        for beta in [0.05,0.1,0.2,0.3,0.4]:

            df = double_exp_smooth(d,extra_periods=extra_periods,
            ↪    alpha=alpha,beta=beta)
            params.append(f'Double Smoothing, alpha: {alpha}, beta:
            ↪    {beta}')
```

```
19              dfs.append(df)
20              MAE = df['Error'].abs().mean()
21              KPIs.append(MAE)
22
23      mini = np.argmin(KPIs)
24      print(f'Best solution found for {params[mini]} MAE of',
        ↵  round(KPIs[mini],2))
25
26      return dfs[mini]
```

You can of course update this function with the following models we will discuss in Part I.

Playing with Our Forecast Engine

First results

Let's now run our function with our dummy demand dataset.

```
1 d = [28,19,18,13,19,16,19,18,13,16,16,11,18,15,13,15,13,11,13,10,12]
2 df = exp_smooth_opti(d)
```

This is what we obtain:

```
1 >> Best solution found for Simple Smoothing, alpha: 0.4 MAE of 2.74
```

As usual, we can now plot the output. See the resulting graph in Figure 6.6.

```
1 df[['Demand','Forecast']].plot(figsize=(8,3),title='Best model found',
   ↵  ylim=(0,30),style=['-','--'])
```

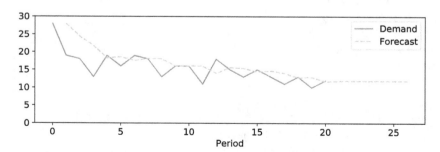

Figure 6.6: Best model selected by our optimization function.

Changing the Objective KPI

In the optimization function, we used MAE to choose the best forecasting model. You can change this by RMSE (or any other KPI) by changing those lines:

```
1  MAE = df['Error'].abs().mean()
2  KPIs.append(MAE)
```

by:

```
1  RMSE = np.sqrt((df['Error']**2).mean())
2  KPIs.append(RMSE)
```

We discussed the impact of choosing RMSE over MAE in Chapter 2. As you will include more and more models in the optimization function (we will discuss new ones in Chapters 7, 9, and 11) and test it on more complex demand datasets, you will see that different optimization KPI will result in the selection of different models.

Parameter Range

Another very important aspect of our function is the range of possible values for alpha and beta. By changing those, you will be able to force the selected model to be more (or less) reactive. A beginner mistake is to allow a very wide range (i. e., from 0 to 1) for both alpha and beta. As we will discuss in the next chapter, this might result in overfitting.

> **Pro-Tip – Acceptable Range for α and β**
>
> A reasonable range for α and β is between 0.05 and 0.6. A value above 0.6 means that the model is allocating nearly no importance to demand history, and the forecast is almost solely based on the latest observations. That would be a hint that something is wrong with the model.

7 Double Smoothing with Damped Trend

7.1 The Idea Behind Double Smoothing with Damped Trend

One of the limitations of the double smoothing model is the fact that the trend is assumed to go on forever. In 1985, Gardner and McKenzie proposed in their paper "Forecasting Trends in Time Series" to add a new layer of intelligence to the double exponential model: a **damping factor, phi (ϕ)**, that will exponentially reduce the trend over time. One could say that this new model **forgets** the trend over time.[1] Or that the model remembers only a fraction (ϕ) of the previous estimated trend.

Practically, the trend (b) will be reduced by a factor ϕ in each period. In theory, ϕ will be between 0 and 1—so that it can be seen as a % (like α and β). Nevertheless, in practice, it is often between 0.7 and 1. At the edge cases if $\phi = 0$, we are back to a simple exponential smoothing forecast; and if $\phi = 1$, the damping is removed and we deal with a double smoothing model.

7.2 Model

We will go back to the double exponential smoothing model and multiply all b_{t-1} occurrences by ϕ. Remember that $\phi \leq 1$, so that the damped trend is a muted version of the double smoothing model. We then have:

$$a_t = \alpha d_t + (1 - \alpha)(a_{t-1} + \boldsymbol{\phi} b_{t-1})$$
$$b_t = \beta(a_t - a_{t-1}) + (1 - \beta)\boldsymbol{\phi} b_{t-1}$$

The forecast for the next period would then be:

$$f_{t+1} = a_t + b_t \phi$$

Or, to be more general, for a forecast made on period t for period $t + \lambda$:

$$f_{t+\lambda} = a_t + b_t \sum_{i=1}^{\lambda} \phi^i$$

Unfortunately, this generalization is not straightforward to implement in Excel. For example, let's imagine you want to forecast period $t + 3$. You would have:

$$f_{t+3} = a_t + b_t \phi + b_t \phi^2 + b_t \phi^3$$

Note that if $\phi = 1$, then we are back to a normal double smoothing model. Setting $\phi = 1$ basically means that the model won't *forget* the trend over time.

---

[1] See Gardner and Mckenzie (1985).

https://doi.org/10.1515/9783110671124-007

7.3 Insights

If we go back to our example from Chapter 5, we obtain the graph shown in Figure 7.1.

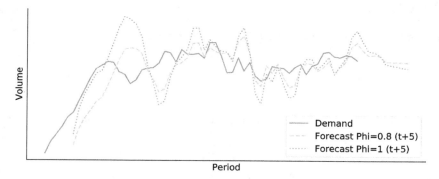

Figure 7.1: Forecast with damped trend.

We have made two forecasts (both for $t + 5$): one with a damping factor of 0.8 and one without damping (i. e., $\phi = 1$). You can observe two things:

– The damping factor smooths extreme forecasts. This is quite helpful in many cases, but results in a poor forecast when the demand is growing with a steady trend (see the left part of the graph).
– The damping factor drastically reduces the impact of the trend for the future forecast. In the end, the future forecast is what we are the most interested in, so this aspect is the most important. With the damped trend, the model will forget the trend and the forecast will remain at a stable level. Without damping, the model risks being over-optimistic or pessimistic, concerning the trend. See in the example how the forecast made without damping is assuming that the (negative) trend goes on forever. If pushed further away in the future, this forecast will eventually predict negative demand.

Limitations

Thanks to the damping factor (ϕ), we solved the main limitation of the vanilla double smoothing model: the trend doesn't go on forever anymore. This damping factor might at first glance seem like a simple idea, but it actually allows us to be much more accurate for mid- and long-term forecasts.

Nevertheless, we still miss the ability for our model to recognize a seasonal pattern and apply it in the future. Many supply chains do face seasonality in one way or another, so we need our forecast models to be smart enough to fit these patterns. In order to do so, we will add a third layer of exponential smoothing in the following chapters.

7.4 Do It Yourself

Let's now implement this damped trend in Excel and Python.

Excel

Let's once again go back to our Excel from the double exponential smoothing, as in Figure 7.2.

	A	B	C	D	E	F	G	H
1	Date	Demand	Forecast	Level (a)	Trend (b)		Alpha:	30%
2	1	37		37	23		Beta:	40%
3	2	60	60	60	23			
4	3	85	83	84	23			
5	4	112	107	108	24			
6	5	132	132	132	24			
7	6	145	156	153	23			
8	7	179	175	176	23			
9	8	198	199	199	23			
10	9	150	222	200	14			
11	10	132	214	190	4			
12	11		194					
13	12		198					
14	13		203					

Figure 7.2: Double exponential smoothing (complete) template in Excel.

From here, you will need to:
1. Add a new cell for the ϕ factor. We will use cell H3 (just below alpha and beta). Let's start with a value of 80% for ϕ.
2. Update the level formula in cell D3:

$$a_t = \alpha d_t + (1 - \alpha)(a_{t-1} + \boldsymbol{\phi} b_{t-1})$$
$$D3 = \$H\$1*B3+(1-\$H\$1)*(D2+\boldsymbol{\$H\$3}*E2)$$

You only need to multiply E2 by $H$3 to update this formula. Once done, simply copy and paste this formula until you reach the end of the table.
3. Update the trend formula in E3 so that:

$$b_t = \beta(a_t - a_{t-1}) + (1 - \beta)\boldsymbol{\phi} b_{t-1}$$
$$E3 = \$H\$2*(D3-D2)+(1-\$H\$2)*\boldsymbol{\$H\$3}*E2$$

As for the level formula, you only need to add $H$3 on the right. Once done, you can copy and paste it until the end of the table.

4. Let's now update the forecast formula in cell C2. We should now have:

$$C2 = D2+E2*\$H\$3$$

$$f_{t+1} = a_t + b_t \phi$$

Again, you will need to copy and paste this formula until the end of the table.

Future Forecast

The easiest way to get a forecast on a longer horizon with a damped trend in Excel is to update the level and the trend for all the future periods. Actually, only the formula for the level needs to change. As of cell D12, change it by:

$$a_{t+1} = a_t + \phi b_t$$

$$C12 = D11+E11*\$H\$3$$

The formula for the trend and the forecast can stay as it is.
You should now have a table as in Figure 7.3.

	A	B	C	D	E	F	G	H
1	Date	Demand	Forecast	Level (a)	Trend (b)		Alpha:	30%
2	1	37		37	23		Beta:	40%
3	2	60	55	57	19		Phi:	80%
4	3	85	72	76	17			
5	4	112	89	96	16			
6	5	132	109	116	16			
7	6	145	128	133	15			
8	7	179	145	155	16			
9	8	198	168	177	16			
10	9	150	190	178	8			
11	10	132	184	169	0			
12	11		169	169	0			
13	12		169	169	0			
14	13		169	169	0			

Figure 7.3: Damped double smoothing template in Excel.

Python

Damped Double Smoothing Function

Just like the double exponential smoothing function, we define a new function double_exp_smooth_damped() that takes a time series d as an input and returns a DataFrame containing the historical demand, the forecast, the level, the trend, and the error. The function can also take parameters alpha and beta as optional inputs.

```
1  def double_exp_smooth_damped(d, extra_periods=1, alpha=0.4, beta=0
   ↪   .4, phi=0.9):
2
3      cols = len(d) # Historical period length
4      d = np.append(d,[np.nan]*extra_periods) # Append np.nan into
   ↪      the demand array to cover future periods
5
6      # Creation of the level, trend, and forecast arrays
7      f,a,b = np.full((3,cols+extra_periods),np.nan)
8
9      # Level & Trend initialization
10     a[0] = d[0]
11     b[0] = d[1] - d[0]z
12
13     # Create all the t+1 forecast
14     for t in range(1,cols):
15         f[t] = a[t-1] + phi*b[t-1]
16         a[t] = alpha*d[t] + (1-alpha)*(a[t-1]+phi*b[t-1])
17         b[t] = beta*(a[t]-a[t-1]) + (1-beta)*phi*b[t-1]
18
19     # Forecast for all extra periods
20     for t in range(cols,cols+extra_periods):
21         f[t] = a[t-1] + phi*b[t-1]
22         a[t] = f[t]
23         b[t] = phi*b[t-1]
24
25     df = pd.DataFrame.from_dict({'Demand':d,'Forecast':f,'Level':a,
   ↪      'Trend':b, 'Error':d-f})
26
27     return df
```

Playing with Our Function

Let's test our new function on the same dummy demand time series as for the previous models. We'll directly use our kpi(df) function from Section 2.5.

```
1  d = [28,19,18,13,19,16,19,18,13,16,16,11,18,15,13,15,13,11,13,10,12]
2  df = double_exp_smooth_damped(d, extra_periods=4)
3  kpi(df)
4  >> Bias: 1.64, 11.02%
5  >> MAPE: 22.75%
```

```
6  >> MAE:  3.48,  23.38%
7  >> RMSE:  4.72,  31.68%
```

We already get some better results than with the traditional double smoothing. You can of course optimize the smoothing parameters (α, β and ϕ) further, thanks to the method described in Chapter 6. See the resulting graph in Figure 7.4.

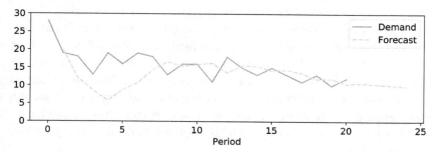

Figure 7.4: Damped double smoothing.

8 Overfitting

With four parameters, I can fit an elephant, and with five, I can make him wiggle his trunk.

John Von Neumann

In Chapter 4, we saw the issue of underfitting a dataset. This happens when a model is not able to learn the patterns present in the training dataset. As we saw, underfitting is most likely due to the model not being smart enough to understand the patterns in the training dataset. This could be solved by using a more complex model.

On the other end of the spectrum, we have the risk for a model to **overfit** a dataset. If a model overfits the data, it means that it has recognized (or learned) patterns from the noise (i. e., randomness) of the training set. As it has learned patterns from the noise, it will reapply these patterns in the future on new data. **This will create an issue as the model will show (very) good results on the training dataset but will fail to make good predictions on the test set**. In a forecasting model, that means that your model will show good accuracy on historical demand but will fail to deliver as good results on future demand.

In other words, overfitting means that you learned patterns that worked **by chance** on the training set. And as these patterns most likely won't occur again on future data, you will make wrong predictions.

Overfitting is the number one enemy of many data scientists for another reason. Data scientists are always looking to make the best models with the highest accuracy. When a model achieves (very) good accuracy, it is always tempting to think that it is simply excellent and call it a day. But a careful analysis will reveal that the model is just overfitting the data. Overfitting can be seen as a mirage: you are tempted to think that there is an oasis in the middle of the desert, but actually, it is just sand reflecting the sky. As we learn more complex models, underfitting will become less of an issue, and overfitting will become the biggest risk. This risk will be especially present with machine learning, as we will see in Part II. Therefore, we will have to use more complex techniques to prevent our models from overfitting our datasets. Our battle against overfitting will reach a peak in Chapters 18 and 24, when we discuss feature optimization.

Let's go over some examples of overfitting and the tools to avoid it.

8.1 Examples

Supply Chain Forecasting

Let's imagine that we have observed the demand of a new product over 20 periods (as shown in Figure 8.1), and now we want to use our optimization algorithm from Chapter 6 to make a forecast.

https://doi.org/10.1515/9783110671124-008

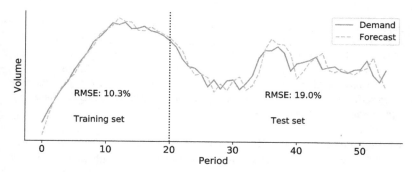

Figure 8.1: Overfitting.

As you can see, based on the optimization until period 20, the algorithm advises us a specific parameter set ($\alpha = 0.7, \beta = 1$, and $\phi = 0.9$) and shows an error of 10%. Can we assume that this accuracy can be obtained for future predictions as well? No.

Unfortunately, around period 30, we get a decrease in accuracy as, the forecast is overreacting to changes in the trend. In our example, the RMSE is nearly doubled from period 20 and onward compared to periods 0 to 20. This is overfitting.

Technically, we would say that the accuracy obtained on the *training* set (periods 0 to 20) is not representative of the one obtained on the *test* set (period 20 and onward).

> **Pro-Tip**
>
> In the case above, the algorithm advised a beta smoothing factor of 1. This is likely too much, as it means that the algorithm entirely updates the trend after each period. You should avoid having alpha and beta higher than 0.6.

Business World

If you torture the data long enough, it will confess to anything.

Ronald Coase[1]

In his book *The Signal and the Noise*, Nate Silver gives a perfect example of overfitting in stock market predictions.[2]

A once-famous "leading indicator" of economic performance, for instance, was the winner of the Super Bowl. From Super Bowl I in 1967 through Super Bowl XXXI in 1997, the stock market gained

---

1 Ronald Coase (1910–2013), Professor of Economics at the University of Chicago Law School, Nobel Memorial Prize in Economic Sciences in 1991.
2 See Silver (2015). Nate Silver is also the author of the blog fivethirtyeight.com

an average of 14 percent for the rest of the year when a team from the original National Football League (NFL) won the game. But it fell by almost 10 percent when a team from the original American Football League (AFL) won instead. Through 1997, this indicator had correctly "predicted" the direction of the stock market in twenty-eight of thirty-one years. A standard test of statistical significance, if taken literally, would have implied that there was only about a 1-in-4,700,000 possibility that the relationship had emerged from chance alone. Whereas of course, there was no relationship at all between the stock market and sports events.

The same effect happens regularly with political elections. One can then often hear in the press that "Someone tested 100+ variables to predict who would win, and they found a perfect model for the last ten elections." That is a perfect example of overfitting. If you look at 100 variables, you will—for sure—find that at least one of them matches whatever output you want to predict.

The website tylervigen.com made a specialty of finding these **random** strange relationships where you find a perfect statistical match. You can see in Figure 8.2 the correlation between movies with Nicolas Cage and people who drowned in pools.

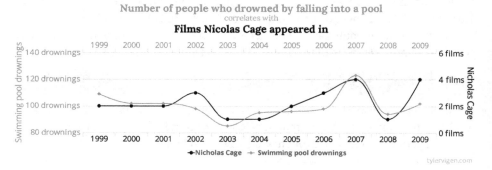

Figure 8.2: Example of spurious correlations from tylervigen.com

8.2 Causes and Solutions

So how do we protect ourselves from this overfitting trap?

Use fewer explanatory variables (or a simpler model). The more explanatory variables the model has, the more possibilities it will have to recognize patterns in the noise. This will become a bigger problem with machine learning models—as we will see in Part II—for which we will have to use many specific techniques to fight overfitting. But it can also happen with exponential smoothing models. We will see two seasonal models in Chapters 9 and 11 that might recognize (and extrapolate) seasonality where there is none. Do not use a too complex model to fit a simple demand pattern.

Use more data. More data will reduce the probability of seeing fake patterns.

Don't fit on the test set. You should never use your test set to select a model or train your model. It should only be used to get a final idea of the accuracy you can expect.

Validate on the test set. You should only validate a model if it performs against the test set. A model that only performs well on a training dataset can't be trusted. Don't blindly assume that the results you obtained on the training set will replicate on unseen data.

9 Triple Exponential Smoothing

9.1 The Idea Behind Triple Exponential Smoothing

With the first two exponential smoothing models we saw, we learned how to identify the level and the trend of a time series and used these pieces of information to populate our forecast. After that, we added an extra layer of intelligence to the trend by allowing the model to partially forget it over time.

Unfortunately, the simple and double exponential smoothing models do not recognize seasonal patterns and therefore cannot extrapolate any seasonal behavior in the future. Seasonal products—with high and low seasons—are common for many supply chains across the globe, as many different factors can cause seasonality. This limitation is thus a real problem for our model.

In order for our model to learn a seasonal pattern, we will add a third layer of exponential smoothing. The idea is that the model will learn **multiplicative seasonal factors** that will be applied to each period inside a full seasonal cycle. As for the trend (β) and the level (α), the seasonal factors will be learned via an exponential weighting method with a new specific learning rate: **gamma (γ)**.

Multiplicative seasonal factors mean, for example, that the model will know that the demand is increased by 20% in January (compared to the yearly average) but reduced by 30% in February.

We will discuss the case of additive seasonality in Chapter 11.

9.2 Model

The main idea is that the forecast is now composed of the level (a) plus the (damped) trend (b) **multiplied by** the seasonal factor (s).

$$\text{Forecast} = (\text{Level} + \text{Trend})\,\text{Season}$$
$$f_{t+1} = (a_t \quad + \phi b_t \quad)\,s_{t+1-p}$$

Pay attention to the fact that, we need to use the seasonal factors that were calculated during the previous season: s_{t-p}, where p (for periodicity) is the season length.[1] The different seasonal factors (s) can be seen as **percentages** to be applied to the level in order to obtain the forecast. For example, for a monthly forecast, the statement, "We sell 20% more in January" would be translated as $s_{\text{january}} = 120\%$.

---

[1] Typically, the periodicity will be 12 for yearly cycles.

https://doi.org/10.1515/9783110671124-009

Component Updates

We calculate the different demand components as such:

$$a_t = \alpha \, \frac{d_t}{s_{t-p}} + (1 - \alpha)(a_{t-1} + \phi b_{t-1})$$

$$b_t = \beta(a_t - a_{t-1}) + (1 - \beta)\phi b_{t-1}$$

$$s_t = \gamma \, \frac{d_t}{a_t} + (1 - \gamma)s_{t-p}$$

Level and Trend
Let's first discuss the level (a) and the trend (b). They are both deseasonalized. Note how the level a is updated based on the most recent demand observation d_t divided by the seasonality s_{t-p}. As the trend is the difference between two consecutive levels, it is also deseasonalized.

Seasonal Factors
The seasonal factor s_t is estimated based on its most recent observation (the demand divided by the level) and its previous estimation (just like a and b). Just like any other smoothing parameter, γ will also determine how much weight is given to the most recent observation compared to the previous estimation. And just like α and β, γ is also theoretically between 0 and 1 (so that it can be seen as a percentage).

> **Pro-Tip – Acceptable Range for γ**
>
> In practice, γ should be rather low (< 0.3). Business-wise, it is rather excep-
> tional to assume that the seasonality could drastically change from one year
> to another. With a high γ, you leave more room for overfitting.

Seasonal Factors Scaling
The seasonal factors determine how the forecast is **allocated** within an entire seasonal cycle. They should not impact the total demand of a full seasonal cycle, as, on average, we will allocate 100% to each period. You can interpret this by saying that if we sell *on average* 20% more than usual in January, we must be selling *on average* 20% less than usual during the rest of the year.

Mathematically, the sum of the seasonal factors over a full seasonal cycle should be p (the number of periods inside a seasonal cycle).

$$\sum_{\text{cycle}} s = p$$

So that, on average, the seasonal factor of each period will be 1 (or 100%, if you interpret them as percentages):

$$\bar{s} = 1 = \frac{1}{p} \sum_{\text{cycle}} s$$

where $\bar{s}$ is seasonal factors average.

This implies that—over a full seasonal cycle—the level is on the same scale as the demand and the forecast, as it is multiplied on average by 1.[2]

Future Forecast

We can generalize the forecast for period $t + 1$ to a forecast for period $t + \lambda$

$$f_{t+\lambda} = \left(a_t + \sum_{i=1}^{\lambda} \phi^i b_t \right) s_{t+\lambda-p}$$

If we don't use a damping factor, we have this simpler equation:

$$f_{t+\lambda} = (a_t + \lambda b_t) s_{t+\lambda-p}$$

Component Initialization

Level and Trend

Remember, a simple initialization technique for the double smoothing model was:

$$a_0 = d_0$$
$$b_0 = d_1 - d_0$$

As the demand is now seasonal, we cannot initialize the level and the trend directly based on first demand observations anymore. We have to deseasonalize the demand first. We then have:

$$a_0 = \frac{d_0}{s_0}$$

$$b_0 = \frac{d_1}{s_1} - \frac{d_0}{s_0}$$

---

2 In practice—in order to simplify the seasonal factors update procedure—you can allow the seasonal factors to slightly drift away from p over time.

Seasonal Factors

There are some discussions in the literature on how to initialize the seasonal factors for exponential smoothing algorithms.[3] Let's just use a simple method here: we will initialize the seasonal factors based on the historical demand.

We will do this in multiple steps.

1. **Compute the historical season averages.**

    You can see in Table 9.1 an example of quarterly seasonal demand over 5 years. We have computed the average demand per quarter on the last column.

Table 9.1: Example of quarterly seasonal demand.

	Y1	Y2	Y3	Y4	Y5	Mean
Q1	14	18	16	18	17	16.6
Q2	10	8	9	11	9	9.4
Q3	6	4	5	4	5	4.8
Q4	2	1	3	2	1	1.8

Unfortunately, we cannot use these historical season averages as seasonal factors for our model, as **they are not scaled**. Remember: the sum of the seasonal factors should be equal to p (4 in our example) so that we can **interpret them as percentages.**

2. **Scale the historical season averages.**

    We will scale our historical averages so that their sum will be equal to 4. In order to do this, we will **divide** our historical season averages by their own mean (8.15), as shown in Table 9.2.

Table 9.2: Seasonal factors.

	Y1	Y2	Y3	Y4	Y5	Mean	Factors
Q1	14	18	16	18	17	16.6	2.04
Q2	10	8	9	11	9	9.4	1.15
Q3	6	4	5	4	5	4.8	0.59
Q4	2	1	3	2	1	1.8	0.22
Mean						8.15	1.00

We now obtain a scaled set of seasonal factors: 2.04, 1.15, 0.59, and 0.22. You can interpret them as saying, "We sell 104% extra units in Q1, and we sell +15% in Q2 but −41% in Q3 and −78% in Q4."

---

3 See Hyndman and Athanasopoulos (2018).

As you can see, these seasonal factors are now properly scaled, as their sum is equal to the periodicity (4) and their average is 1. This is perfect, as it means that the level (a) will be, on average, multiplied by 1 to obtain a forecast, so that they are both on the same scale.

> **Pro-Tip**
>
> Instead of taking the mean of the historical seasonal values, you can try to take the median. As discussed in Chapter 2, using the median instead of the mean will help you to smooth out historical outliers.

Other Methods

As supply chain scientists, we love to experiment, so you could also try your own methods. Here are some ideas:

- Initialize the seasonal factors simply as the first historical season.
- Use common seasonal factors for similar products (that could help against overfitting).
- Apply any seasonal factors that you think are correct based on your business experience.
- In Excel, you can allow Solver to tweak the initial seasonal factors directly to optimize them. Pay attention to the fact that by doing so, you face the risk of overfitting.

Strictly speaking, there is no better method. In order to find the most appropriate one for your dataset, you will have to use a scientific approach: test different methods and see which one gives the best result. In any case, do not forget to scale the seasonal factors so that their sum is equal to p, so that they can be interpreted as percentages.

> **Going Further**
>
> Note that if you have an important trend in the historical demand, you might face an issue and you should potentially remove the trend in your data before computing the seasonal factors.

9.3 Insights

First Example

To see how this works in practice, you can observe in Figure 9.1 an example based on our dummy data:

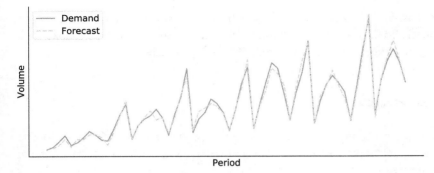

Figure 9.1: Example for seasonal forecast.

We have used $\alpha = 0.8$, $\beta = 0.1$, and $\gamma = 0.4$. We see on this dummy dataset how close the forecast at $t + 1$ is to the demand, even though the demand is drastically changing over time.

Let's plot in Figure 9.2 the seasonal factors to see how they change over time.

Actually, it seems that seasonal factors do not change so much over time. Let's see in Figure 9.3 how the trend evolves.

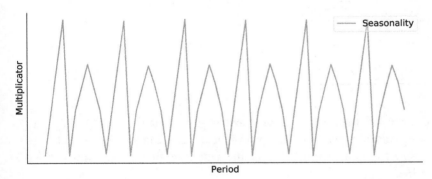

Figure 9.2: Seasonal factors.

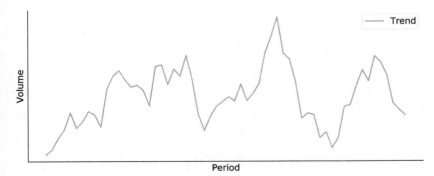

Figure 9.3: Trend.

The model behaves as expected: the seasonality doesn't vary much over time. Instead, it is the level and the trend that evolve more over time. This is perfect, as it makes little sense to expect the seasonality of a product to change much over time.

Intermittent Products

One of the issues of a multiplicative seasonality appears when you deal with low demand: the model might overreact to level changes if the level is too close to 0. Remember that the seasonality is defined as such:

$$s_t = \gamma \frac{d_t}{a_t} + (1 - \gamma)s_{t-p}$$

A small absolute demand variation (from one piece to five pieces) can result in a huge difference of seasonality (100% to 500%). Let's take an example as shown in Table 9.3.

Table 9.3: Quarterly demand.

	Y1	Y2	Y3	Y4	Y5	Y6
Q1	14	18	16	18	17	?
Q2	10	8	9	11	9	?
Q3	6	4	5	4	5	?
Q4	2	1	3	2	1	?

Most likely, you saw that in Q1, we could expect something between 16 and 18, then a demand around 10 pieces for Q2, 5 pieces for Q3, and 2 pieces for Q4. Let's see in Figure 9.4 how our model handles this (using a model with $\alpha = 0.4$, $\beta = 0.4$, $\phi = 0.9$, and $\gamma = 0.3$).

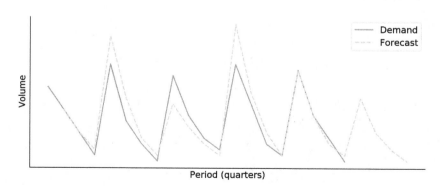

Figure 9.4: Quarterly forecast.

We see that even though the demand is very stable, the forecast seems too low for Y6. Actually, if you look at the seasonal factors, they are pretty stable at around $[2.0, 1.2, 0.6, 0.2]$. The error lies in how the level is massively impacted by Q4 (see periods 15–20 in Figure 9.5).

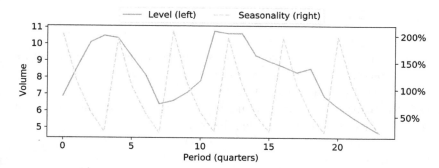

Figure 9.5: Level and seasonality evolution.

We will come back to this example later (in Chapter 11) with our next model: an additive seasonality.

Undefined Models
A worst case can even happen if any of the initial seasonal parameters is estimated to be 0. Remember that the level estimation is made by dividing the current demand observation by a seasonal factor. If any of the seasonal factors is 0, this level estimation will fail, as the model will have to do a division by 0.

Conclusion
This new triple exponential smoothing is a fantastic model, as we can now deal with seasonal products. Unfortunately, as discussed, the multiplicative part of the model might result in (mathematical) errors if the demand level or the seasonality factors are too close to 0. This means that this model is unfortunately not suited for all products. To solve this, we will next work on a model with an additive seasonality.

9.4 Do It Yourself

Excel

As an Excel model is more complicated for a triple exponential smoothing, we will start from scratch on a simple example for a quarterly demand. We won't implement a

Table 9.4: Quarterly demand.

	Y1	Y2	Y3	Y4	Y5
Q1	14	18	16	18	17
Q2	10	8	9	11	9
Q3	6	4	5	4	5
Q4	2	1	3	2	1

damped trend to focus on the seasonal part. We will work on the demand dataset we used in the previous examples (as shown in Table 9.4).

Let's open a new Excel sheet to create our model.

1. **Table Preparation**   Let's start creating the table layout for our data, as shown in Figure 9.6. We will use the following columns:

Date in column A
Demand in column B
Forecast in column C
Level in column D
Trend in column E
Season in column F

	A	B	C	D	E	F	G	H	I
1	Date	Demand	Forecast	Level (a)	Trend (b)	Season (s)		Alpha:	80%
2	1	14						Beta:	10%
3	2	10		First Cycle				Gamma:	40%
4	3	6							
5	4	2							
6	5	18							
7	6	8							
8	7	4							
9	8	1							
10	9	16							
11	10	9							
12	11	5							
13	12	3		Historical Periods					
14	13	18							
15	14	11							
16	15	4							
17	16	2							
18	17	17							
19	18	9							
20	19	5							
21	20	1							
22	21								
23	22			Future Forecast					
24	23								
25	24								

Figure 9.6: Triple smoothing template in Excel.

Next to these, let's add the cells with our different parameters:

Alpha in cell I1

Beta in cell I2

Gamma in cell I3

with their respective names in column H.

2. **Model Initialization**   Once this is done, we need to initialize our model. We have to do this for the level, the trend, and the seasonality. Let's keep it simple for this example.

Seasonality For the first year, it is initialized as [2.0; 1.2; 0.6; 0.2] in cells F2:F5 (as we computed in Section 9.2)

Level We initialize the level on $t = 1$ as:

$$D2 = B2/F2$$

$$a_{t=1} = \frac{d_{t=1}}{s_{t=1}}$$

Trend We initialize the trend on $t = 1$ as:

$$E2 = B3/F3-B2/F2$$

$$b_{t=1} = \frac{d_{t=2}}{s_{t=2}} - \frac{d_{t=1}}{s_{t=1}}$$

3. **First Cycle** We can now start to compute our forecast during the first year (i. e., the first seasonal cycle).

Level Usually, the level is computed as:

$$a_t = \alpha \frac{d_t}{s_{t-p}} + (1 - \alpha)(a_{t-1} + b_{t-1})$$

But we will have to use s_t instead of s_{t-p} for the first seasonal cycle. We have then:

$$a_t = \alpha \frac{d_t}{s_t} + (1 - \alpha)(a_{t-1} + b_{t-1})$$

$$D3 = \$I\$1*B3/F3+(1-\$I\$1)*(D2+E2)$$

You can then drag this formula until cell D5 (which is the end of the first seasonal cycle).

Trend As of cell E3, we use the same formula as for the double smoothing model:

$$b_t = \beta(a_t - a_{t-1}) + (1 - \beta)b_{t-1}$$

$$E3 = \$I\$2*(D3-D2)+(1-\$I\$2)*E2$$

You can copy and paste this until you reach the end of the table—even for future forecast—as it is independent from the seasonal factors.

Forecast Just as for the level, the forecast is usually computed as:

$$f_t = (a_{t-1} + b_{t-1})s_{t-p}$$

But for the first cycle, we will define it based on the first seasonal cycle. In cell C3, you can type:

$$C3 = (D2+E2)*F3$$
$$f_t = (a_{t-1} + b_{t-1})s_t$$

and copy and paste it until cell C5.

4. **Historical Cycles** We can now populate the forecast from the second year until the end of the historical period.

Level As of the 5th quarter, we should use the previous-year seasonal factors.

$$D6 = \$I\$1*B6/F2+(1-\$I\$1)*(D5+E5)$$
$$a_t = \alpha\frac{d_t}{s_{t-p}} + (1-\alpha)(a_{t-1} + b_{t-1})$$

You can then copy and paste it until the end of the historical period.

Trend We use the same formula as from cell E3.

Season We need to update the seasonal factors based on:

$$F6 = \$I\$3*(B6/D6)+(1-\$I\$3)*F2$$
$$s_t = \gamma\frac{d_t}{a_t} + (1-\gamma)s_{t-p}$$

and copy and paste it until the end of the table.

Forecast We can now compute the forecast as:

$$f_t = (a_{t-1} + b_{t-1})s_{t-p}$$
$$C6 = (D5+E5)*F2$$

Just as for the trend and the season, this formula will hold even for future forecasts, so you can drag it until the end of the table.

5. **Future Cycles** We can now populate the future forecast that will be based on the latest seasonality factors.

Level We will update the level at each new period by the trend. You can type =D21+E21 in cell D22.

Trend We use the same formula as from cell E3.

Season We will simply copy the latest seasonal factors and extrapolate them. You can simply input =F18 in cell F22.

Forecast We use the same formula as from cell C6.

Once this is done, you can copy and paste the cells D22 : F22 downwards to get your future forecast!

You should now obtain a similar table as in Figure 9.7.

	A	B	C	D	E	F	G	H	I
1	Date	Demand	Forecast	Level (a)	Trend (b)	Season (s)		Alpha:	80%
2	1	14		7,0	1,3	200%		Beta:	10%
3	2	10	10	8,3	1,3	120%		Gamma:	40%
4	3	6	6	9,9	1,4	60%			
5	4	2	2	10,3	1,3	20%			
6	5	18	23	9,5	1,1	196%			
7	6	8	13	7,4	0,7	115%			
8	7	4	5	7,0	0,6	59%			
9	8	1	2	5,5	0,4	19%			
10	9	16	12	7,7	0,6	200%			
11	10	9	10	7,9	0,6	114%			
12	11	5	5	8,5	0,6	59%			
13	12	3	2	14,3	1,1	20%			
14	13	18	31	10,3	0,6	190%			
15	14	11	12	9,9	0,5	113%			
16	15	4	6	7,5	0,2	57%			
17	16	2	2	9,6	0,4	20%			
18	17	17	19	9,1	0,3	189%			
19	18	9	11	8,2	0,2	112%			
20	19	5	5	8,7	0,2	57%			
21	20	1	2	5,7	- 0,1	19%			
22	21		11	5,6	- 0,1	189%			
23	22		6	5,5	- 0,1	112%			
24	23		3	5,4	- 0,1	57%			
25	24		1	5,3	- 0,1	19%			

Figure 9.7: Triple smoothing in Excel.

As you can see, we are starting to reach a point where Excel does not seem to be the most appropriate tool anymore. Our Python functions will be much easier to implement, correct, and update.

Python

Seasonal Factors Initialization
First, let's create a function to compute our (multiplicative) seasonal factors. In the future, if you want to play with the initialization method (maybe based on the different ideas in Section 9.2), this will make your life easier.

```
1  def seasonal_factors_mul(s,d,slen,cols):
2      for i in range(slen):
3          s[i] = np.mean(d[i:cols:slen]) # Season average
4      s /= np.mean(s[:slen]) # Scale all season factors (sum of ⌐
       ↪  factors = slen)
5      return s
```

Python Mastery – Indexing with Step-size

You can index an array (or a list) using a step-size using the following notation: array[start:stop:step-size] (excluding the stop index).

```
1  array = [1,2,3,4,5,6,7,8,9,10]
2  print(array[2:8:3])
3  >> [3, 6]
```

Indeed, array[2] is 3, array[5] is 6 and array[8] is not printed as the stop index is not excluded.

Triple Smoothing

As usual, we will create a function triple_exp_smooth_mul() that will take a time series d and the season length slen as inputs. The function will also take as optional inputs the different smoothing parameters (alpha, beta, gamma and phi) and extra_periods (the number of extra periods we want to forecast in the future). The function will return a pandas DataFrame that contains the demand, forecast, level, trend, seasonal factors, and the error.

```
1  def triple_exp_smooth_mul(d, slen=12, extra_periods=1, alpha=0.4, ⌐
   ↪  beta=0.4, phi=0.9, gamma=0.3):
2
3      cols = len(d) # Historical pteriod length
4      d = np.append(d,[np.nan]*extra_periods) # Append np.nan into ⌐
       ↪  the demand array to cover future periods
5
6      # components initialization
7      f,a,b,s = np.full((4,cols+extra_periods),np.nan)
8      s = seasonal_factors_mul(s,d,slen,cols)
9
```

```
10      # Level & Trend initialization
11      a[0] = d[0]/s[0]
12      b[0] = d[1]/s[1] - d[0]/s[0]
13
14      # Create the forecast for the first season
15      for t in range(1,slen):
16          f[t] = (a[t-1] + phi*b[t-1])*s[t]
17          a[t] = alpha*d[t]/s[t] + (1-alpha)*(a[t-1]+phi*b[t-1])
18          b[t] = beta*(a[t]-a[t-1]) + (1-beta)*phi*b[t-1]
19
20      # Create all the t+1 forecast
21      for t in range(slen,cols):
22          f[t] = (a[t-1] + phi*b[t-1])*s[t-slen]
23          a[t] = alpha*d[t]/s[t-slen] + (1-alpha)*(a[t-1]+phi*b[t-1])
24          b[t] = beta*(a[t]-a[t-1]) + (1-beta)*phi*b[t-1]
25          s[t] = gamma*d[t]/a[t] + (1-gamma)*s[t-slen]
26
27      # Forecast for all extra periods
28      for t in range(cols,cols+extra_periods):
29          f[t] = (a[t-1] + phi*b[t-1])*s[t-slen]
30          a[t] = f[t]/s[t-slen]
31          b[t] = phi*b[t-1]
32          s[t] = s[t-slen]
33
34      df = pd.DataFrame.from_dict({'Demand':d,'Forecast':f,'Level':a,
        ↪  'Trend':b, 'Season':s,'Error':d-f})
35
36      return df
```

You can then call this function to obtain a DataFrame with all the different components.

```
1  d = [14,10,6,2,18,8,4,1,16,9,5,3,18,11,4,2,17,9,5,1]
2  df = triple_exp_smooth_mul(d, slen=12, extra_periods=4, alpha=0.3,
   ↪  beta=0.2, phi=0.9, gamma=0.2)
```

If you use our kpi(df) function from Section 2.5, this is what you should obtain:

```
1  kpi(df)
2  >> Bias: -0.19, -2.39%
3  >> MAPE: 9.30%
```

```
4  >> MAE:  0.64,  8.12%
5  >> RMSE:  0.92,  11.74%
```

Visualization

We can use the method `.plot()` on our DataFrame to plot our time series and its components. Nevertheless, such a graph would be messy due to the number of components and their different scales (see Figure 9.8).

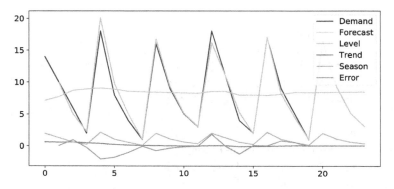

Figure 9.8: Messy graph of our time series.

To overcome this, we have two solutions: we can plot our time series and its components, as follows:

– with different y-axes/scales, thanks to the following command (see Figure 9.9):

```
1  df[['Level','Trend','Season']].plot(secondary_y=['Season'])
```

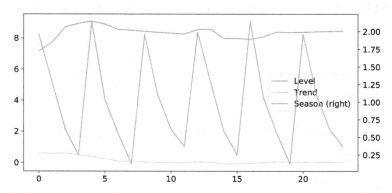

Figure 9.9: Plot with two axes.

- with one subplot per component, thanks to the following command (see Figure 9.10):

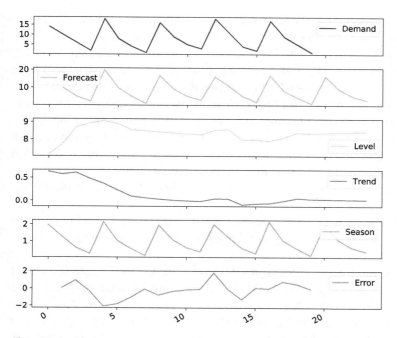

Figure 9.10: Subplots.

10 Outliers

I shall not today attempt further to define this kind of material ... and perhaps I could never succeed in intelligibly doing so. But I know it when I see it.

Potter Stewart

In 1964, Potter Stewart was a United States Supreme Court Justice. He was discussing not outliers, but whether the movie *The Lovers* was obscene or not.

As you work on forecasts with the different models we saw—and the following models we will see later—you will notice that your dataset has outliers. And even though *I know it when I see it* might be the only practical definition, these outliers pose a real threat to supply chains. These high (or low) points will result in overreactions in your forecast or your safety stocks, ultimately resulting in (at best) manual corrections or (at worst) dead stocks, losses, and a nasty bullwhip effect. Actually, when you look at blogs, books, articles, or software on forecasting, the question of outlier detection is often eluded. This is a pity. **Outlier detection is serious business.**

These outliers pop out all the time in modern supply chains. They are mostly due to two main reasons:

Mistakes and Errors These are obvious outliers. If you spot such kind of errors or encoding mistakes, it calls for process improvement to prevent these from happening again.

Exceptional Demand Even though some demand observations are real, it does not mean they are not *exceptional* and shouldn't be cleaned or smoothed. This kind of exceptional sales is actually not so uncommon in supply chains. Think about promotions, marketing, strange customer behaviors, or destocking. Typically, you might not want to take into account for your forecast the exceptional −80% sales you did last year to get rid of an old, nearly obsolete inventory.

If you can spot outliers and smooth them out, you will make a better forecast. I have seen numerous examples where the forecast error was reduced by a couple of percentages, thanks to outlier cleaning. Flagging outliers manually is a time-intensive, error-prone, and un rewarding process; few demand planners will take the time necessary to review those. Therefore, the bigger the dataset, the more important it is to *automate* this detection and cleaning. As data scientists, we automate tasks to scale our processes. Let's see how we can do this for outliers detection.

In the following pages, we will discuss three and a half ideas to spot these outliers and put them back to a reasonable level.

10.1 Idea #1 – Winsorization

As we said, an outlier is an exceptionally high or low value. Based on this simple definition, a first idea to detect outliers would be to simply cut down the top x highest

https://doi.org/10.1515/9783110671124-010

Table 10.1: Simple demand history.

Month	M1	M2	M3	M4	M5	M6	M7	M8	M9	M10	M11	M12
Y1	17	12	7	5	4	9	13	14	11	11	10	12
Y2	6	11	14	15	8	12	14	14	11	10	7	15
Y3	9	8	5	12	10	8	9	10	8	16	8	10

Table 10.2: Simple demand history with an outlier (Y2 M7).

Month	M1	M2	M3	M4	M5	M6	M7	M8	M9	M10	M11	M12
Y1	17	12	7	5	4	9	13	14	11	11	10	12
Y2	6	11	14	15	8	12	100	14	11	10	7	15
Y3	9	8	5	12	10	8	9	10	8	16	8	10

and lowest points of the dataset. Let's see how this would work on the two (dummy) datasets in Tables 10.1 and 10.2.

This first technique will simply decrease the top/down x% values of our historical demand down to the limit of the **xth percentile.**

> ### xth Percentile
>
> The xth percentile (also known as quantile) is a value below which x% of the observations in a group will fall. For example, 99% of the demand observations for a product will be lower than its 99th percentile.

This technique of simply shrinking the demand down to a certain percentile is called **winsorization.**[1]

If we look at the 1st and 99th percentile on our two dummy datasets (10.1 and 10.2), this is what we obtain:

Table 10.3: Outlier detection with winsorization.

Dataset	Lower limit	Higher limit
#1	4.4	16.6
#2	4.4	70.9

Table 10.3 tells us that in both datasets, all the low values would be increased up to 4.4. You can see in Figure 10.1 that this cuts a part of our dataset. The high values would

---

1 The name comes from Charles P. Winsor, a statistician from the first half of the 20th century.

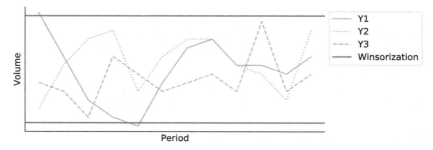

Figure 10.1: Winsorization on simple dataset.

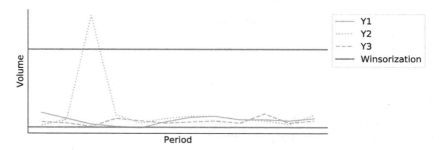

Figure 10.2: Winsorization on an extreme dataset.

be decreased down to 16.6 on the dataset without outliers (Figure 10.1) and down to 70.9 for the dataset with an outlier (Figure 10.2).

You might have noticed that the winsorization didn't give us round results such as 4 or 5, but instead we got this 4.4. Actually, as we don't have an exact value that cuts the dataset by 99%, it does a linear approximation based on the two closest values. This is how we got these numbers instead of round numbers.

So, are we happy with this technique? No we're not.

- We have spotted fake outliers on a dataset without outliers.
- On the dataset with outliers, we haven't sufficiently reduced the outlier (it went from 100 to 70.9).

Of course, one could simply propose to decrease the higher limit of the winsorization from 99% to 95% to further reduce the outlier on dataset #2. Unfortunately, this would still also affect dataset #1. This is not a good solution. One could also propose to remove this lower limit so that we don't increase our demand to 4.4. But what if we have periods with missing demand? Shouldn't we clean these as well, if there are any?

Do It Yourself

Excel

You can easily get the different percentiles of a range of cells in Excel by using the formula =PERCENTILE.INC(range,limit). Of course, you'll have to use this formula once for the upper limit (with a value around 0.95–0.99) and once for the lower limit (with a value around 0.01–0.05).

Python

We can easily winsorize our dataset in Python, thanks to NumPy. We can compute the different percentiles of an array, thanks to the np.percentile(array, percentile) function.

```
1 higher_limit = np.percentile(array, 99)
2 lower_limit = np.percentile(array, 1)
```

Note that the percentile function takes a percentile expressed as a value between 0 and 100, and not a ratio (i. e., a value between 0 and 1) as in Excel.

We can then simply cut the array to these lower and higher limits, thanks to the function np.clip(array, a_min, a_max):

```
1 array = np.clip(array, a_min=lower_limit, a_max=higher_limit)
```

10.2 Idea #2 – Standard Deviation

As we just saw, winsorization wasn't the perfect way to exclude outliers, as it would take out high and low values of a dataset even if they weren't exceptional, per se.

Another approach would be to look at the demand variation around the historical average and exclude the values that are *exceptionally* far from this average.

Let's define the demand standard deviation as σ:

$$\sigma = \sqrt{\frac{\sum_n (d - \bar{d})^2}{n}}$$

where $\bar{d}$ is the demand average and n is the amount of demand observations we have.

If we assume that our demand is normally distributed around the historical mean,[2] **we can compute the probability for the demand to be between two**

---

2 The exact mathematics involved here are beyond the scope of this book, and unfortunately, more often than not, the assumption of normality is not strictly respected. See Vandeput (2020) for a detailed discussion about demand normality (and gamma distributed demand).

thresholds. These two thresholds will be centered on the demand average (μ) with a spread of x times the standard deviation (σ) in both directions. The more chaotic the demand (i. e., σ is big), the wider the thresholds.

Min. threshold	<	Probability	<	Max. threshold
$\mu - 1.28\sigma$	<	95%	<	$\mu + 1.28\sigma$
$\mu - 2.33\sigma$	<	98%	<	$\mu + 2.33\sigma$
$\mu - 2.58\sigma$	<	99%	<	$\mu + 2.58\sigma$

For example, we have a 98% probability to be in the **range**: demand average $\pm$ 2.33 times the standard deviation (as in Figure 10.3). If we wanted to remove the top 1% of both high and low values, we would restrict the demand to $\mu \pm 2.33\sigma$.

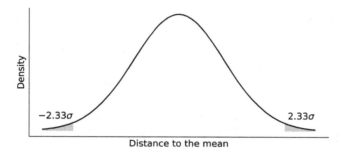

Figure 10.3: Normal curve excluding top and bottom 1% of values.

Note that this means that we have a 99% probability to be **lower** than $\mu + 2.33\sigma$. And a 99% probability to be **higher** than $\mu - 2.33\sigma$.

If we applied this to our example datasets (see Tables 10.1 and 10.2), we would get the limits as shown in Table 10.4.

Table 10.4: Outlier detection based on standard deviation.

Dataset	Lower limit	Higher limit
#1	3.0	17.8
#2	−22.2	47.9

Let's see how these new *normal* limits behave compared to the winsorization limits.

This is already much better than the results we got with winsorization:

– On the dataset without outliers (see Figure 10.4), we don't change any demand observation (perfect!—just as we wanted).

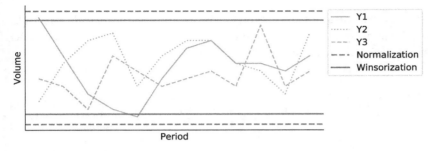

Figure 10.4: Simple dataset.

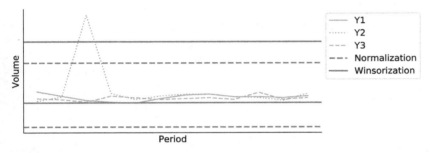

Figure 10.5: Extreme dataset.

– On the dataset with an outlier, we don't change the low-demand points but only the actual outlier (see Figure 10.5).

Still, even though we reduce the outlier to a more manageable amount (47.9) than with the winsorization (70.9), it might not be enough yet.

So, are we happy now? Not quite yet. As you might remember, we assumed the error to be around the historical mean. This is fine for products with flat demand, but the actual limitation will arise when you have a product with a trend or a seasonality. For example, in Table 10.5, the highest (or lowest) points are no longer the outliers you want to remove.

Table 10.5: Seasonal demand with an outlier (Y2 M11).

Month	M1	M2	M3	M4	M5	M6	M7	M8	M9	M10	M11	M12
Y1	11	24	15	11	9	11	8	8	7	7	7	4
Y2	18	22	14	20	7	9	7	3	8	6	**19**	3
Y3	17	21	22	12	11	12	12	8	8	6	3	4

You can see how winsorization and normalization work on the seasonal demand in Figure 10.6. It simply doesn't make sense: both techniques flag the season peaks as outliers but they skip the *real* outlier, which is Y2 M11.

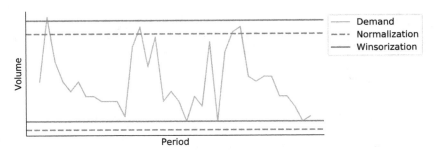

Figure 10.6: Winsorization and normalization on seasonal dataset.

We will solve this with our next technique.

Do It Yourself

Excel
You can compute the standard deviation of a range of cells, thanks to the formula =STDEV.P(range). As always, you can compute the mean by using =AVERAGE(range). Once you have these two, you can compute the higher and lower limits by using =NORM.INV(percentile, mean, stdev). Typically, you will want the high percentile to be around 0.99 and the low one around be around 0.01.

Python
You can calculate the standard deviation via np.std(array) for an array-like (e. g., a list, a DataFrame, etc.) or for a DataFrame directly via the method .std(). So that if you have a DataFrame df you can simply type:

```
m = df.mean()
s = df.std()
```

We will then once again use the SciPy library to compute the normal probabilities. We'll then use the .clip() method on our DataFrame to cap it to our limits.

```
from scipy.stats import norm
limit_high = norm.ppf(0.99,m,s)
```

```
3  limit_low = norm.ppf(0.01,m,s)
4  df = df.clip(lower=limit_low, upper=limit_high, axis=1)
```

As extra information, you can easily print the percentile of each demand observation with the following command. As expected, if you run it after .clip(), the maximum value should correspond to the upper limit.

```
1  print(norm.cdf(df.values, m, s).round(2))
```

10.3 Idea #3 – Error Standard Deviation

The second idea we had to flag outliers was to compare each observation against the mean of the demand. We saw that it didn't make sense if we had a trend or a seasonality, as the difference between an observation and the historical mean wasn't relevant.

Well, let's go back to the definition of an outlier: *an outlier is a value that you didn't expect.*[3] That is to say that an outlier is a value far away from your prediction (i. e., your forecast). To spot outliers, we will therefore analyze the forecast error and see which periods are *exceptionally* wrong. To do that, we'll use the standard deviation approach that we used previously.

Let's take another look at the example we used in Table 10.5. We will compare the historical demand to a simple (but seasonal) forecast we have for it (see Figure 10.7).

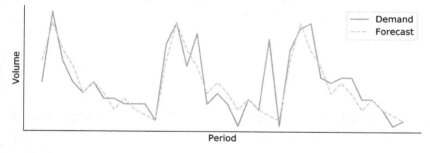

Figure 10.7: Seasonal demand.

If we computed the error we have for such a forecast (which is simply an average of the historical demand), we would obtain a mean error of 0.4 and a standard deviation of 3.2 (this is of course heavily impacted by the error we have for Y2 M11). If we took a 99% confidence interval around this mean, we would shrink forecast errors into −0.4±

---

3 Just like the Spanish Inquisition in Monty Python shows.

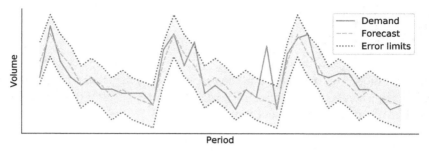

Figure 10.8: Outlier detection via forecast error.

2.33 × 3.2 = [−8, 7]. You can see in Figure 10.8 how these limits around the forecast perfectly fit the seasonal demand.

We can now correct our outlier from Y2 M11. The demand was 19, but the forecast was 5 for this period. The maximum *acceptable* value is then 5 + 7 = 12. This means that we can replace the outlier of Y2 M11 (19) by this new value (12).

Conclusion

With this smarter detection method—analyzing the forecast error deviation instead of simply the demand variation around the mean—we will be able to flag outliers much more precisely and replace them with a plausible amount. As you saw in Figure 10.6, normalization and winsorization couldn't achieve any meaningful results for this seasonal demand.

The fine-tuning of this method (*how many standard deviations should you take as a limit?*) is—of course—left to you to experiment...

Do It Yourself

Python

If you have a pandas DataFrame with one column as the forecast and another one as the demand (the typical output from our exponential smoothing models), you can use this code:

```
1  df['Error'] = df['Forecast'] - df['Demand']
2  m = df['Error'].mean()
3  s = df['Error'].std()
4  limit_high = norm.ppf(0.99,m,s) + df['Forecast']
5  limit_low = norm.ppf(0.01,m,s) + df['Forecast']
6  df['Updated'] = df['Demand'].clip(lower=limit_low,upper=limit_high)
```

10.4 Go the Extra Mile!

If you think back to our idea to analyze the forecast error and make a threshold of acceptable errors, we actually still have a minor issue. The threshold we compute is based on the dataset including the outliers. This outlier drives the error variation upward so that the acceptable threshold is biased and overestimated. To correct this, one could actually shrink the outlier not to the threshold calculated based on the original demand dataset, but to **a threshold calculated on a dataset without this specific outlier**. Here's the method:

1. Populate an initial forecast against the historical demand.
2. Compute the error, the error mean, and the error standard deviation.
3. Compute the lower and upper acceptable thresholds (based on the error mean and standard deviation).
4. Identify outliers just as previously explained.
5. Re-compute the error mean and standard deviation, but this time, exclude the outliers.
6. Update the lower and upper acceptable thresholds based on these new values.
7. Update the outlier values based on the new thresholds.

In our example from Table 10.5, we initially had a forecast error mean of 0.4 and a standard deviation of 3.22. If we remove the point Y2 M11, we obtain an error mean of −0.1 and a standard deviation of 2.3. This means that the thresholds around the forecast are now [−5.3, 5.2]. Our outlier in Y2 M11 would then be updated to 10 (instead of 12 with our previous technique).

Do It Yourself

Let's reuse our code from Section 10.3 and add a new step to update the error mean and standard deviation values.

```
1  df['Error'] = df['Forecast'] - df['Demand']
2  m = df['Error'].mean()
3  s = df['Error'].std()
4  prob = norm.cdf(df['Error'], m, s)
5  outliers = (prob > 0.99) | (prob < 0.01)
6  m2 = df.loc[~outliers,'Error'].mean()
7  s2 = df.loc[~outliers,'Error'].std()
8  limit_high = norm.ppf(0.99,m2,s2) + df['Forecast']
9  limit_low = norm.ppf(0.01,m2,s2) + df['Forecast']
10 df['Updated'] = df['Demand'].clip(lower=limit_low, upper=limit_high)
```

11 Triple Additive Exponential Smoothing

11.1 The Idea Behind Triple Additive Exponential Smoothing

So far, we have discussed four different exponential smoothing models:
- Simple exponential smoothing
- Double exponential smoothing with (additive) trend
- Double exponential smoothing with (additive) damped trend
- Triple exponential smoothing with (additive) damped trend and multiplicative seasonality

The last model we saw is potent but still has some limitations due to its seasonality's multiplicative aspect. The issue of multiplicative seasonality is how the model reacts when you have periods with very low volumes. Periods with a demand of 2 and 10 might have an absolute difference of 8 units. Still, their relative difference is 500%, so the seasonality (which is expressed in relative terms) could drastically change. We will then replace this multiplicative seasonality with an additive one.

    With multiplicative seasonality, we could interpret the seasonal factors as a percentage increase (or decrease) of the demand during each period. One could say "We sell 20% more in January but 30% less in February." Now, the seasonal factors will be absolute amounts to be added to the demand level. One could say "We sell 150 units more than usual in January but 200 less in February."

11.2 Model

The model idea is that the forecast is now composed of the level plus the (damped) trend, **plus** an additive seasonal factor s.

$$\text{Forecast} = \text{Level} + \text{Trend} + \text{Season}$$
$$f_{t+1} = a_t \quad + \phi b_t \quad + s_{t+1-p}$$

Pay attention—like for the multiplicative model, we use the seasonal factors from the previous cycle: s_{t-p} (where p denotes the season length—p for periodicity). The seasonal factors can now be read as an amount to add (or subtract) from the period level to obtain the forecast. For example, if $s_{\text{january}} = 20$, it means you will sell 20 pieces more in January than in an average month.

Component Updates

We calculate the different components as such:

$$a_t = \alpha\,(d_t - s_{t-p}) + (1 - \alpha)\,(a_{t-1} + \phi b_{t-1})$$

https://doi.org/10.1515/9783110671124-011

$$b_t = \beta\,(a_t - a_{t-1}) + (1 - \beta)\,\phi b_{t-1}$$
$$s_t = \gamma\,(d_t - a_t) \quad + (1 - \gamma)\,s_{t-p}$$

Note that the level and the trend are deseasonalized, whereas the forecast and the demand are seasonal. Again, s_{t-p} means that we use the seasonal factor as computed in the last season. Moreover, note that the trend is updated just as it was for the multiplicative and the double smoothing models.

> **Pro-Tip – Acceptable Range for γ**
>
> As for the multiplicative model, γ should stay rather low. But we are now dealing with additive seasonal factors, which are not automatically scaled to a possibly changing level. It might then make sense to allow γ to be a bit higher than for the multiplicative model.

Seasonal Factors Scaling

The seasonal factors must impact how the forecast is spread across each period *within* a full seasonal cycle. We do not want the seasonal factors to impact the *total forecast* of the full cycle. For example, we want these seasonal factors to allocate, and more or less forecast, to each month of a year, but the seasonal factors' impact over the full year should be 0. If we sell 150 units more than usual in January, we should sell 150 units less than usual during the rest of the year.

If we translate this in mathematical terms, we have:

$$\sum_{cycle} s = 0$$

This is important, as it implies that the level, the forecast, and the demand are on the same scale, as the sum of the seasonal factors over a full season cycle is 0.[1]

Future Forecast

Any future forecast can then be computed as:

$$f_{t+\lambda} = a_t + \sum_{i=1}^{\lambda} \phi^i\,b_t + s_{t+\lambda-p}$$

or, if you don't use a damping factor:

$$f_{t+\lambda} = a_t + \lambda b_t + s_{t+\lambda-p}$$

---

[1] In practice—in order to simplify the seasonal factor update procedure—you can allow the seasonal factors to slightly drift away from 0 over time.

Component Initialization

Level and Trend

As for the multiplicative triple model, we will have to deseasonalize the demand in order to initialize the level and the trend.

$$a_0 = d_0 - s_0$$
$$b_0 = (d_1 - s_1) - (d_0 - s_0)$$

Seasonal Factors

Let's take another look at the initialization method we used for the multiplicative seasonality (i. e., initialize the seasonal weights based on the historical period—see Section 9.2) and adapt it for additive seasonal factors.

1. **Compute the historical season averages.**

   Let's reuse our dummy quarterly dataset from Chapter 9, as shown in Table 11.1.

   Table 11.1: Example of quarterly seasonal demand.

	Y1	Y2	Y3	Y4	Y5	Mean
Q1	14	18	16	18	17	16.6
Q2	10	8	9	11	9	9.4
Q3	6	4	5	4	5	4.8
Q4	2	1	3	2	1	1.8

2. **Scale the historical season averages.**

   We will scale our historical averages so that their sum will be equal to 0. In order to do this, as shown in Table 11.2, we will **subtract** from our historical season averages their own mean (8.15).

   Table 11.2: Seasonal factors.

	Y1	Y2	Y3	Y4	Y5	Mean	Factors
Q1	14	18	16	18	17	16.6	8.45
Q2	10	8	9	11	9	9.4	1.25
Q3	6	4	5	4	5	4.8	−3.35
Q4	2	1	3	2	1	1.8	−6.35
Mean						8.15	0.00

We now obtain a scaled set of seasonal factors: 8.45, 1.25, −3.35, and −6.35. They are now scaled, as their sum is equal to 0. You can easily interpret them by saying that "We sell 8.45 units more than usual in Q1 and 1.25 more than usual in Q2; in Q3 and Q4, we sell respectively 3.35 and 6.35 units less than usual."

Other Methods

Do not hesitate to apply the initialization methods for the multiplicative seasonal factors discussed in Section 9.2 to the additive seasonal factors. In any case, do not forget to scale the seasonal factors so that their sum is equal to 0.

As for the multiplicative seasonal factors, if you have an important trend in the historical demand, you might face an issue. A possible solution would be to first remove the trend in your data before computing the seasonal factors.

> **Going Further**
>
> If you are looking for more information on the different exponential smoothing models, you can check the reference book *Forecasting: Principles and Practice*, which is freely available online on otexts.org/fpp2. It is written by Rob J. Hyndman and George Athanasopoulos, two of the very, best world-class leaders in the field of forecasting.

11.3 Insights

Comparison with the Multiplicative Model

Let's take another look at our example from the multiplication triple model in Table 11.3.

Table 11.3: Quarterly demand.

	Y1	Y2	Y3	Y4	Y5	Y6
Q1	14	18	16	18	17	?
Q2	10	8	9	11	9	?
Q3	6	4	5	4	5	?
Q4	2	1	3	2	1	?

Let's populate a forecast with our new additive model (with parameters alpha = 0.4, beta = 0.4, phi = 0.9 and gamma = 0.3) and see the differences compared to the multiplicative model.

As you can see in Figure 11.1, the additive model is much more accurate than the multiplicative model (MAE of, respectively, 0.70 and 1.87), and gives a much more reasonable future prediction. Actually, if we look at how each model estimates the de-

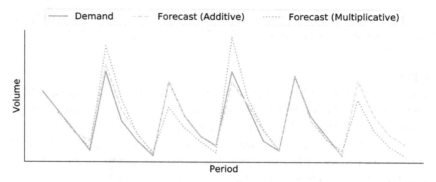

Figure 11.1: Additive forecast.

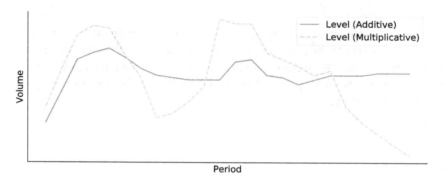

Figure 11.2: Level estimation.

mand level (see Figure 11.2), it is quite clear that the multiplicative model has an issue compared to the additive one.

Limitations

Of course, like any other exponential smoothing model, the first limitation is the inability to deal with any external input (marketing budget, pricing impact, etc.). But there is actually a second one. We will face an issue for items with a significant trend.

Remember that the seasonality is defined by absolute amounts to be added to or removed from the (deseasonalized) level. If the demand level grows (or shrinks) over time, these absolute seasonal factors will **not** scale with the level. For example, let's imagine that in year 1 you have a product with an average demand of 10 pieces per month. You observe a seasonality ranging from −5 to +5. If you start to increase your sales at a rhythm of +10% per month as of Y2, your seasonality factors will soon be negligible compared to the demand level. The way the triple exponential smoothing model is defined does not allow for the seasonality to quickly evolve through time!

This new additive model is **best suited for items with stable or low demand**. The two seasonal models (additive and multiplicative) are complementary and should allow you to forecast any seasonal product. The best way to know which one you should use is, of course, to experiment.

11.4 Do It Yourself

Excel

We will reuse the table we made for the multiplicative model at the end of Chapter 9 (as shown in Figure 11.3) and change it for an additive model.

	A	B	C	D	E	F	G	H	I
1	Date	Demand	Forecast	Level (a)	Trend (b)	Season (s)		Alpha:	80%
2	1	14						Beta:	10%
3	2	10		First Cycle				Gamma:	40%
4	3	6							
5	4	2							
6	5	18							
7	6	8							
8	7	4							
9	8	1							
10	9	16							
11	10	9							
12	11	5							
13	12	3		Historical Periods					
14	13	18							
15	14	11							
16	15	4							
17	16	2							
18	17	17							
19	18	9							
20	19	5							
21	20	1							
22	21								
23	22			Future Forecast					
24	23								
25	24								

Figure 11.3: Triple smoothing template in Excel.

1. **Level**

   First, we need to update the initialization by changing the formula in cell D2:

   $$a_0 = d_0 - s_0$$
   $$D2 = B2 - F2$$

   From there, we have to update the first year by updating the formula in cell D3 as:

   $$a_t = \alpha (d_t - s_t) + (1 - \alpha)(a_{t-1} + b_{t-1})$$
   $$D3 = \$I\$1*(B3-F3)+(1-\$I\$1)*(D2+E2)$$

From here, you can copy it until D5. As of cell D6, you should then use:

$$a_t = \alpha \, (d_t - s_{t-p}) + (1 - \alpha) \, (a_{t-1} + b_{t-1})$$

$$D6 = \$I\$1*(B6-\textbf{F2})+(1-\$I\$1)*(D5+E5)$$

Which we copy and paste until cell D21.

2. **Trend**

We only need to initialize the trend in cell E2 as:

$$b_0 = (d_1 - s_1) - (d_0 - s_0)$$

$$E2 = (B3-F3)-(B2-F2)$$

No need to change the other formula, as the trend is the same as the one for the multiplicative model:

$$b_t = \beta \, (a_t - a_{t-1}) + (1 - \beta) \, b_{t-1}$$

3. **Season**

Let's initialize our seasonal factors as $[8.5, 1.3, -3.4, -6.4]$ in cells F2:F5. In cell F6, you can use the formula:

$$s_t = \gamma \, (d_t - a_t) + (1 - \gamma) \, s_{t-p}$$

$$F6 = \$I\$3*(B6-D6)+(1-\$I\$3)*F2$$

which is the same formula as the one for the multiplicative model, except for the (B6-D6) part. You can then copy and paste this formula until the end of the historical period (cell F21).

4. **Forecast**

It is now simply defined as the sum of the previous level, trend, and season. In cell C3, you can type:

$$f_{t+1} = a_t + b_t + s_t$$

$$C3 = D2+E2+F2$$

and copy and paste it until the end of the first year (cell C5). You can then define C6 as:

$$f_{t+1} = a_t + b_t + s_{t-p}$$

$$C6 = D5+E5+F2$$

and copy and paste this until the end of the table.

Python

Seasonal Factor Initialization

Just as we did for the multiplicative model, let's first create a function to compute our additive seasonal factors. Do not hesitate to play with different initialization methods until you find the one that works best for you.

```python
1  def seasonal_factors_add(s,d,slen,cols):
2      for i in range(slen):
3          s[i] = np.mean(d[i:cols:slen]) # Calculate season average
4      s -= np.mean(s[:slen]) # Scale all season factors (sum of ⌋
       ↪   factors = 0)
5      return s
```

Triple Additive Smoothing

As we did for the other models, we will create a function called `triple_exp_smooth_add()` that will take a time series d and a season length `slen` as inputs. The function takes as other optional inputs the different parameters `alpha`, `beta`, `gamma`, and `phi` and the number of extra periods that we want to forecast. The function will return a pandas DataFrame that will contain the historical demand, the forecast, the level, the trend, the seasonal factors, and the forecast error.

```python
1  def triple_exp_smooth_add(d, slen=12, extra_periods=1, alpha=0.4, ⌋
      ↪   beta=0.4, phi=0.9, gamma=0.3):
2
3      cols = len(d) # Historical pteriod length
4      d = np.append(d,[np.nan]*extra_periods) # Append np.nan into ⌋
       ↪   the demand array to cover future periods
5
6      # components initialization
7      f,a,b,s = np.full((4,cols+extra_periods),np.nan)
8      s = seasonal_factors_add(s,d,slen,cols)
9
10     # Level & Trend initialization
11     a[0] = d[0]-s[0]
12     b[0] = (d[1]-s[1]) - (d[0]-s[0])
13
14     # Create the forecast for the first season
15     for t in range(1,slen):
16         f[t] = a[t-1] + phi*b[t-1] + s[t]
17         a[t] = alpha*(d[t]-s[t]) + (1-alpha)*(a[t-1]+phi*b[t-1])
```

```
18          b[t] = beta*(a[t]-a[t-1]) + (1-beta)*phi*b[t-1]
19
20      # Create all the t+1 forecast
21      for t in range(slen,cols):
22          f[t] = a[t-1] + phi*b[t-1] + s[t-slen]
23          a[t] = alpha*(d[t]-s[t-slen]) + (1-alpha)*(a[t-1]+phi*b[t-1])
24          b[t] = beta*(a[t]-a[t-1]) + (1-beta)*phi*b[t-1]
25          s[t] = gamma*(d[t]-a[t]) + (1-gamma)*s[t-slen]
26
27      # Forecast for all extra periods
28      for t in range(cols,cols+extra_periods):
29          f[t] = a[t-1] + phi*b[t-1] + s[t-slen]
30          a[t] = f[t]-s[t-slen]
31          b[t] = phi*b[t-1]
32          s[t] = s[t-slen]
33
34      df = pd.DataFrame.from_dict({'Demand':d,'Forecast':f,'Level':a,
        ↪  'Trend':b, 'Season':s,'Error':d-f})
35
36      return df
```

Once again, we can easily plot the model by simply calling df.plot() and we can easily calculate any forecast KPI by using kpi(df), as defined in Section 2.5.

scikit-learn - 2010

pandas - 2008

NumPy - 2005

Python - 1991

Damped trends - 1985

Winters - 1960

Holt - 1957

Python

Exponential
Smoothing

Part II: **Machine Learning**

12 Machine Learning

Tell us what the future holds, so we may know that you are gods.

Isaiah 41:23

What Is Machine Learning?

Until now, we have been using old-school statistics to predict demand. But with the recent rise of machine learning algorithms, we have new tools at our disposal that can easily achieve outstanding performance in terms of forecast accuracy for a typical supply chain demand dataset. As you will see in the following chapters, these models will be able to learn many relationships that are beyond the ability of traditional exponential smoothing models. For example, we will discuss how to add external information to our model in Chapters 20 and 22.

So far, we have created different algorithms that have used a predefined model to populate a forecast based on historical demand. The issue was that these models couldn't adapt to historical demand. If you use a double exponential smoothing model to predict a seasonal product, it will fail to interpret the seasonal patterns. On the other hand, if you use a triple exponential smoothing model on a non-seasonal demand, it might overfit the noise in the demand and interpret it as a seasonality.

Machine learning is different. Here, the algorithm (i. e., the machine) will learn relationships from a training dataset (i. e., our historical demand) and then apply these relationships on new data. Whereas a traditional statistical model will apply a predefined relationship (model) to forecast the demand, a machine learning algorithm will not assume *a priori* a particular relationship (like seasonality or a linear trend); it will **learn** these patterns directly from the historical demand.

For a machine learning algorithm to learn how to make predictions, we will have to feed it with both the inputs and the desired respective outputs. It will then automatically understand the relationships between these inputs and outputs.

Another important difference between using machine learning and exponential smoothing models to forecast our demand is that machine learning algorithms will **learn patterns from our entire dataset**. Exponential smoothing models will treat each item individually and independently from the others. Because it uses the entire dataset, a machine learning algorithm will apply what works best to each product. One could improve the accuracy of an exponential smoothing model by increasing the length of each time series (i. e., providing more historical periods for each product). Using machine learning, we will be able to increase our model's accuracy by providing more of the products' data to be ingested by the model.

Welcome to the world of machine learning.

https://doi.org/10.1515/9783110671124-012

12.1 Machine Learning for Demand Forecasting

To make a forecast, the question we will ask the machine learning algorithm is the following: *Based on the last* n *periods of demand, what will the demand be during the next period(s)?*

We will train the model by providing it with the data in a specific layout:
- *n* consecutive periods of demand as input.
- the demand of the (very) next period(s) as output.

Let's see an example (with a quarterly forecast to simplify the table):

Table 12.1: Historical demand formatting for machine learning.

Product	Inputs Year 1				Output Year 2
	Q1	Q2	Q3	Q4	Q1
#1	5	15	10	7	6
#2	7	2	3	1	1
#3	18	25	32	47	56
#4	4	1	5	3	2

For our forecasting problem, we will basically show our machine learning algorithm different extracts of our historical demand dataset as inputs and, as a desired output, what the very next demand observation was. In our example in Table 12.1, the algorithm will learn the relationship between the last four quarters of demand, and the demand of the next quarter. The algorithm will *learn* that if we have 5, 15, 10, and 7 as the last four demand observations, the next demand observation will be 6, so that its prediction should be 6. Next to the data and relationships from product #1, the algorithm will also learn from products #2, #3, and #4. In doing so, the idea is for the model to use *all* the data provided to give us better forecasts.

Most people will react to this idea with two very different thoughts. Either people will think that "it is simply impossible for a computer to look at the demand and make a prediction" or that "as of now, the humans have nothing left to do." Both are wrong.

As we will see later, machine learning can generate very accurate predictions. And as the human controlling the machine, we still have to ask ourselves many questions, such as:
- Which data should we feed to the algorithm for it to understand the proper relationships? We will discuss how to include other data features in Chapters 20, 22, and 23; and how to select the relevant ones in Chapters 18 and 24.
- Which machine learning algorithm should be used? There are many different ones: we will discuss new models in Chapters 13, 15, 17, 19, 21, and 25.

- Which parameters should be used in our model? As you will see, each machine learning algorithm has some parameters that we can tweak to improve its accuracy (see Chapter 14).

As always, there is no definitive, one-size-fits-all answer. Experimentation will help you find what is best for your dataset.

12.2 Data Preparation

The first step of any machine learning algorithm project is to properly clean and format the data. In our case, we need to format the historical demand dataset to obtain one similar to Table 12.1.

Naming Convention

During our data cleaning process, we will use the standard data science notation and call the inputs X and the outputs Y. Specifically, the datasets X_train and Y_train will contain all the historical demand that we will use to **train** our algorithm (X_train being the inputs and Y_train the outputs). The datasets X_test and Y_test will be used to **test** our model.

You can see in Table 12.2 an example of a typical historical demand dataset you should have at the beginning of a forecasting project.

Table 12.2: Typical example of historical demand dataset.

Product	Year 1				Year 2				Year 3			
	Q1	Q2	Q3	Q4	Q1	Q2	Q3	Q4	Q1	Q2	Q3	Q4
#1	5	15	10	7	6	13	11	5	4	11	9	4
#2	7	2	3	1	1	0	0	1	3	2	4	5
#3	18	25	32	47	56	70	64	68	72	67	65	58
#4	4	1	5	3	2	5	3	1	4	3	2	5

We now have to format this dataset to something similar to Table 12.1. Let's say for now that we want to predict the demand of a product during one quarter based on the demand observations of this product during the previous four quarters.[1] We will populate the datasets X_train and Y_train by going through the different products we have, and, each time, create a data sample with four consecutive quarters as X_train

---

[1] We'll discuss variations of this in Chapters 18 and 24.

and the following quarter as Y_train. This way, the machine learning algorithm will learn the relationship(s) between one quarter of demand and the previous four.

You can see in Table 12.3 an illustration for the first iterations. Loop #1 uses Y1Q1 to Y1Q4 to predict Y2Q1, Loop #2 is shifted by one quarter: we use Y1Q2 to Y2Q1 to forecast Y2Q2, etc.

Table 12.3: Training and test sets creation.

Loop	Product	Year 1				Year 2				Year 3			
		Q1	Q2	Q3	Q4	Q1	Q2	Q3	Q4	Q1	Q2	Q3	Q4
#1	#1	5	15	10	7	6							
#1	#2	7	2	3	1	1							
#1	#3	18	25	32	47	56							
#1	#4	4	1	5	3	2							
#2	#1		15	10	7	6	13						
#2	#2		2	3	1	1	0						
#2	#3		25	32	47	56	70						
#2	#4		1	5	3	2	5						
#3	#1			10	7	6	13	11					
...	...			...	...	...	...	...					
#8	#1									5	4	11	9	4
#8	#2									1	3	2	4	5
#8	#3									68	72	67	65	58
#8	#4									1	4	3	2	5

Our X_train and Y_train datasets will look like Table 12.4.

Table 12.4: Training set.

Loop	Product	X_train				→	Y_train
#1	#1	5	15	10	7	→	6
#1	#2	7	2	3	1	→	1
#1	#3	18	25	32	47	→	56
#1	#4	4	1	5	3	→	2
#2	#1	15	10	7	6	→	13
#2	#2	2	3	1	1	→	0
#2	#3	25	32	47	56	→	70
...	...	...	...	...	...	→	...

Remember that our algorithm will learn relationships in X_train to predict Y_train. So we could write that as X_train → Y_train.

In order to validate our model, we need to keep a test set aside from the training set. Remember, the data in the test set won't be shown to the model during its training phase. The test set will be kept aside and used after the training to evaluate the model accuracy against *unseen* data (as a final test).[2]

In our example, if we keep the last loop as a test set (i. e., using demand from Y2Q4 to Y3Q3 to predict Y3Q4) we would have a test set as shown in Table 12.5.

Table 12.5: Test set.

X_test				Y_test
5	4	11	9	4
1	3	2	4	5
68	72	67	65	58
1	4	3	2	5

That means that our algorithm won't see these relationships during its training phase. It will be tested on the accuracy it achieved on these specific prediction exercises. We will measure its accuracy on this test set and assume its accuracy will be similar when predicting future demand.

Dataset Length

It is important for any machine learning exercise to pay attention to how much data is fed to the algorithm. The more, the better. On the other hand, the more periods we use to make a prediction (we will call this x_len), the fewer we will be able to loop through the dataset. Also, if we want to predict more periods at once (y_len), it will cost us a part of the dataset, as we need more data (Y_train is longer) to perform one loop in our dataset.

Typically, if we have a dataset with n periods, we will be able to make $1+n-x\_len-y\_len$ loops through it.

$$loops = 1 + n - x\_len - y\_len$$

Also keep in mind that you will have to keep some of those loops aside as a test set. Optimally, you should have enough loops of test set to cover a full season (so that you are sure that your algorithm captures all demand patterns properly).

$$train\_loops = 1 + n - x\_len - y\_len - s\_len$$
$$test\_loops = s\_len$$

---

2 See Chapters 4 and 8 for a discussion about training and test sets, as well as underfitting and overfitting, respectively.

For the training set, a best practice is to keep—at the very least—enough runs to loop through two full years. Overall, for a monthly dataset, you should then have at least $35 + \text{x\_len} + \text{y\_len}$ periods (as shown below) in order for the algorithm to have two full seasonal cycles to learn any possible relationships and a full season to be tested on.

$$\text{train\_loops} = 1 + n - \text{x\_len} - \text{y\_len} - \text{s\_len}$$
$$24 = 1 + n - \text{x\_len} - \text{y\_len} - 12$$
$$n = 23 + \text{x\_len} + \text{y\_len} + 12$$

12.3 Do It Yourself – Datasets Creation

Data Collection

The dataset creation and cleaning is a crucial part of any data science project. To illustrate all the models we will create in the next chapters, we will use the historical sales of cars in Norway from January 2007 to January 2017 as an example dataset. You can download this dataset on supchains.com/download.[3] You will get a csv file called norway_new_car_sales_by_make.csv. This dataset, graphed in Figure 12.1, contains the sales of 65 carmakers across 121 months. On average, a bit more than 140,000 new cars are sold in Norway per year. If we assume that the price of a new car is around $30,000 on average in Norway, the market can be roughly estimated to be worth $4B.

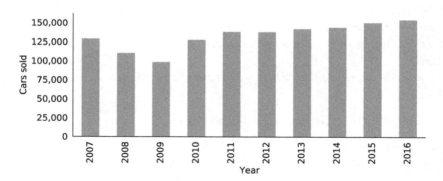

Figure 12.1: Cars sold per year in Norway.

---

3 The data is compiled by the Opplysningsrådet for Veitrafikken (OFV), a Norwegian organization in the automotive industry. It was initially retrieved by Dmytro Perepølkin and published on Kaggle.

> **Attention Point**
>
> This dataset is modest in terms of size, allowing for fast training and manipulation. This is perfect for a learning exercise and trying out new models and ideas. But this dataset is not big enough to showcase all the power of advanced machine learning models—they should show better results on bigger datasets.

> **Bring Your Own Dataset**
>
> In the next chapters, we will discuss various different models and apply them to this example dataset. But what we are actually interested in is **your own dataset.** Do not waste any time, and start gathering some historical demand data so that you can test the following models on your own dataset as we progress through the different topics. It is recommended that you start with a dataset of at least 5 years of data and more than a hundred different products. The bigger, the better.
>
> We will discuss in the following chapters many models and ideas and apply them to this dataset. The thought processes we will discuss can be applied to any demand dataset; but the results obtained, as well as the parameters and models selected, won't be the same on another dataset.

We will make a function `import_data()` that will extract the data from this csv and format it with the dates as columns and the products (here car brands) as lines.

```
1  def import_data():
2      data = pd.read_csv('norway_new_car_sales_by_make.csv')
3      data['Period'] = data['Year'].astype(str) + '-' + data['Month'] ↵
       ↪ .astype(str).str.zfill(2)
4      df = pd.pivot_table(data=data,values='Quantity',index='Make', ↵
       ↪  columns='Period',aggfunc='sum',fill_value=0)
5      return df
```

We used two special functions:
`.str.zfill(x)` adds leading zeros to a string until it reaches a length of x.[4]
`pd.pivot_table()` creates a pivot table from a DataFrame. The main inputs are:
    data the DataFrame used
      index which column(s) from the DataFrame should be used as the rows of the pivot table

---

4 See www.w3schools.com/python/ref_string_zfill.asp for more information and examples.

columns which column(s) from the DataFrame should be used as the columns of the pivot table

values what value to show in the pivot

aggfunc how to aggregate the values

fill_value fill-in value in case of missing data

You can print the results in an Excel file for later reference by using df.to_excel('demand.xlsx', index=False). It is always good practice to visually check what the dataset looks like to be sure that the code worked as intended.

This is what you should obtain if you print df.

```
1  print(df)
2  >> Period        2007-01  2007-02  2007-03  ...  2016-11  2016-12  2017-01
3  >> Make                                      ...
4  >> Alfa Romeo         16        9       21  ...        4        3        6
5  >> Aston Martin        0        0        1  ...        0        0        0
6  >> Audi              599      498      682  ...      645      827      565
7  >> BMW               352      335      365  ...     1663      866     1540
8  >> Bentley             0        0        0  ...        0        0        0
9  >> ...               ...      ...      ...  ...      ...      ...      ...
10 >> Think               2        0        0  ...        0        0        0
11 >> Toyota           2884     1885     1833  ...     1375     1238     1526
12 >> Volkswagen       2521     1517     1428  ...     2106     2239     1688
13 >> Volvo             693      570      656  ...      754     1235     1158
14 >> Westfield           0        0        0  ...        0        0        0
15 >>
16 >> [65 rows x 121 columns]
```

Training and Test Sets Creation

Now that we have our dataset with the proper formatting, we can create our training and test sets. For this purpose, we will create a function datasets that takes as inputs:

df our historical demand dataset

x_len the number of historical periods we will use to make a prediction

y_len the number of future periods we want to predict

test_loops the number of loops (iterations) we want to leave out as a final test. If you want to populate a future forecast (i. e., you are not running an optimization exercise), you have to set test_loops to 0.

The function will return X_train, Y_train, X_test, and Y_test.

```
1   def datasets(df, x_len=12, y_len=1, test_loops=12):
2       D = df.values
3       rows, periods = D.shape
4
5       # Training set creation
6       loops = periods + 1 - x_len - y_len
7       train = []
8       for col in range(loops):
9           train.append(D[:,col:col+x_len+y_len])
10      train = np.vstack(train)
11      X_train, Y_train = np.split(train,[-y_len],axis=1)
12
13      # Test set creation
14      if test_loops > 0:
15          X_train, X_test = np.split(X_train,[-rows*test_loops],axis=0)
16          Y_train, Y_test = np.split(Y_train,[-rows*test_loops],axis=0)
17      else: # No test set: X_test is used to generate the future
     ↵      forecast
18          X_test = D[:,-x_len:]
19          Y_test = np.full((X_test.shape[0],y_len),np.nan) #Dummy value
20
21      # Formatting required for scikit-learn
22      if y_len == 1:
23          Y_train = Y_train.ravel()
24          Y_test = Y_test.ravel()
25
26      return X_train, Y_train, X_test, Y_test
```

Let's discuss a few of the artifices we had to use in our function.

np.split(array, indices, axis) cuts an array at specific indices along an axis.

In our function, we use it to cut train in two pieces at the column x_len in order to create X_train and Y_train (see row 11). We also use it (along the row axis this time) to cut the test set out of the training set (see rows 14 and 15).

array.ravel() reduces the dimension of a NumPy array to 1D (see rows 23 and 24).

Y_train and Y_test are always created by our function as 2D arrays (i. e., arrays with rows and columns). If we only want to predict one period at a time, these arrays will then only have one column (and multiple rows). Unfortunately, the functions we will use later (from the scikit-learn library) will need 1D arrays if we forecast only one period.

We can now easily call our new function datasets(df) as well as import_data().

```
1 df = import_data()
2 X_train, Y_train, X_test, Y_test = datasets(df, x_len=12, y_len=1, ⌐
  ↪   test_loops=12)
```

We obtain the datasets we need to feed our machine learning algorithm (X_train and Y_train) and the datasets we need to test it (X_test and Y_test). Note that we set test_loops as 12 periods. That means that we will test our algorithm over 12 different loops (i. e., we will predict 12 times the following period [y_len=1] based on the last 12 periods [x_len=12]).

Forecasting Multiple Periods at Once
You can change y_len if you want to forecast multiple periods at once. In the following chapters, we will keep y_len = 1 for the sake of simplicity.

Future Forecast
If test_loops==0, the function will return the latest demand observations in X_test (and Y_test set as a dummy value), which will allow you to populate the future forecast, as we will see in Section 12.5.

What About Excel?
So far, Excel could provide us an easy way to see the data and our statistical model relationships. But it won't get us any further. Unfortunately, Excel does not provide the power to *easily* format such datasets into the different parts we need (X_train, X_test, Y_train, and Y_test). Moreover, with most of our machine learning models, the dataset size will become too large for Excel to handle correctly. Actually, another major blocking point is that Excel does not provide any machine learning algorithm.

12.4 Do It Yourself – Linear Regression

Now that we have created our training and test sets, let's create a forecast benchmark. We want to have an indication of what a simple model could do in order to compare its accuracy against our more complex models. Basically, if a model got an error of x percent, we will compare this against the error of our benchmark in order to know if x is a good result or not.

We will use a simple linear regression as a benchmark. If you are not familiar with the concept of linear regression, you can just picture it as a straight line that will match historical demand and project it into the future. Many Python libraries propose models to compute linear regressions, but we will choose scikit-learn, as we will later use this library for all our machine learning models. Let's stay consistent from one model to another.

```
1  from sklearn.linear_model import LinearRegression
2  reg = LinearRegression() # Create a linear regression object
3  reg = reg.fit(X_train,Y_train) # Fit it to the training data
4  # Create two predictions for the training and test sets
5  Y_train_pred = reg.predict(X_train)
6  Y_test_pred = reg.predict(X_test)
```

As you can see, we created a model object called reg that we fit to our training data (X_train, Y_train), thanks to the method .fit() (remember, we should fit our model to the training set and not to the test set). We then populated a prediction based on X_train and X_test via the method .predict().

KPI Function

We can now create a KPI function kpi_ML() that will display the accuracy of our model. This function will be similar to the one defined in Chapter 2. Here, we use a DataFrame in order to print the various KPI in a structured way.

```
1  def kpi_ML(Y_train, Y_train_pred, Y_test, Y_test_pred, name=''):
2      df = pd.DataFrame(columns = ['MAE','RMSE','Bias'],index=['Train',
       ↪  'Test'])
3      df.index.name = name
4      df.loc['Train','MAE'] = 100*np.mean(abs(Y_train -
       ↪  Y_train_pred))/np.mean(Y_train)
5      df.loc['Train','RMSE'] = 100*np.sqrt(np.mean((Y_train -
       ↪  Y_train_pred)**2))/np.mean(Y_train)
6      df.loc['Train','Bias'] = 100*np.mean((Y_train - Y_train_pred))/np
       ↪  .mean(Y_train)
7      df.loc['Test','MAE'] = 100*np.mean(abs(Y_test - Y_test_pred))/np
       ↪  .mean(Y_test)
8      df.loc['Test','RMSE'] = 100*np.sqrt(np.mean((Y_test -
       ↪  Y_test_pred)**2))/np.mean(Y_test)
9      df.loc['Test','Bias'] = 100*np.mean((Y_test - Y_test_pred))/np
       ↪  .mean(Y_test)
10     df = df.astype(float).round(1) #Round number for display
11     print(df)
```

This is what we obtain:

```
1  kpi_ML(Y_train, Y_train_pred, Y_test, Y_test_pred, name='Regression')
2  >>                  MAE   RMSE Bias
3  >> Regression
4  >> Train          17.8% 43.9% 0.0%
5  >> Test           17.8% 43.7% 1.6%
```

You can see that the RMSE is much worse than the MAE. This is usually the case, as demand datasets contain a few exceptional values that drive the RMSE up.[5]

Car sales per month, per brand, and at national level are actually easy to forecast, as those demand time series are stable without much seasonality. This is why the linear benchmark provides such good results here. On top of that, we only predict one month at a time and linear approximation works well in the short term. On a different dataset, with a longer forecast horizon (and more seasonality), linear regressions might not be up to the challenge. Therefore, don't be surprised to face much worse results on your own datasets. We will discuss in the following chapters much more advanced models that will be able to keep up with longer-term forecasting horizons, seasonality, and various other external drivers.

> **Attention Point**
>
> Do not worry if the MAE and RMSE of your dataset is much above the example benchmark presented here. In some projects, I have seen MAE as high as 80 to 100%, and RMSE well above 500%. Again, we use a linear regression benchmark precisely to get an order of magnitude of the complexity of a dataset.

12.5 Do It Yourself – Future Forecast

In Section 12.3, we created a function datasets() to populate a training and a test set. In Section 12.4, we used our training and test sets to evaluate a (simple) model. We can now change our hat from data scientist—working with training and test sets to evaluate models—to demand planner—using a model to populate a baseline forecast.

We will create a future forecast—the forecast to be used by **your** supply chain—by using our datasets() function and set test_loops to 0. The function will then return X_test filled-in with the latest demand observations—thus we will be able to use it to predict *future* demand. Moreover, as we do not keep data aside for the test set, the

---

5 See Chapter 2 for a thorough discussion about forecast KPI and the impact of outliers and extreme values.

training dataset (X_train and Y_train) will include the whole historical demand. This will be helpful, as we will use as much training data as possible to feed the model.

```
1  X_train, Y_train, X_test, Y_test = datasets(df, x_len=12, y_len=1,
   ↵   test_loops=0)
2  reg = LinearRegression()
3  reg = reg.fit(X_train,Y_train)
4  forecast = pd.DataFrame(data=reg.predict(X_test), index=df.index)
```

The DataFrame forecast now contains the forecast for the future periods.

```
1  print(forecast.head())
2  >>                        0
3  >> Make
4  >> Alfa Romeo        6.187217
5  >> Aston Martin      1.032483
6  >> Audi            646.568622
7  >> BMW            1265.032834
8  >> Bentley           1.218092
```

Now that we have a proper dataset, a benchmark to beat, and we know how to generate a future forecast, let's see how far machine learning can get us.

13 Tree

It's a dangerous business, Frodo, going out your door. You step onto the road, and if you don't keep your feet, there's no knowing where you might be swept off to.

J. R. R. Tolkien, *The Lord of the Rings*

As a first machine learning algorithm, we will use a **decision tree**. Decision trees are a class of machine learning algorithms that will create a map (a tree, actually) of questions to make a prediction. We call these trees **regression trees** if we want them to predict a number, or **classification trees** if we want them to predict a category or a label.

> **Regression**
>
> Regression problems require an estimate of a numerical output based on various inputs. For example, forecasting is a regression problem.

> **Classification**
>
> Classification problems require you to classify data samples in different categories. For example, identifying pictures as cat or dog is a classification problem.

In order to make a prediction, the tree will start at its foundation with a yes/no question, and based on the answer, it will continue asking new yes/no questions until it gets to a final prediction. Somehow you might see these trees as a big game of "Guess Who?" (the famous '80s game): the model will ask multiple consecutive questions until it gets to a good answer.[1]

In a decision tree, each question is called a **node**. For example, in Figure 13.1, "Does the person have a big nose?" is a node. Each possible final answer is called a **leaf**. In Figure 13.1, each leaf contains only one single person. But that is not mandatory. You could imagine that multiple people have a big mouth and a big nose. In such case, the leaf would contain multiple values.

The different pieces of information that a tree has at its disposal to split a node are called the **features**.

> **Feature**
>
> A feature is a type of information that a model has at its disposal to make a prediction.

---

1 If you do not think an algorithm can easily make a prediction based on a few yes/no questions, I advise you to check out Akinator—a genius who will find any character you can think of within a few questions (en.akinator.com).

https://doi.org/10.1515/9783110671124-013

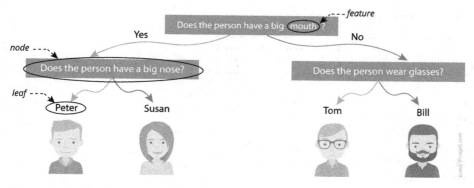

Figure 13.1: Decision tree for *Guess Who?*

For example, the tree we had in Figure 13.1 for the game "Guess Who?" could split a node on the three features: mouth, nose, and glasses.

13.1 How Does It Work?

To illustrate how our tree will grow, let's go back to Table 13.1, our quarterly dummy dataset.

Table 13.1: Training dataset.

X_train				Y_train
5	15	10	7	6
15	10	7	6	13
10	7	6	13	11
7	6	13	11	5
6	13	11	5	4
13	11	5	4	11
11	5	4	11	9
7	2	3	1	1

Based on this training dataset, a **smart** question to ask yourself in order to make a prediction is: *Is the first demand observation >7?*

As shown in Table 13.2, this is a useful question, as you know that the answer (Yes/No) will provide an interesting indication of the behavior of the demand for the next quarter. If the answer is *yes*, the demand we try to predict is likely to be rather high (≥ 8), and if the answer is *no*, then the demand we try to predict is likely to be low (≤ 7).

Table 13.2: Useful question.

X_train				Y_train	Is the first demand observation >7?
5	15	10	7	6	No
15	10	7	6	13	Yes
10	7	6	13	11	Yes
7	6	13	11	5	No
6	13	11	5	4	No
13	11	5	4	11	Yes
11	5	4	11	9	Yes
7	2	3	1	1	No

In Table 13.3, you can see an example of a **bad** question.

Table 13.3: Useless question.

X_train				Y_train	Is the third demand observation <6?
5	15	10	7	6	No
15	10	7	6	13	No
10	7	6	13	11	No
7	6	13	11	5	No
6	13	11	5	4	No
13	11	5	4	11	Yes
11	5	4	11	9	Yes
7	2	3	1	1	Yes

This does not really help, as this question does not separate our dataset into two *different* subsets (i. e., there is still a lot of variation inside each subset). If the answer to the question *Is the third demand observation <6?* is *yes*, we still have a range of demand going from 1 to 11, and if the answer is *no*, the range goes from 4 to 13. This question is simply not helpful to forecast the future demand.

Without going too much into detail about the tree's mathematical inner workings, the algorithm to grow our tree will—as shown in Figure 13.1—at each node, choose a question (i. e., perform a **split**) using one of the available **features** (i. e., the previous quarters). A good question will create a split that will minimize the prediction error across the two new data subsets (**leaves**).

> **A Brief History of Decision Trees**
>
> The first algorithm proposed to create a decision tree was published in 1963 by Morgan and Sonquist.[a] Many different algorithms on how to grow a decision tree were developed since the 1960s, and they all follow the objective of asking the most meaningful questions about the different features of a dataset in order to split it into different subsets, until some criterion is reached.
>
> ───────
>
> *a* See Morgan and Sonquist (1963).

Parameters

It's important to realize that without a criterion to stop the growth of our tree, it will grow until each data observation (otherwise called **sample**) has its own leaf. This is a really bad idea as, even though you will have perfect accuracy in your training set, you will not be able to replicate these results in new data. This is a perfect example of **extreme overfitting**: achieving perfect results on the training set while no replication of those results is achieved on the test set. Therefore, we need to limit the growth of our tree with the help of some criterion. Let's take a look at the most important ones (while already using the scikit-learn naming convention).

`max_depth` The maximum amount of consecutive questions (nodes) the tree can ask. More questions means that the algorithm can do a better job at distinguishing cases in the training set, henceforth achieving a better accuracy. But you will also be facing the risk of overfitting the training set.

`min_samples_split` The minimum amount of samples that are required in a node to trigger a new split. If you set this to 6, a node with only 5 observations left won't be split further. Reducing `min_samples_split` will also allow you to achieve a better accuracy on the training test, which could result in overfitting it.

`min_samples_leaf` The minimum amount of observations that need to be in a leaf. This is a very important parameter. The closer this is to 0, the higher the risk of overfitting—your tree will actually grow until it asks enough questions to treat each observation separately.

Of course, depending on your dataset, you might want to give different values to these parameters. We will discuss how to choose the best parameters in the following chapter.

13.2 Do It Yourself

We will use the scikit-learn Python library (www.scikit-learn.org) to grow our first tree. This is a well-known open-source library that is used all over the world by data scientists. It is built on top of NumPy so that it interacts easily with the rest of our code.

The first step is to use the scikit-learn library and create an *instance* of a regression tree.

> **Instance**
>
> An (object) instance is a technical term for an occurrence of a *class*. You can see a class as a blueprint, and an instance as a specific realisation of this blueprint. The class (blueprint) will define what each instance will look like (which variables will constitute it) and what it can do (what methods or functions it will be able to perform).
>
> In our case, tree is an instance of the class DecisionTreeRegressor.

Once this is done, we have to train it based on our X_train and Y_train arrays.

```
from sklearn.tree import DecisionTreeRegressor
# Instantiate a Decision Tree Regressor
tree = DecisionTreeRegressor(max_depth=5, min_samples_split=15,
    min_samples_leaf=5)
# Fit the tree to the training data
tree.fit(X_train,Y_train)
```

In the code extract used here, we created a tree with a maximum depth of 5 (i. e., maximum 5 yes/no consecutive questions are asked to classify one sample), where each tree leaf has a minimum of 5 samples, and a node can be split only if it has at least 15 samples.

We now have a tree trained to our specific demand history. We can already measure its accuracy on the training and the test set using the kpi_ML() function defined in Section 12.4.

```
Y_train_pred = tree.predict(X_train)
Y_test_pred = tree.predict(X_test)
kpi_ML(Y_train, Y_train_pred, Y_test, Y_test_pred, name='Tree')
>>            MAE   RMSE  Bias
>> Tree
>> Train   18.1   43.4  -0.0
>> Test    21.1   52.6   3.2
```

See the difference of accuracy (both for MAE, RMSE, and bias) between the training and the test set? This means that our regression tree is overfitted to the historical demand.

Our benchmark (the linear regression we did at the end of Chapter 12) obtained a training and test MAE of 17.8%! Which means that our regression tree is (unfortunately) less good than a simple linear regression.

Before we look at how we can improve this further, let's discuss MAE and RMSE.

Going Further

You can plot your tree, using the code below, out of curiosity to see what happens under the hood.[a] It might be hardly helpful for a forecasting exercise, but this might come in handy if you want to perform data analysis using machine learning.

```
1  from sklearn.tree import plot_tree
2  import matplotlib.pyplot as plt
3  fig = plt.figure(figsize=(15,6), dpi=300)
4  ax = fig.gca()
5  plot_tree(tree, fontsize=3, feature_names=[f'M{x-12}' for x in ↵
   ↪    range(12)], rounded=True, filled=True, ax=ax)
6  fig.savefig('Regression Tree.PNG')
```

You will obtain a vizualization of your tree in a pdf file (similar to Figure 13.2). As the layout of tree—even with a maximum depth of 5 layers—can be massive, I advise you to use a pdf reader to inspect it.

Figure 13.2: Visualisation of a regression tree.

---

a See scikit-learn.org/stable/modules/generated/sklearn.tree.plot_tree.html for more details.

MAE vs. RMSE

We discussed in Chapter 2 the advantages (and disadvantages) of using either the root mean square error (RMSE) or the mean absolute error (MAE) as a KPI to assess our forecast accuracy. Thanks to scikit-learn we can choose to build our tree in a way that minimizes one or the other (thanks to the parameter criterion). Unfortunately, due to the inner workings of the algorithm used to grow regression trees, the optimization for MAE is going to take much longer than the one for RMSE.

Let's record how long it takes to optimize a tree that minimizes MAE and another one that minimizes MSE (most of the machine learning algorithms optimize the mean square error [MSE] rather than the root mean square error, as it is easier to compute and manipulate). In order to do so, we will use the time library, which can give us the current time via time.time().

```
1   import time
2   for criterion in ['mse','mae']:
3       start_time = time.time()
4       tree = DecisionTreeRegressor(max_depth=5, min_samples_split=15, ⏎
        ↳  min_samples_leaf=5, criterion=criterion)
5       tree.fit(X_train,Y_train)
6       Y_train_pred = tree.predict(X_train)
7       Y_test_pred = tree.predict(X_test)
8       kpi_ML(Y_train, Y_train_pred, Y_test, Y_test_pred, name=f'Tree ⏎
        ↳  {criterion}')
9       print('{:0.2f} seconds'.format(time.time() - start_time))
10      print()
```

These are the results we obtain:

```
1   >>               MAE   RMSE   Bias
2   >> Tree mse
3   >> Train       18.1   43.4   -0.0
4   >> Test        21.1   52.6    3.2
5   >> 0.02 seconds
6   >>
7   >>               MAE   RMSE   Bias
8   >> Tree mae
9   >> Train       17.9   47.0    2.3
10  >> Test        21.5   58.5    5.2
11  >> 0.79 seconds
```

As you can see, on this dataset, MAE optimization is around 40 times slower than MSE optimization. This difference might even grow bigger as our dataset grows. This means that unfortunately, to optimize our tree (and later, our Forest and extremely randomized trees), we will need to stick to MSE instead of MAE. Note that, by default, scikit-learn uses MSE to fit its different models.

Another interesting aspect is that the optimization for MAE results in a slightly worse MAE on the final test set than the one for MSE. This is surprising but not unusual, as we haven't optimized our parameters yet and we can have, from time to time, a dataset that is much more fitted to MSE or to MAE. Once again, only experimentation will tell.

As discussed in Chapter 2, note how optimizing RMSE (or MSE) results in a lower bias than an optimization of the MAE.

14 Parameter Optimization

When we created our regression tree in Chapter 13, we chose some parameters:

```
1  tree = DecisionTreeRegressor(max_depth=5, min_samples_split=15, ⌐
   ↪  min_samples_leaf=5)
```

But are we sure these are the best? Maybe if we set `max_depth` to 7, we could improve our model accuracy? It is unfortunately impossible to know *a priori* what the best set of parameters is. But that's fine—we are supply chain data scientists, we love to run experiments.

14.1 Simple Experiments

As a first technique, we will run through different values for the maximum depth, test each of them, and select the best one. As you can see in Figure 14.1, increasing the maximum depth of our tree (i. e., allowing it to ask more consecutive questions) continuously improves the accuracy over the *training* set. But we reach a plateau for the *test* set accuracy as of around six consecutive questions. Actually, the accuracy on the test set is even a bit worse if the maximum depth is 14 rather than 6. It is important to understand that if we allow our model to ask eight consecutive questions or more, we overfit it to the training set, and it won't perform well on the test set. So should we choose `max_depth=6` and call it a day? No.

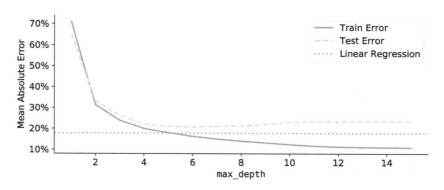

Figure 14.1: Experimentation for maximum depth optimization.

If we did this, we would actually be optimizing this parameter directly against the test set. We would then face the risk of overfitting the model to the test set and not being able to replicate similar results against new data.

https://doi.org/10.1515/9783110671124-014

Risk of Overfitting

Our initial idea to optimize a parameter was to train different versions of our model on the training set and keep the one that performed best against our test set.

This was a terrible idea. You would get outstanding but **artificial** results. Remember that the test set should only be used to *validate* the results of your model at the very end of the process, not to cherry-pick a set of parameters. If you do that, you are actually optimizing your model to fit the test set.

We will then have to use another experiment that does not require us to use our test set.

14.2 Smarter Experiments

Let's design a new experimentation method that is both efficient and doesn't risk overfitting. This method will rely on two concepts:

K-fold Cross-validation to avoid overfitting.

Random Search to efficiently find a (very) good parameter set among different possibilities.

K-fold Cross-Validation

K-fold cross-validation is a validation technique used to assess a model's accuracy over a dataset without overfitting.

Algorithm – K-fold Cross-validation

1. Divide our (training!) dataset into k different subsets (each of which is called a **fold**).
2. Train our model based on all the folds but one.
3. Use the remaining fold as a **validation** set to assess the model's performance.
4. As we have k folds, we can repeat steps 2 and 3 k times (each time, changing the validation set) and keep the average performance obtained as the final result.

You can see an example in Table 14.1 with five folds ($k = 5$). We cut the initial dataset into two parts: the training set (itself subdivided into five subsets) and the test set.

Based on our initial training set, we can then run 5 different experiments (as shown in Table 14.2). For each of them, we will train the model with 4 folds and keep the fifth one to test its performance. We will call this fifth fold the **validation dataset**.

Table 14.1: Dataset for 5-fold cross-validation.

Training Set					Test Set
Fold #1	Fold #2	Fold #3	Fold #4	Fold #5	Final test set

Table 14.2: 5-fold cross-validation.

Experiment	Training Set				Validation Set
#1	Fold #1	Fold #2	Fold #3	Fold #4	Fold #5
#2	Fold #2	Fold #3	Fold #4	Fold #5	Fold #1
#3	Fold #3	Fold #4	Fold #5	Fold #1	Fold #2
#4	Fold #4	Fold #5	Fold #1	Fold #2	Fold #3
#5	Fold #5	Fold #1	Fold #2	Fold #3	Fold #4

Validation Set

This is a random subset of the training set that is kept aside during the training in order to validate a model against unseen data.

We will then measure the accuracy of a model (created with a specific set of parameters) as the average accuracy achieved against the validation set over each of these 5 experiments. Finally, we will keep the best model—among all those tested—by selecting the one that achieved the best accuracy against those validation sets.

Our new k-fold cross-validation method allows us to test many different parameter sets and keep the best one without overfitting. Remember that with the cross-validation method, we keep the best model based on results achieved over different validation sets which are all part of the initial training dataset. It means that **we optimize our model directly on the training set and leave the test set for the final results**.

Searching Across a Parameter Space

Now that we have a method to test different parameter sets against a training set, we should ask ourselves the question: *which parameter sets should we try?* As the complexity of our model grows, we will have more and more different parameters that need to be optimized. We cannot optimize each parameter independently of the others, as there might be an interaction between them, so that we could actually come up with thousands—millions?—of possible different parameter sets. Therefore, we have to find a smart way to test *some* parameter sets and keep the best one.

Grid Search

One way to attack this problem is to define a space with all the possible values for each parameter we want to try. As shown in Figure 14.2, we can then test a certain number of possibilities of this space by uniformly choosing points across it.

Let's imagine a very simple example in which you want to choose the best parameters among two inputs (max_depth and min_samples_split). You assume that max_depth could vary between 5 and 15, and that min_samples_split could vary between 2 and 12. As you have 11 potential values for each parameter, that's a total of 121 different models to test. If you only have the time to test 25 models out of these 121 possibilities, you would uniformly spread these tests among the space of possibilities, as shown in Figure 14.2.

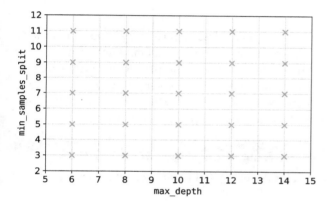

Figure 14.2: Grid search.

This uniform search (called *grid search* in scikit-learn) is a straightforward technique to look for a good parameter set among many possibilities. But actually, there is a smarter—yet less obvious—way.

Random Search

The second idea is to cover the space of possibilities **not by searching uniformly** among the parameters but **by random spot tests.** You could think that this is a bad idea, as we risk missing an interesting output by lack of chance. But there is actually an interesting fact about this technique. With the uniform search example, you would only test 5 different values for each parameter, but if you take each test at random, you will test many more values for each parameter. In Figure 14.3, you can see that by doing 25 random tests, we tried 10 different values for max_depth and 9 different values for min_samples_split.

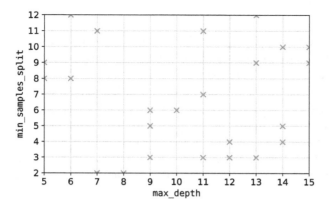

Figure 14.3: Random search.

Now imagine that one parameter's influence is less important than the other (but we do not know which one). In such a situation, with the random search, you will have tested more different values of the interesting parameter than with a grid search. Of course, this example with only two parameters is rather simple. As you will have to optimize more and more parameters at once, this effect will become increasingly important, as some parameters will be much more important than others.

> **Pro-Tip – Double Search**
>
> I recommend that you search for the best set of parameters in a two-step approach:
>
> 1. Start by doing a random search on a broad space of parameters.
> 2. Launch a new random search on a more refined space around the best value found in step 1.
>
> This should help you to cover a lot of space efficiently and help you to avoid missing a very good value.

14.3 Do It Yourself

Doing a k-fold cross-validation random search with scikit-learn is easy, as the library has very practical functions to perform it all automatically.

We will start by creating a dictionary param_dist that will contain all the parameter sets we want to test.

```
1  max_depth = list(range(5,11)) + [None]
2  min_samples_split = range(5,20)
```

```
3  min_samples_leaf = range(2,20)
4  param_dist = {'max_depth': max_depth,
5                'min_samples_split': min_samples_split,
6                'min_samples_leaf': min_samples_leaf}
```

We also append None to max_depth. If the maximum depth of a tree is set to None, it simply means that the tree is not restricted by any maximum depth.

Of course, feel free to experiment with the parameter ranges given in the example.

We can then launch our experiment and test all these different parameter sets against our training set.

```
1  from sklearn.model_selection import RandomizedSearchCV
2  tree = DecisionTreeRegressor()
3  tree_cv = RandomizedSearchCV(tree, param_dist, n_jobs=-1, cv=10,
    ↪    verbose=1, n_iter=100, scoring='neg_mean_absolute_error')
4  tree_cv.fit(X_train,Y_train)
5  print('Tuned Regression Tree Parameters:',tree_cv.best_params_)
```

We start by creating a tree instance. Then we create an instance of a Randomized-SearchCV object.[1] This object takes as an input a specific model type (here, our tree) and a parameter distribution (that we did above). We can also input other parameters, such as the following:

n_jobs (default=1)

This very useful parameter is the number of processors Python will allocate to run the model. Each processor will work in parallel to run a different tree. You can set it to n_jobs=-1 to allocate all your processors—and drastically reduce the computation time!

cv (default=3)

This is the number of folds we want to create (the k factor from the k-fold cross-validation).

verbose (default=0)

The higher the parameter, the more information the function will print out when you launch it.

n_iter (default=10)

This is the number of parameter sets you want to test. The higher, the better, as you will test more different parameter sets. But this will be done at the expense of a longer computation time.

---

[1] For a grid search in scikit-learn, see scikit-learn.org/stable/modules/generated/sklearn.model_selection.GridSearchCV.html

scoring (default None)

This gives the scoring metric (i. e., KPI) that will be used to select the best model. Typically, we want to use either `neg_mean_absolute_error` which is MAE or `neg_mean_squared_error` for MSE. Note that there is a difference between this scoring that is used to select the best model among all the ones that were tested and the `criterion` that is the KPI used to optimize each tree individually. Basically, this means that we can optimize our trees for MSE (via `criterion`) and then select the one that got the best MAE (via `scoring`).

The function will then print the best parameters that it has found. Finally, you can display the accuracy achieved over the training and the test sets, thanks to our `kpi_ML()` function from Section 12.4:

```
1  Y_train_pred = tree_cv.predict(X_train)
2  Y_test_pred = tree_cv.predict(X_test)
3  kpi_ML(Y_train, Y_train_pred, Y_test, Y_test_pred, name='Tree')
```

In our example, we got these results:

```
1  >> Fitting 10 folds for each of 100 candidates, totalling 1000 fits
2  >> [Parallel(n_jobs=-1)]: Using backend LokyBackend with 8 ⌐
   ↵  concurrent workers.
3  >> [Parallel(n_jobs=-1)]: Done   34 tasks      | elapsed:    2.0s
4  >> [Parallel(n_jobs=-1)]: Done 560 tasks      | elapsed:    4.3s
5  >> [Parallel(n_jobs=-1)]: Done 985 out of 1000 | elapsed:    6.2s ⌐
   ↵  remaining:    0.0s
6  >> [Parallel(n_jobs=-1)]: Done 1000 out of 1000 | elapsed:    6.2s ⌐
   ↵  finished
7  >> Tuned Regression Tree Parameters: {'min_samples_split': 17, ⌐
   ↵  'min_samples_leaf': 17, 'max_depth': 6}
8  >>
9  >>          MAE   RMSE  Bias
10 >> Tree
11 >> Train   17.3  42.2   0.0
12 >> Test    18.9  46.8   2.9
```

Note in Table 14.3 how the accuracy on the test set improved, going from 21.1% (on our original tree) to 18.9%. This is much better, of course, but still less than a simple linear regression.

Table 14.3: Results.

Models	MAE		RMSE		Bias	
	Train	Test	Train	Test	Train	Test
Regression	17.8	**17.8**	43.9	**43.7**	0.0	**1.6**
Tree (initial)	18.1	21.1	43.4	52.6	−0.0	3.2
Tree (optimized)	**17.3**	18.9	**42.2**	46.8	0.0	2.9

Note that the accuracy on the training set is now around 17%—so still much lower than our test set results. To reduce the overfitting a bit more, we could do the randomized search on a larger space of parameters along with a higher number of k-folds (note that cv=10 is already considered as a high value), but this will drastically increase the computation time. Unfortunately, we will never be able to take this overfitting away completely. As discussed in Chapter 8, we will face this issue more often as we use more complex models.

Pro-Tip

When doing a random search with scikit-learn, you can easily retrieve the metrics obtained for each set of tested parameters.

```
1  df = pd.DataFrame(tree_cv.cv_results_)
```

The resulting DataFrame contains a column params that contains, in a dictionary, the set of parameters of each fit. We can unpack them in various columns before exporting the DataFrame to Excel.

```
1  df_params = pd.DataFrame(df['params'].values.tolist())
2  df = pd.concat([df_params,df],axis=1)
3  df.to_excel('Results.xlsx')
```

14.4 Recap

As machine learning models have many parameters, we learned how to combine a random search with k-fold cross-validation, which is a powerful and easy way to test many different parameter sets with a limited risk of overfitting. As we tested many parameter sets, we improved the performance of our tree. But not enough to beat the benchmark yet.

Let's see what else we can do.

15 Forest

15.1 The Wisdom of the Crowd and Ensemble Models

In social choice theory[1] there is a concept called **the wisdom of the crowd**. This idea explains that the average opinion of a group of people is going to be more precise (on average) than the opinion of a single member of the group. Let's explore a simple example: if you want to make a forecast for the demand of a product next month, it is better to ask the opinion of many different team members (salespeople, marketing, CEO, supply chain planners, financial analysts) and take the average of the different forecasts, rather than to trust only one team member blindly.

> ### A Brief History of the Wisdom of the Crowd
>
> In 1906, Francis Galton, an English scientist, went visiting a livestock fair. He witnessed a contest: the villagers were invited to guess the weight of an ox. Eight hundred people took part in this contest, all noting down their guess on tickets. Galton noted that "the hope of a prize and the joy of competition prompted each competitor to do his best. The competitors included butchers and farmers, some of whom were highly expert in judging the weight of cattle." After the event, he was able to perform a statistical analysis of the various guesses. To his surprise, averaging all the guesses resulted in a virtually perfect weight estimation.[a] Moreover, this average guess was beating the actual winner of the contest, and the guesses made by experts.
>
> ---
>
> *a* See Wallis (2014) for more information.

In their (excellent) book *Superforecasting: The Art and Science of Prediction*, Philip E. Tetlock and Dan Gardner explain how one can harness the power of the wisdom of the crowd among a team to predict anything from stock-price value to presidential elections.[2] For wisdom to emerge out of a crowd, you need three main elements. First, each individual needs independent sources of information. Second, they must make independent decisions (not being influenced by the others). And third, there must be a way to gather and weigh those individual predictions into a final one (usually taking the average or median of the various predictions).

---

1 The social choice theory is the science of combining different individual choices into a final global decision. This scientific field emerged in the late 18th century with the voting paradox. It states that a group's collective preference can be cyclic (i. e., A is preferred to B, B is preferred to C, and C is preferred to A) even if none of the preferences of each individual are cyclic.
2 See Tetlock and Gardner (2016).

https://doi.org/10.1515/9783110671124-015

Actually, this idea—gathering different opinions to get a better prediction—works in most situations. For example, you may able to diagnose cancers using pigeons. In an experiment, scientists trained pigeons to detect breast tumors by looking at biopsies and rewarding correct prediction (i. e., if the tumor is either benign or malignant) them with food.[3] The results were the following: around 85% prediction accuracy for a single trained pigeon, and 99% accuracy for a pigeon-team (that's the level of accuracy obtained by a professional).

> **Ensemble**
>
> An ensemble model is a (meta-)model constituted of many sub-models.

Can we use this concept with our tree? Yes, of course.

15.2 Bagging Trees in a Forest

In 1995, Tin Kam Ho proposed an idea to bring the power of the wisdom of the crowd to regression trees.[4] Let's imagine that we could populate *different* regression trees from our *single* training dataset. All accurate but all slightly different. Being different is what makes them all relevant. We could then make a better prediction by taking the average of all the different trees' predictions. We will call this ensemble of regression trees a... forest!

> **Bagging**
>
> Bagging (a short word for *Bootstrap Aggregation*) is a method for aggregating multiple sub-models into an ensemble model by averaging their predictions with equal weighting.
>
> For example, a forest is an *ensemble* model that aggregates the results of *base learners* (trees) by *bagging*.

Generally speaking, to obtain the best possible bagging ensemble model (forest), we need each of the base learners (tree) to be as good and as different from each other as possible.[5]

---

3 See Levenson et al. (2015) for the initial article, or Stetka (2015) for the newspaper story.

4 See Ho (1995) for the original paper. Her initial algorithm was later improved by other teams, see for example Breiman (2001).

5 In other words, as stated in Breiman (2001), "The generalization error of a forest of tree classifiers depends on the strength of the individual trees in the forest and the correlation between them."

This means we have to create (slightly) different (accurate) regression trees from a single training dataset. In order to do so, we will use two main ideas, varying their respective training set and the way each tree is constructed.[6]

Idea #1 – Using Different Training Sets

The first main idea is that we want to train each tree (in the forest) based on a slightly different training set. We will randomly create a variety of training sets from our initial main training set by using two techniques:

Bootstrapping This means that each tree will receive a random selection from the initial training dataset. This random selection is done *with replacement*.[7] In practice, it means that you could find the same data points multiple times in the training set used by each tree, and you could simply not use some other data points.

As you will see in the next section, you can activate bootstrapping in scikit-learn by setting `bootstrapping` to `True` (and let scikit-learn perform the random selection).

Limit the Number of Samples The second idea is to limit the amount of data given to each tree. By doing so, you limit their training, but you make each tree a bit more different.

The number of samples can be set in scikit-learn with the parameter `max_samples`. Usually, a ratio is set (for example, `0.9`) so that a (random) fraction of the initial training set is kept.

Thanks to our two ideas, we will create a unique, random training set for each single tree.

Idea #2 – Restrain the Maximum Amount of Features

Recall from Section 13.1 that the regression tree will choose at each node the best feature (i. e., input) to create a split on. If we limit the maximum number of features that the algorithm can choose from at each node (`max_features` in scikit-learn), and the features are chosen randomly each time, **we will then obtain different trees at each fitting**. What is interesting is that by restricting how the different trees can grow, they become more different from each other than simply by bootstrapping and limiting the number of samples (even if it is done at the expense of their own accuracy).

---

6 Or, as summarized in Breiman et al. (1998), "Unstable methods can have their accuracy improved by perturbing and combining, that is, generate multiple versions of the predictor by perturbing the training set or construction method, then combine these multiple versions into a single predictor."

7 In statistics and probability science, *sampling with replacement* is a sample selection method where each sample that has already been selected is still a possible target for selection.

15.3 Do It Yourself

Random Forest

We will import the RandomForestRegressor from the sklearn.ensemble library.[8] See how easy it is to create one forest with sklearn. Scikit-learn allows us to create forests as easily as trees.

```
1  from sklearn.ensemble import RandomForestRegressor
2  forest = RandomForestRegressor(bootstrap=True, max_samples=0.95, ⌋
   ↳   max_features=11, min_samples_leaf=18, max_depth=7)
3  forest.fit(X_train,Y_train)
```

Let's take a look at the accuracy before we discuss the different parameters:

```
1  Y_train_pred = forest.predict(X_train)
2  Y_test_pred = forest.predict(X_test)
3  kpi_ML(Y_train, Y_train_pred, Y_test, Y_test_pred, name='Forest')
4  >>           MAE  RMSE  Bias
5  >> Forest
6  >> Train   15.7  40.0  -0.0
7  >> Test    18.3  47.1   3.6
```

We now obtain an MAE of around 18.3%. That is currently not as good as our benchmark (17.8%), but is better than our optimized tree (18.9%).

Now that we have a working model, let's discuss the different parameters.

Parameters

Before we improve our model further, let's take some time to discuss the different parameters.

bootstrap (default=True)

This parameter indicates if the random forest will use bootstrapping. As explained, bootstrapping allows each tree to grow differently, as they use a randomized training dataset. It is then advised to keep this to True.

max_depth (default=None)

Just as for the regular tree, this is the maximum depth of each tree (i. e., the maximum number of consecutive yes/no questions). A higher value will result in better

---

8 See scikit-learn.org/stable/modules/generated/sklearn.ensemble.RandomForestRegressor.html

accuracy on the training set (as the forest can distinguish more cases), but will increase the likelihood of overfitting.

max_features (default=n_features)

This is the maximum amount of features that a tree can choose from when it has to split a node. Note that the set of available features to choose from randomly changes at each node. As explained, it is important to create some variations among the different trees, and the feature restriction is a good way to create this randomness. The lower max_features, the more variation among the trees of the forest (resulting in a better forest), but the more constrained each tree will be (resulting in a lower individual accuracy).

> **Attention Point**
>
> Pay attention that if max_features is input as an integer (e. g., 1, 2, 10...), this will be the exact number of features to be selected. If it is input as a float from 0.0 to 1.0,[a] this ratio will be applied to the total number of features in the dataset. For example, max_features=0.5 means that you want the maximum number of features to be equal to half of the dataset features; max_features=1.0 means that you want the maximum number of features to be equal to the number of features (that is to say that there is no maximum).
>
> ———
> **a** Pay attention that 1 will be considered as an integer and 1.0 as a float. You can expect totally different results.

min_samples_leaf (default=1)

Just as for a normal tree, this is the minimum number of samples each leaf has to contain. A low value will allow the tree to grow further, resulting (most likely) in a better accuracy on the training dataset at the expense of a risk of overfitting.

min_samples_split (default=1)

Just as for a normal tree, this is the minimum number of samples a node has to contain to be split. Just as for the min_samples_leaf, a low value will most likely result in a higher accuracy on the training set but might not improve the test set, or may even harm it. Typically, a good k-fold cross-validation will help us determine the right trade-off between too deep and too shallow.

n_estimators (default=10)

This is simply the number of trees in the forest. The higher, the better; at the expense of a longer computation time. At some point, the extra running time will not be worth the incremental minimal improvement.

criterion (default='mse')

This is the KPI that the algorithm will minimize. Choose 'mse' to optimize MSE or 'mae' for MAE. As we discussed for the tree, the algorithm to create a random forest will take a much longer time to optimize itself for MAE than for MSE.

Optimization

Just as for a single tree, we will optimize our random forest via a random search and a k-fold cross-validation. The code is similar to the one that we used to optimize our regression tree. Note that we won't optimize the number of trees in our forest (n_estimators) for now—we will discuss this later in Section 15.4.

```
1  max_depth = list(range(5,11)) + [None]
2  min_samples_split = range(5,20)
3  min_samples_leaf = range(2,15)
4  max_features = range(3,8)
5  bootstrap = [True] #We force bootstrap
6  max_samples = [.7,.8,.9,.95,1]
7
8  param_dist = {'max_depth': max_depth,
9                'min_samples_split': min_samples_split,
10               'min_samples_leaf': min_samples_leaf,
11               'max_features': max_features,
12               'bootstrap': bootstrap,
13               'max_samples': max_samples}
14
15 forest = RandomForestRegressor(n_jobs=1, n_estimators=30)
16 forest_cv = RandomizedSearchCV(forest, param_dist, cv=6, n_jobs=-1, ⌐
   ↪  verbose=2, n_iter=400, scoring='neg_mean_absolute_error')
17 forest_cv.fit(X_train,Y_train)
```

> **Pro-Tip – Bootstrapping by Default**
>
> We limit the search here to bootstrap=True as this is usually the best setup. If we don't use bootstrapping, the tree's variability is only relying on max_samples and max_features, which is often not enough. Therefore, in order to make our search more efficient, we limit it to bootstrap=True.

Once this is done, we can print the optimal parameters and the accuracy achieved by our brand-new model.

```
1  print('Tuned Forest Parameters:', forest_cv.best_params_)
2  print()
3  Y_train_pred = forest_cv.predict(X_train)
4  Y_test_pred = forest_cv.predict(X_test)
5  kpi_ML(Y_train, Y_train_pred, Y_test, Y_test_pred, name='Forest ⌐
   ↪  optimized')
```

You should obtain something similar to this:

```
1  >> Tuned Forest Parameters: {'min_samples_split': 15, ⌋
   ↪  'min_samples_leaf': 4, 'max_samples': 0.95, 'max_features': 4, ⌋
   ↪  'max_depth': 8, 'bootstrap': True}
2  >>
3  >>                    MAE   RMSE  Bias
4  >> Forest optimized
5  >> Train             14.3  35.5   0.0
6  >> Test              17.9  45.9   3.2
```

Keep in mind that the forests are random and you will, therefore, get (slightly) different results each time you run your model—even with the exact same parameters! On top of this, a random search does not test all the possible combinations of parameters—that would take too much time!—so you might get a different set of parameters.

> **Pro-Tip – Faster Search**
>
> When doing a random search, it is usually faster to set n_jobs=1 for the forest and n_jobs=-1 for the random search. This means that the computer will process different forests simultaneously (allocating a thread to each of them) rather than working on a single forest at one time (allocating all its threads to one forest).

15.4 Insights

Differences Compared to a Single Tree

Note how the optimal max_depth changed from the original optimal *lonely* tree from Chapter 13 to the optimal tree in our (random) forest (it was 6 and now it is 10). The trees in the forest are now deeper. These deeper trees are more prone to overfitting, but the forest compensates for this by the number of trees and the features limitation (5, in our example). With fewer features to choose from at each node, our model will simply have to ask more questions to get to a proper forecast.

Number of Trees in the Forest

In order to save some computation time for our random search, we reduced the number of trees in the forest (n_estimators) to 30 trees. Typically, the first parameter that you will want to increase to improve the accuracy of your forest is the number of trees. The more, the better. Of course, we could input a very high number, but that would come at the cost of computation time and wouldn't provide so much extra accuracy as of a certain number of trees. **There is a trade-off to be made between computation time and forecast accuracy.** The best way to know when it is worth increasing the amount of trees is to plot the model accuracy based on the amount of trees.

Remember we are data scientists: we experiment.

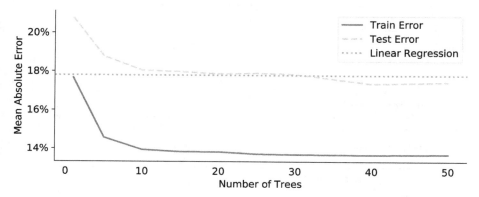

Figure 15.1: Accuracy based on number of trees.

As you can see in Figure 15.1, as of around 20 trees, the incremental accuracy for any new tree is limited. But it seems, nevertheless, that the error decreases (very) slightly over time.

In order to get the best out of our forest—without increasing computation time too much—let's run a forest with our new optimal parameters and n_estimators=200. We can easily allow ourselves 200 trees due to the dataset limited size.

```
1  forest = RandomForestRegressor(n_estimators=200, n_jobs=-1, ⌋
   ↳  **forest_cv.best_params_)
2  forest = forest.fit(X_train, Y_train)
3  Y_train_pred = forest.predict(X_train)
4  Y_test_pred = forest.predict(X_test)
5  kpi_ML(Y_train, Y_train_pred, Y_test, Y_test_pred, name='Forestx200')
```

As the optimal parameters are contained in a dictionary (forest_cv.best_params_), we can pass them easily to our new model by unpacking them with ** (as discussed below).

Python Mastery – Packing/Unpacking Inputs

You can pass multiple arguments to a function at once, thanks to a dictionary. You need first to wrap them in a dictionary where the keys will be the parameter names. You can then pass the dictionary to a function with **dic; this will unpack each key-value pair contained in the dictionary as separate arguments to the function. Basically:

```
1  function('param1'=1,'param2'=2)
```

is the same as:

```
1  dic = {'param1':1,'param2':2}
2  function(**dic)
```

And this is what we get:

```
1  >>               MAE  RMSE  Bias
2  >> Forestx200
3  >> Train        14.1  35.0  -0.0
4  >> Test         17.6  44.9   2.7
```

As you can see in Table 15.1, the MAE improved only by 0.1% compared to the forest with 30 trees—and the RMSE worsened. Anyway, we are happy, as our forest is now beating the linear regression.

Table 15.1: Results.

Models	MAE		RMSE		Bias	
	Train	Test	Train	Test	Train	Test
Regression	17.8	17.8	43.9	**43.7**	0.0	1.6
Tree	17.3	18.9	42.2	46.8	0.0	2.9
Forest	**14.1**	**17.6**	**35.0**	44.9	−0.0	2.7

So, can we further improve our forecast?

Yes, we can.

16 Feature Importance

In some ways, AI is comparable to the classical oracle of Delphi, which left to human beings the interpretation of its cryptic messages about human destiny.

Henry A. Kissinger, Eric Schmidt, Daniel Huttenlocher[1]

Statistical models are interesting, as they can show us the interactions between the different input variables and the output. **Such models are easy to understand and to interpret.** In the first part of the book, we worked with many different exponential smoothing models: we could analyze them by simply looking at their level, trend, or seasonality over time. Thanks to them, we can easily answer questions such as *Do we have a seasonality?* or *Is there a trend?* And if the forecast for a specific period is strange, we can look at how the sub-components (level, trend, seasonality) are behaving to understand where the error comes from.

This is unfortunately not the case with machine learning. These models are very difficult to interpret. A forest will never give you an estimation of the level, trend, or seasonality of a product. You won't even know if the model *sees* a seasonality or a trend. Nevertheless, we have one tool at our disposal to understand how our machine learning algorithm thinks: the feature importance.

As you remember, we created a machine learning algorithm that looked at the last 12 months of historical car sales in Norway to predict the sales in the following month. In order to do that, we trained our model by showing it many different sequences of 13 months so that it could learn from these sequences how to predict the 13th month based on the 12 previous ones.

Before we continue with new models and further optimization, let's discuss the importance of these inputs. We do not know yet which of these 12 historical months is the most important to predict the sales of the 13th.

We would like to answer questions such as:
- Is M-1 more important than M-12?
- Is M-5 of any help?

When we grow a tree or a forest, we can get an idea of each feature's importance (in our specific case, each feature is one of the 12 previous periods). There are different definitions and ways to compute each feature's importance; we will focus on the one used by the scikit-learn library. Basically, the importance of a feature is the reduction it brings to the objective that the algorithm tries to minimize. In our case, we want to bring the MAE or the RMSE down. Therefore, the **feature importance** is measured as the forecast accuracy brought by each feature. The feature importance is then normalized (i. e., each feature importance is scaled so that the sum of all features importance is 1).

---

1 See Kissinger et al. (2019).

https://doi.org/10.1515/9783110671124-016

Before we discuss the implementation in Python, let's plot the feature importance we get from our random forest. Data visualization is a very important part of any data science project.

As we can see in Figure 16.1, the recent months (M-1 to M-3) are critical to forecast M+1. More than half of the total information comes from these three months. We then have two relatively helpful months: M-12 (this is the same month as M+1 but on Y-1) and M-6 (may be used to check if there is a seasonality, as this month is at the exact opposite in the calendar). The other months (M-11 to M-7) are virtually useless.

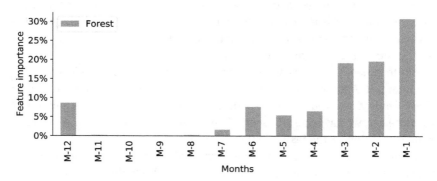

Figure 16.1: Feature importance.

Feature importance will be a useful technique to prevent our model from overfitting, as we are now able to see which feature brings an added value or not. We will discuss this further in Chapter 14, when we optimize the number of historical months that our model will use to make a forecast, and in Chapter 24, when we will analyze the added value of many extra features (that we will add through Chapters 20, 22, and 23).

As a general piece of advice, do not hesitate to plot the feature importance of any new model you create. If you see that some features have minimal importance, try to exclude them (as we will do later in Chapter 24). This might make your model faster and more precise (as it will have a limited risk of overfitting).

16.1 Do It Yourself

Let's create the code to make a feature importance graph like Figure 16.1.

We start by creating a list (features) that will contain each feature name.

```
1  cols = X_train.shape[1] # number of columns in our training sets
2  features = [f'M-{cols-col}' for col in range(cols)]
```

We can then extract the feature importance from our forest model, thanks to its attribute feature_importances_ and reshape this to a vertical array (thanks to re-shape(-1,1)).

```
1   data = forest.feature_importances_.reshape(-1,1)
```

We can then save these features and their respective importance into a DataFrame.

```
1   imp = pd.DataFrame(data=data, index=features, columns=['Forest'])
```

Finally, we can simply plot it and obtain a figure such as Figure 16.1.

```
1   imp.plot(kind='bar')
```

17 Extremely Randomized Trees

The random forest idea was that we could obtain a better forecast accuracy by taking the average prediction of many *different* trees. To create those slightly different trees from the same initial training dataset, we used two tricks. The first was to limit the number of features the algorithm could choose from each node split. The second trick was to create different random subsets of the initial training dataset (thanks to bootstrapping and only keeping a subset of the initial samples).

In 2006, Belgian researchers Pierre Geurts, Damien Ernst, and Louis Wehenkel introduced a third idea to further increase the differences between each tree.[1] At each node, the algorithm will now choose a split point **randomly** for each feature and then select the best split among these. It means that, for our Norwegian car sales dataset, this new method will draw at each node one random split point for each of the 12 previous months (our features) and, among these 12 potential splits, choose the best one to split the node. The fact that an Extremely Randomized Trees (or ETR) draws split points randomly seems counter intuitive. Still, this will increase further the *difference* between each tree in the ETR, resulting in better overall accuracy. Remember, an ensemble model (such as the ETR or the forest) is more accurate, as its sub-models are different.

17.1 Do It Yourself

We will once again use the scikit-learn library, so our code will be very similar to the one we used for the random forest.

```
from sklearn.ensemble import ExtraTreesRegressor
ETR = ExtraTreesRegressor(n_jobs=-1, n_estimators=200,
    min_samples_split=15, min_samples_leaf=4, max_samples=0.95,
    max_features=4, max_depth=8, bootstrap=True)
ETR.fit(X_train,Y_train)
```

The input parameters we use (n_jobs, n_estimators, max_depth, max_features, min_samples_leaf, min_samples_split) are the same as for the random forest.

Let's print the results.

```
Y_train_pred = ETR.predict(X_train)
Y_test_pred = ETR.predict(X_test)
kpi_ML(Y_train, Y_train_pred, Y_test, Y_test_pred, name='ETR')
```

1 See Geurts et al. (2006).

https://doi.org/10.1515/9783110671124-017

```
4  >>            MAE   RMSE  Bias
5  >> ETR
6  >> Train   17.8  43.7  -0.0
7  >> Test    18.9  47.1   3.2
```

The results we obtain are not as good as those we had with the forest (MAE of 17.6% on the test set). Our previous forest parameters do not seem appropriate for our new ETR model. Let's optimize them.

Optimization

As for the random forest, we could be tempted to increase the number of trees to improve the test set's accuracy. As the ETR trees are more different from each other, ETR should benefit slightly more from an increased number of trees than the forest. Nevertheless, as shown in Figure 17.1, the impact will be limited when going over about 30 trees.

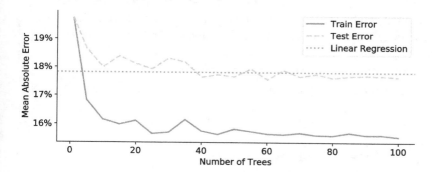

Figure 17.1: Impact of the number of trees for the extremely randomized trees model.

The best way to improve the accuracy further is actually to optimize the parameters via a random search (as discussed in Chapter 14). We will do a random search on our ETR model just as we did for our forest. Note that we changed the parameter ranges slightly.

```
1  max_depth = list(range(6,13)) + [None]
2  min_samples_split = range(7,16)
3  min_samples_leaf = range(2,13)
4  max_features = range(5,13)
5  bootstrap = [True] #We force bootstrap
6  max_samples = [.7,.8,.9,.95,1]
7
```

```
8  param_dist = {'max_depth': max_depth,
9                'min_samples_split': min_samples_split,
10               'min_samples_leaf': min_samples_leaf,
11               'max_features': max_features,
12               'bootstrap': bootstrap,
13               'max_samples': max_samples}
14
15 ETR = ExtraTreesRegressor(n_jobs=1, n_estimators=30)
16 ETR_cv = RandomizedSearchCV(ETR, param_dist, cv=5, verbose=2, ↵
   ↪ n_jobs=-1, n_iter=400, scoring='neg_mean_absolute_error')
17 ETR_cv.fit(X_train,Y_train)
```

Pro-Tip – Double Search

As you can see in the previous code, we updated the parameter ranges compared to those we used for the forest in Chapter 15. This is normal; these models are slightly different and will thus find their sweet spot in a different region. As mentioned previously, I advise you to first start to look across a wide space, and then do a second, more precise search around the first optimal parameter set found.

We can now show the optimal parameters and compute the accuracy they achieved.

```
1  print('Tuned Forest Parameters:', ETR_cv.best_params_)
2  print()
3  Y_train_pred = ETR_cv.predict(X_train)
4  Y_test_pred = ETR_cv.predict(X_test)
5  kpi_ML(Y_train, Y_train_pred, Y_test, Y_test_pred, name='ETR ↵
   ↪ optimized')
```

You should obtain something similar to:

```
1  >> Tuned ETR Parameters: {'min_samples_split': 14, 'min_samples_leaf': ↵
   ↪ 2, 'max_samples': 0.9, 'max_features': 12, 'max_depth': 12, ↵
   ↪ 'bootstrap': True}
2  >>
3  >>                  MAE   RMSE   Bias
4  >> ETR optimized
5  >> Train          14.4   36.5   0.1
6  >> Test           17.6   44.3   2.6
```

Randomness

As for the forest, the results of an ETR are slightly random. This means that you might get different KPI values if you run this experiment on your computer. Remember that the random search does not test all the parameter possibilities (and uses random k-fold subsets). This means that running the random search twice for the ETR might give you slightly different parameter sets.

Differences Compared to a Forest

As you can see, the maximum number of features came from 4 with the forest to 12 with the ETR—those are all the features (as we used 12 months). This was expected, as the ETR cannot choose the optimal split point for each feature; instead, it has to deal with random split points. As the split points are random, the risk of overfitting is reduced so that the ETR can use more features at once compared to the forest.

Final Results

Before computing the final results, don't forget to run your ETR with 200 trees to slightly improve the results.

```
1  >> ETR = ExtraTreesRegressor(n_estimators=200, n_jobs=-1, **ETR_cv
   ↵    .best_params_).fit(X_train, Y_train)
2  >> Y_train_pred = ETR.predict(X_train)
3  >> Y_test_pred = ETR.predict(X_test)
4  >> kpi_ML(Y_train, Y_train_pred, Y_test, Y_test_pred, name='ETRx200')
5  >>            MAE  RMSE  Bias
6  >> ETRx200
7  >> Train      14.2  35.8  -0.0
8  >> Test       17.5  44.4   2.5
```

We now obtain an MAE of 17.5% in the test set. This is better than the 17.8% obtained via the linear regression, and similar to the one obtained via the forest (as shown in Table 17.1).

Table 17.1: Results.

Models	MAE		RMSE		Bias	
	Train	Test	Train	Test	Train	Test
Regression	17.8	17.8	43.9	**43.7**	0.0	**1.6**
Tree	17.3	18.9	42.2	46.8	0.0	2.9
Forest	**14.1**	17.6	**35.0**	44.9	−0.0	2.7
ETR	14.2	**17.5**	35.8	44.4	−0.0	2.5

As ETR is often better and—as we will see in the next section—as fast as a forest. Do not hesitate to use it as your first go-to model for any new project.

17.2 Speed

Another advantage of the extremely randomized trees algorithm compared to a regular random forest is the training speed. As you can see in Figure 17.2, it is actually faster than the random forest (around 30% less of computation time). This is due to the fact that the ETR goes faster to choose the split at each node, as it only has a few possibilities.

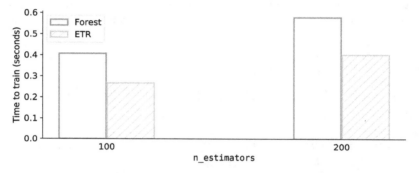

Figure 17.2: ETR vs. forest training time, both with the same parameters (optimal ones from Chapter 15).

But this speed advantage only holds if the parameters are the same. As we discussed earlier, an ETR is likely to have fewer feature restrictions than a forest, resulting in a slower model. If you compare the speed of an ETR and a forest using both their optimal parameters, you obtain very close results (as shown in Figure 17.3).

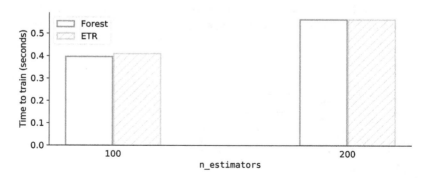

Figure 17.3: ETR vs. forest training time, both with their respective optimal parameters.

18 Feature Optimization #1

The more you know about the past, the better prepared you are for the future.

Theodore Roosevelt

So far, we have created three different models (a regression tree, a random forest, and a set of extremely randomized trees), and we have optimized each of them via a random search automatically running through some possible parameter sets and testing them via k-fold cross-validation.

We took the time to choose a model and optimize its parameters. There is one thing that we haven't optimized (yet): the features that we use.

The different models that we used so far have an interesting feature: once fitted to a training dataset, they can show each input's (i. e., feature) importance. Remember that, in our case, the input features are the different historical periods that we use to populate our forecast. For our car sales in Norway, we used the last 12 months of sales to predict the next month: these are our features. We previously looked at the feature importance of our random forest and saw that M-1 was the most critical month, leaving half of the other months useless. As you can see in Figure 18.1, if we do the same exercise with the ETR model, we obtain a much flatter curve.

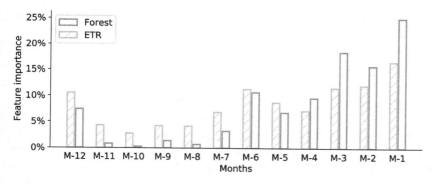

Figure 18.1: Feature importance.

How can we explain this? As you might remember, the difference between the extra trees model and the random forest lies in the fact that the split point chosen at each node is not the optimal one, but can only be selected from a set of random points for each selected feature. So even though M-1 should be the most useful feature, in many cases, the random split point proposed for this feature is not the best across the different possibilities the algorithm can choose from.

Based on this graph, we can then ask ourselves an important question: *what if we used 13 months instead of 12 to make a forecast?* To answer this question, we will have to do a lot of experiments (on our training set).

https://doi.org/10.1515/9783110671124-018

18.1 Idea #1 – Training Set

The first experiment we will perform will consist of fitting our forest and our ETR models on a training set based on 6 to 50 months and plot the results. You can see them in Figure 18.2.

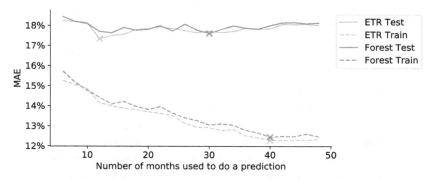

Figure 18.2: Feature optimization.

We see in this graph that, as we increase the number of months the model considers to make a prediction, the error over the training set is reduced. This effect only seems to slow down from around 40 months for the forest and seems to continue for the ETR. We actually have two effects here:

1. More input features allow our model to learn more patterns from the noise of the training set (as we discussed in Chapter 8). This drives the error down. But only in the training set, unfortunately. **This is pure overfitting.**

2. More input features also means fewer data available, as we cannot make as many loops through the original dataset as before (as we discussed in Chapter 12). This will increase the test set error, as the model has fewer data to learn from. **As there is fewer data in the training set, it is also easier for the model to overfit it.** Fortunately, this Norwegian car sales dataset is very long. We have nearly 10 years of history. So this effect is actually somewhat limited for us, in this specific example. Pay attention that it might not be the case in another dataset. Shorter historical datasets (3 to 5 years) will suffer a lot from this.

Note that both effects will drive the overfitting up, as we have at the same time fewer data to train on and more input features to learn from. This is what we observe in Figure 18.2: we clearly see that even as the training error is reduced over and over as we increase the number of features, the error in the test set seems to decrease until around 14–16 months and then increase slowly. This means that as of a certain number of input features, our model will not learn anything meaningful anymore and will just overfit the training set.

What should we do then? Could we just look at the results over the test set and take from there the optimal number of months that we should take into account?

No, we cannot. We would be overfitting the test set. Don't do this. Remember that the test set should only be used to note the final accuracy obtained on fully unseen data. If we used the test set to choose the optimal parameter set, we would generate some outstanding results today that we would not be sure to be able to replicate to-morrow. This is very bad, as we would be relying on luck to achieve the same results on new data and—based on these excellent results—we would be overcommitting our model.

The experiment that we designed simply does not give us the appropriate answer to our initial question: *how many months should we take into account?* We will have to design a new one. But before that, let's see how we can implement this first technique.

Do It Yourself

We will create a loop that runs our two models—forest and ETR—for each possible x_len and measure their accuracy on both the training set and the test set. Let's divide this into multiple steps.

First, we will define the parameters that we want to have for both the forest (forest_features) and the ETR (ETR_features), as well as the range of historical horizons (n_months) that we want to investigate.

```
1  df = import_data()
2  forest_features = {'n_jobs':-1, 'n_estimators':200, ↵
   ↪   'min_samples_split': 15, 'min_samples_leaf': 4, 'max_samples': 0↵
   ↪   .95, 'max_features': 0.3, 'max_depth': 8, 'bootstrap': True}
3  forest = RandomForestRegressor(**forest_features)
4  ETR_features = {'n_jobs':-1, 'n_estimators':200, 'min_samples_split': ↵
   ↪   14, 'min_samples_leaf': 2, 'max_samples': 0.9, 'max_features': 1.0,↵
   ↪   'max_depth': 12, 'bootstrap': True}
5  ETR = ExtraTreesRegressor(**ETR_features)
6  models = [('Forest',forest), ('ETR',ETR)]
```

We have defined forest_features and ETR_features as two dictionaries so we can pass them to the functions. Note that you have to set max_features as a ratio and not as an absolute number (remember, scikit-learn will interpret 1.0 as "Use all features" and not as "Use 1 feature").

We will also define a function model_mae() that will return the mean absolute error obtained by a model against a dataset Y. This function will be useful to simplify our code in the following sections. Feel free to update it to return RMSE instead of MAE if you want to.

```
1  def model_mae(model, X, Y):
2      Y_pred = model.predict(X)
3      mae = np.mean(np.abs(Y - Y_pred))/np.mean(Y)
4      return mae
```

We are now ready to loop through all the possible historical horizons. We will create a list (`results`) to record our results.

```
1  n_months = range(6,50,2)
2  results = []
3  for x_len in n_months: # We loop through the different x_len
4      X_train, Y_train, X_test, Y_test = datasets(df, x_len=x_len)
5      for name, model in models: # We loop through the models
6          model.fit(X_train,Y_train)
7          mae_train = model_mae(model, X_train, Y_train)
8          mae_test = model_mae(model, X_test, Y_test)
9          results.append([name+' Train',mae_train,x_len])
10         results.append([name+' Test',mae_test,x_len])
```

We now have a list (`results`) that contains all our results. Let's format it a bit so that we can make a figure similar to Figure 18.2.

```
1  data = pd.DataFrame(results,columns=['Model','MAE%','Number of Months'])
2  data = data.set_index(['Number of Months','Model']).stack() ↵
   ↪  .unstack('Model')
3  data.index = data.index.droplevel(level=1)
4  data.index.name = 'Number of months'
```

We can then simply plot `data` using the method `.plot()` to obtain something similar to Figure 18.2.

```
1  data.plot(color=['orange']*2+['black']*2,style=['-','--']*2)
```

You can also populate a summary table with the optimal number of months that was obtained on each dataset, thanks to this one line of code:

```
1  print(data.idxmin())
```

18.2 Idea #2 – Validation Set

We saw that our first experiment didn't give us the result we wanted, as our model overfitted the training set; the error in the training set did not give us any meaningful information about the expected error in the test set. In Chapter 14, we saw that we could use the k-fold cross-validation method to properly test each parameter set. The idea was to cut the training set into k subsets; and run k trials with each one of these subsets kept as a validation set. The final error would then be the average of the error obtained over each validation set. Let's do the same here and run, for each different possible number of features, k different trials, each one with a different validation set. You can see in Figure 18.3 the accuracy obtained in the validation set.

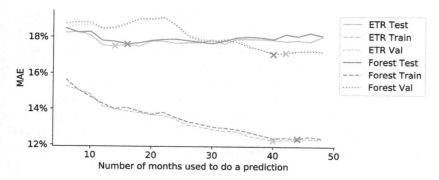

Figure 18.3: Feature optimization: Validation set.

These results are already much better! The accuracy obtained in the validation set is much more aligned with the one in the test set compared to the training set. Nevertheless, suppose that we look at the optimal number of input features (see Table 18.1). In that case, we see that the optimal number of months is fairly different for the validation set (around 40 months) and the test set (about 12–18!).

Table 18.1: Optimal results.

	ETR	Forest
Train	40	44
Validation	42	40
Test	14	16

We observe some interesting behaviors:
1. We have to use a relatively high number of k-folds (8, in this example) to reduce the result's randomness (due to the variability of each subset). A higher number of

k-folds will also limit the reduced amount of data available for our model to learn from. With 8 k-folds, the model only loses 12.5% of its training dataset, which is already a small penalty. On the other hand, as we use more k-folds, the computation time explodes.

2. The initial error of the validation set is higher than the one of the test set. This can be explained, as the test set is a rather "easy" dataset. We know this by using the regression that we used as a benchmark: it obtained a better score in the test set than in the training set.

3. As we use more months to make our prediction, the error in the validation set goes down, and the error in the test set grows bigger. Until they cross each other at around 40 months.

This last point is rather interesting: how does the validation error shrink with a higher number of months, whereas the test set error grows?

A possible explanation may come from the fact that each year is a bit different. In a typical business, you might face some unusual years. Maybe January last year was excellent, or you had an issue in April. These can be due to new legislation, the apparition of new competitors—or the bankruptcy of some others—the introduction of a breakthrough new product, and so on. As our machine learning models gain more input features, they start to remember these small demand bumps. As the validation set is composed of random extracts of the training dataset, it contains years that the model already knows, so that the model doesn't just predict any month but recognizes that we want it to predict *specifically* April 2015, which was 5% higher than usual. Somehow, the model is overfitting the validation set, as it learns historical patterns that won't happen again in the future.

Once again, we will have to find a new, experimental method to overcome this overfitting. But first, let's take a look at how you can implement this technique.

Do It Yourself

We will use the KFold function from the scikit-learn library. This will allow us to randomly split our training dataset into a validation set and a new training set. In our code, we will create kf as an instance of a KFold object (see line 11). It will be used to cut our training dataset into 8 splits.

```
1  from sklearn.model_selection import KFold
2  results = []
3  for x_len in n_months:
4      X_train, Y_train, X_test, Y_test = datasets(df, x_len=x_len)
5      for name, model in models:
6          mae_kfold_train = []
```

```
7    mae_kfold_val = []
8    for train_index, val_index in KFold(n_splits=8)
     ↪    .split(X_train):
9        X_train_kfold, X_val_kfold = X_train[train_index],
         ↪    X_train[val_index]
10       Y_train_kfold, Y_val_kfold = Y_train[train_index],
         ↪    Y_train[val_index]
11       model.fit(X_train_kfold, Y_train_kfold)
12       mae_train = model_mae(model, X_train_kfold,
         ↪    Y_train_kfold)
13       mae_kfold_train.append(mae_train)
14       mae_val = model_mae(model, X_val_kfold, Y_val_kfold)
15       mae_kfold_val.append(mae_val)
16   results.append([name+' Val',np.mean(mae_kfold_val),x_len])
17   results.append([name+' Train',np.mean(mae_kfold_train),x_len])
18
19   model.fit(X_train,Y_train)
20   mae_test = model_mae(model, X_test, Y_test)
21   results.append([name+' Test',mae_test,x_len])
```

As we did for the first experiment from Section 18.1, we can also clean our results in order to plot them.

```
1  data = pd.DataFrame(results,columns=['Model','MAE%','Number of Months'])
2  data = data.set_index(['Number of Months','Model']).stack()
   ↪    .unstack('Model')
3  data.index = data.index.droplevel(level=1)
4  data.index.name = 'Number of months'
5  data.plot(color=['orange']*3+['black']*3,style=['-','--',':']*2)
6  print(data.idxmin())
```

Your plot should be similar to Figure 18.3.

18.3 Idea #3 – Holdout Dataset

As we saw in our previous experiments, despite our best efforts with a powerful k-fold method, our model could overfit the validation set itself. We have to think of a smarter way to find the best model.

Why Do We Use a Test Set in the First Place?

The initial idea behind the test set is to keep a set of data aside so that we can run our model against it (once we have chosen one and optimized it) as if it were real, unseen data. With our example dataset, we kept the last 12 months as the test set (February 2016 to January 2017). We took the implicit assumption that the accuracy we would obtain on this 2016–2017 period would be similar to the accuracy we would achieve on a future forecast made on the remaining part of 2017 (assuming we would today be somewhere in February 2017).

A Second Test Set?

A smart new method is to create a second test set (based on 2015, for example) and keep the best model based on the 2015 results. We would somehow create a *pre-test* set. We can then assume that the model that achieves the best results over 2015 would also perform well against 2016 and in the future as well. We will call this new test set the **holdout set**.

> **Holdout Set**
>
> A holdout set is a subset of the training set that is kept aside during the training in order to validate a model against unseen data. The holdout set is made of the last periods of the training set in order to replicate a test set.

Results

In Figure 18.4, you can see the results that we obtain if we use a holdout dataset for each iteration of our models.

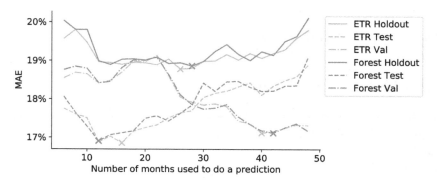

Figure 18.4: Results with a holdout dataset.

We observe two main behaviors:
1. The error in the validation set seems to decrease as the number of months increases.
2. The very good news is that the overall accuracy obtained in the holdout dataset behaves more or less the same as the one obtained in the test set.

First Observe, Then Conclude

As you might have noticed, the results shown in Tables 18.1 and 18.2 do not match exactly. This is normal, as the results vary from one simulation to another: both models contain a part of randomness, and the validation set is also random—even if it is done based on eight folds! One way to reduce randomness would be to increase the number of trees and folds in both models, but that would come at the expense of computation time. Also, as 2015 is not the same as 2016 (i. e., our test and holdout sets are not the same), the optimum on one of these two can be different from the other.

Table 18.2: Optimal results.

	ETR	Forest
Train	40	40
Validation	40	42
Holdout	26	28
Test	16	12

The question that we asked ourselves was: *How many months should we take into account to make a prediction?* Even though we found a good method to answer this question, the answer does not seem black and white, due to all this randomness. This will often be the case with machine learning. It means that we cannot find a definitive answer to our simple question, but we can nevertheless draw some trends and refine the search space from these first trends. It will take a few iterations to reach excellent results. But, keep in mind that—due to the randomness—you will unfortunately never select a **perfect** model.

The best model for 2015 might not be the best one for 2016, which might not be the best one for 2017, and so on. Therefore, it is important to understand that we should not draw definitive conclusions by saying that if one set of parameters is the best for 2015, it will also be the best in the future. What if we were just lucky?

Back to Feature Importance

A conscientious observation of the results and the main trends, as well as some experience in modeling, might help us to find a **very good** model—which might not be the **best** model on this holdout dataset. To do this analysis, let's plot in Figure 18.5 the feature importance for a model for 26 months.

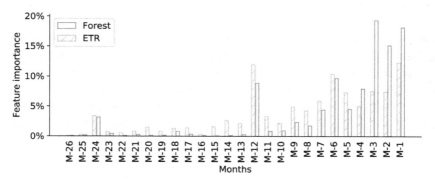

Figure 18.5: Feature importance for 26 months.

We are looking here for patterns rather than definitive, direct conclusions. We observe that:
1. The first year (months M-1 to M-12) is much more important than the second.
2. The very first months of -Y2 and -Y3 (M-13 and M-25) are nearly useless (for the forest).
3. M-12 and M-24 seem to be more important than the months just next to them. This is normal: we only want to predict one month in the future, and these are the same months from one and two years ago. Basically, if we want to forecast January 2017, these are January 2016 and January 2015.

Based on these observations, we can restrict the number of possible models to either 12 or 24 months. Remember that the parameters that we used for our models were initially given by a random search we did for models with 12 months. It means that the models with 24 months might be better with a (slightly) different set of parameters.

Finally, to decide to use either one or two years of input data, we should launch a new random search on the models that take 24 months as input for those models to be properly optimized. We should then use the results of these models against a holdout set to determine if we want to keep a forest and an ETR with 12 or 24 months.

That is a lot of work, but careful optimization has a cost. Hopefully, Python will allow us to automate most of this.

It is imperative to note here that the conclusion we drew for this dataset might not apply to your dataset. But the process and the logic of the search will still be applicable. Also, this conclusion only holds for a prediction at M+1. If you want to create predictions at M+6, you might need to keep 18 months instead of 12 months. Machine learning feature optimization calls for many experiments.

Recap

Thanks to our holdout dataset, we could finally create an experiment that behaved similarly to the test set. Based on initial broad search, we could restrict the potential number of months we should use as an input. We could then investigate these few possibilities in depth before choosing the best one.

Do It Yourself

We first have to define a new function datasets_holdout() to populate a holdout subset, along with the training and test sets (see Section 12.3 for the initial datasets() function). datasets_holdout() will take as an input holdout_loops, which is the number of periods that we will keep aside in the holdout dataset (see lines 14 to 18).

```
1   def datasets_holdout(df, x_len=12, y_len=1, test_loops=12,
    ↵    holdout_loops=0):
2       D = df.values
3       rows, periods = D.shape
4
5       # Training set creation
6       train_loops = periods + 1 - x_len - y_len - test_loops
7       train = []
8       for col in range(train_loops):
9           train.append(D[:,col:col+x_len+y_len])
10      train = np.vstack(train)
11      X_train, Y_train = np.split(train,[-y_len],axis=1)
12
13      # Holdout set creation
14      if holdout_loops > 0:
15          X_train, X_holdout = np.split(X_train,[-rows*holdout_loops],
            ↵    axis=0)
16          Y_train, Y_holdout = np.split(Y_train,[-rows*holdout_loops],
            ↵    axis=0)
17      else:
18          X_holdout, Y_holdout = np.array([]), np.array([])
19
20      # Test set creation
21      if test_loops > 0:
22          X_train, X_test = np.split(X_train,[-rows*test_loops],axis=0)
```

```
23      Y_train, Y_test = np.split(Y_train,[-rows*test_loops],axis=0)
24    else: # No test set: X_test is used to generate the future
         forecast
25      X_test = D[:,-x_len:]
26      Y_test = np.full((X_test.shape[0],y_len),np.nan) #Dummy value
27
28    # Formatting required for scikit-learn
29    if y_len == 1:
30      Y_train = Y_train.ravel()
31      Y_test = Y_test.ravel()
32      Y_holdout = Y_holdout.ravel()
33
34    return X_train, Y_train, X_holdout, Y_holdout, X_test, Y_test
```

We can now use this new function in our main loop (we will take the same structure as previously).

```
1  results = []
2  for x_len in n_months:
3      X_train, Y_train, X_holdout, Y_holdout, X_test, Y_test =
           datasets_holdout(df, x_len=x_len, holdout_loops=12)
4      for name, model in models:
5          model.fit(X_train,Y_train)
6          mae_train = model_mae(model, X_train, Y_train)
7          mae_holdout = model_mae(model, X_holdout, Y_holdout)
8          mae_test = model_mae(model, X_test, Y_test)
9          results.append([name+' Train',mae_train,x_len])
10         results.append([name+' Test',mae_test,x_len])
11         results.append([name+' Holdout',mae_holdout,x_len])
```

We can also plot the results.

```
1  data = pd.DataFrame(results,columns=['Model','MAE%','Number of Months'])
2  data = data.set_index(['Number of Months','Model']).stack()
        .unstack('Model')
3  data.index = data.index.droplevel(level=1)
4  data.index.name = 'Number of months'
5  data.plot(color=['orange']*3+['black']*3,style=['-','--',':']*3)
6  print(data.idxmin())
```

Your plot should be similar to Figure 18.4.

19 Adaptive Boosting

> **Note to the Reader**
>
> We introduce the Adaptive Boosting model in this chapter more as an essential historical step in the path of machine learning rather than as a plea to use it. We will see in Chapter 21 a more powerful model—and one that is simpler to use, which can be seen as the evolution of Adaptive Boosting.

Can a set of weak learners create a single strong learner?

Michael Kearns, Leslie Valiant

19.1 A Second Ensemble: Boosting

In Chapters 15 and 17, two models—the forest and the extremely random trees—that both created a very good prediction by averaging many slightly different, good models. These models were called *ensemble bagging* models: *ensemble* as they use an ensemble of different models to make a prediction; *bagging* as they use the average of many sub-models to make a prediction.

In the late 1980s, Michael Kearns and Leslie Valiant asked the following question, *"Can a set of weak learners create a single strong learner?"*[1]

> **Weak Model**
>
> A weak model (or weak learner) is a model that is slightly more accurate than random guessing—typically, a simple, shallow tree.

If we reframe this question, we could say: *Can we obtain a good forecasting model by using only (very) simple trees?* In 1990, Robert E. Schapire answered this positively. In 1997, Yoav Freund and Robert E. Schapire published an algorithm together that could create a strong learner based on weak ones.[2] To do so, they used another *ensemble* technique called **boosting**.

---

[1] See Kearns (1988), Kearns and Valiant (1989). In his work, Kearns noted that "the resolution of this question is of theoretical interest and possibly of practical importance." As you will see, boosting algorithms further pushed the frontiers of machine learning power.

[2] See Schapire (1990), Freund and Schapire (1997) for the original papers. For a detailed review and discussion between multiple academic authors, see Breiman et al. (1998) (available here: projecteuclid.org/download/pdf_1/euclid.aos/1024691079). Those initial papers discussed Adaptive Boosting for classification problems; the first implementation of AdaBoost for regression problems was published by Drucker (1997), which is the algorithm used in scikit-learn.

https://doi.org/10.1515/9783110671124-019

> **Boosting**
>
> Boosting is a class of ensemble algorithms in which models are added *sequentially*, so that later models in the sequence will correct the predictions made by earlier models in the sequence.

Their idea is based on the fact that it is better to use 100 *complementary* models rather than to average 100 good but rather *similar* models.

OK, so how do we create complementary models?

19.2 AdaBoost

Rather than to aggregate many different models, Freund and Schapire's idea was to first run a simple model (typically a simple, shallow tree) and see what it got wrong. Then, the second step was to create a second one that emphasizes the mistakes that the first model made, then a third one that puts more emphasis on the errors made by the first two, and so on. You can end up, for example, with 100 trees built one after another, specialized each time on the current model mistakes so far (we say that they are *stacked*). In the end, you will not have 100 good generalistic models, but rather, 100 models that *complement* each other by each time focusing on the mistakes made by the previous models.

Their model is called **Adaptive Boosting**—or AdaBoost. The algorithm is schematized in Figure 19.1.[3]

> **Algorithm – Adaptive Boosting**
>
> 1. Allocate uniform *weights* to each of the training samples. Simply put, each training sample is as likely to appear during the first weak model training.
> 2. Train a *weak model* (base_estimator in scikit-learn) on a random selection (with replacement) of the training set.
> 3. Compute the weak model *prediction error* on the (whole) training set using a *loss function* such as squared error or absolute error (loss in scikit-learn).
> 4. Compute the weak model *confidence* based on its average prediction error (as computed in step 3). The lower its error, the higher its confidence.
> 5. Update the training set weights based on the weak model errors, its confidence, and its learning rate (learning_rate in scikit-learn). The lower the

---

3 See the online article by Bourret Sicotte (2018) for a detailed—and illustrated—review of a classification AdaBoost (available here: xavierbourretsicotte.github.io/AdaBoost.html).

learning rate, the lower the impact on training set weights. In other words, a low learning rate will slow down the weight updates, thereby requiring more trees to impact the training set distribution significantly. Data samples with the highest prediction errors will get a heavier weight, while data samples with the lowest prediction errors will see their weight reduced.

6. Repeat steps 2–5 until a given number of weak models (n_estimators in scikit-learn) has been fitted.

The ensemble model's final prediction is given as the weighted median prediction of all the weak learners.

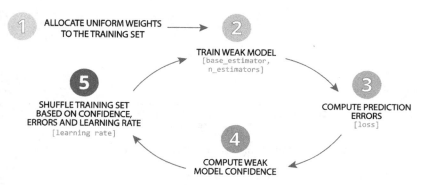

Figure 19.1: AdaBoost algorithm (with scikit-learn parameters).

19.3 Insights

The AdaBoost algorithm implementation in scikit-learn has four parameters:[4]

base_estimator This is the weak learner we want to boost. Typically, we will use a tree with a specified max_depth.

n_estimators The number of weak learners generated.

learning_rate A coefficient that reduces the overall impact of each weak model on the weighting of the training set.

loss The loss function when updating the weight allocation given to each sample before reshuffling.

Let's discuss these new parameters one by one.

---

4 See scikit-learn.org/stable/modules/generated/sklearn.ensemble.AdaBoostRegressor.html

Number of Estimators (n_estimators)

Let's first play with the number of estimators we will use. Each extra estimator means that the model gets a new weak predictor that is going to be fitted with a greater emphasis on the model's current mistakes. That's an extra chance to get these mistakes right. As you can see in Figure 19.2, the error on the training set keeps on decreasing as we throw more and more trees against it. That's normal, of course, as each new tree is fitted to compensate for the errors of the model's training set.

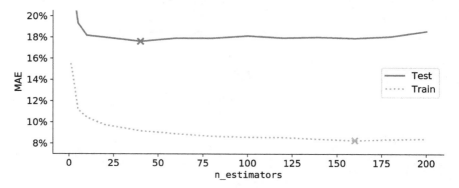

Figure 19.2: Adaboost vs. training set (with `learning_rate=0.25, max_depth=8, loss='linear'`).

What about the error on the test set? We see that its decrease is not as steep: as of a certain number of trees, it does not decrease anymore. This means we can't rely on the training set to give meaningful indications on how to optimize parameters or their impact. We could be tempted to directly look at the forecast error on the test set to set the optimal number of estimators. That would be overfitting: remember, we cannot directly use the results obtained against the test set to choose the best parameter set. Instead, we will again use a *validation set*[5] to analyze the impact of our model (and select the best parameters later). In the following figures, to obtain some insights about AdaBoost, we will plot both the error on the test set and the validation set. Later, in Section 19.4, we will discuss a proper method to optimize the parameters using a cross-validation random search (as used in Chapter 14).

As you can see in Figure 19.3, the test error follows the same curves as the error in the validation set. We see a small increase in forecast error as of a certain number of trees.

---

5 A validation set is a random subset of the training set that is kept aside to validate a model. See Section 18.2.

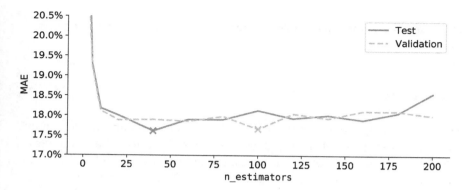

Figure 19.3: Adaboost vs. test set (with `learning_rate=0.25, max_depth=8, loss='linear'`).

Learning Rate (`learning_rate`)

The AdaBoost implementation allows us to apply a learning rate to each tree. In short, the learning rate reduces the impact of each new estimator in the shuffling of the training set. Typical values range from 0.01 to 0.3. The impact is shown in Figure 19.4.

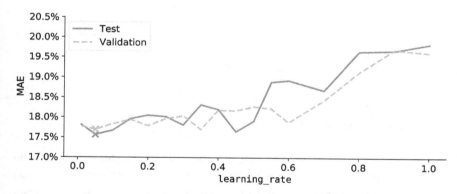

Figure 19.4: Learning rate impact (with `n_estimators=100, max_depth=8, loss='linear'`).

Together with the number of trees, the learning rate is a good parameter to tackle the speed issue. The higher it is, the faster your model will evolve, therefore requiring fewer base learners. But this will be done at the expense of a higher risk of overfitting. Generally speaking, it is always better to increase the number of estimators and reduce the learning rate proportionally. This allows the model to get to a very good spot in a smooth way. Unfortunately, this will drive you into a (too) long training time. A good technique here would be to set an arbitrary number of trees that you are willing to train (for example, 100) based on how fast you want your model to be. Once you have decided on the number of estimators you want, you can optimize the other parameters!

Loss Function (loss)

The loss function is used to compute each weak learner's error against the training set to update its weights. Depending on the loss function selected (either absolute error, squared error, or exponential error), the training set will be reshuffled differently, as different samples will get more or less importance. Based on Figure 19.5, it seems difficult to draw any conclusion.

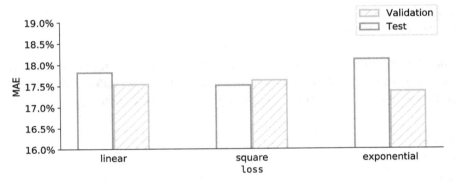

Figure 19.5: Loss function (with `max_depth=8`, `learning_rate=0.25`, `n_estimators=100`).

Playing with Trees (base_estimator)

As mentioned, an AdaBoost model only gets a few parameters—the base estimator, the number of estimators, the learning rate, and the loss function—so you might think that it is easy to find the best combination. Unfortunately, nothing could be further from the truth.

The question of how we optimize the base estimator (a tree in our case) is as open as the optimization of a single tree on its own (as we did in Chapter 14). Let's focus on one main parameter of a tree: its maximum depth. In Figure 19.6, you can see the results we obtain based on different maximum depths.

As you can see, it seems that a maximum depth of 12 is a good value. Deeper trees do not result in a lower error in the validation and test sets—they result in more error. The model is actually overfitting the training set, learning erroneous patterns from it. We do not want this, especially as deeper trees are slower to run.

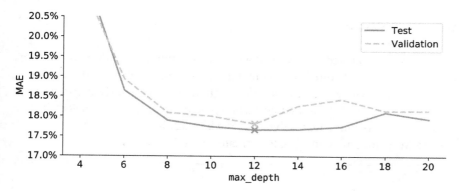

Figure 19.6: Maximum depth of the base estimator (with `max_depth=8`, `learning_rate=0.25`, `n_estimators=100`).

19.4 Do It Yourself

Simple Model

Let's start with some simple code to run our first Adaptive Boosting model.

```
1  from sklearn.tree import DecisionTreeRegressor
2  from sklearn.ensemble import AdaBoostRegressor
3  ada = AdaBoostRegressor(DecisionTreeRegressor(max_depth=8), ⌐
   ↳  n_estimators=100, learning_rate=0.25, loss='square')
4  ada = ada.fit(X_train,Y_train)
```

As usual, we can now measure the accuracy of our new model.

```
1  Y_train_pred = ada.predict(X_train)
2  Y_test_pred = ada.predict(X_test)
3  kpi_ML(Y_train, Y_train_pred, Y_test, Y_test_pred, name='AdaBoost')
```

You should obtain something similar to:

```
1  >>             MAE  RMSE  Bias
2  >> AdaBoost
3  >> Train      10.1  21.4  -0.3
4  >> Test       17.7  47.5   2.6
```

Parameter Optimization

Unfortunately, our beloved RandomizedSearchCV function from scikit-learn won't allow us to automatically run through different regression tree designs (i. e., different maximum depths). We will have to loop through different tree designs and for each run, a RandomizedSearchCV on AdaBoost's parameters. We then have to select the tree design (i. e., the maximum depth) that gave the best result.

Before we go for our main loop, let's create our main variables.

```
1  #n_estimators = [100]
2  learning_rate = [0.005,0.01,0.05,0.1,0.15,0.2,0.25,0.3,0.35]
3  loss = ['square','exponential','linear']
4  param_dist = {#'n_estimators': n_estimators,
5                'learning_rate': learning_rate,
6                'loss':loss}
```

We will also use the function model_mae() we created initially in Chapter 18.

```
1  def model_mae(model, X, Y):
2      Y_pred = model.predict(X)
3      mae = np.mean(np.abs(Y - Y_pred))/np.mean(Y)
4      return mae
```

Let's now go into our optimization loop. In results, we will record the best score and parameters obtained for each max_depth tried (see lines 7–9) by using ada_cv.best_score_ and ada_cv.best_params_.

```
1  from sklearn.model_selection import RandomizedSearchCV
2  results = []
3  for max_depth in range(2,18,2):
4      ada = ↵
        ↪   AdaBoostRegressor(DecisionTreeRegressor(max_depth=max_depth))
5      ada_cv = RandomizedSearchCV(ada, param_dist, n_jobs=-1, cv=6, ↵
        ↪   n_iter=20, scoring='neg_mean_absolute_error')
6      ada_cv.fit(X_train,Y_train)
7      print('Tuned AdaBoost Parameters:',ada_cv.best_params_)
8      print('Result:',ada_cv.best_score_)
9      results.append([ada_cv.best_score_,ada_cv.best_params_, ↵
        ↪   max_depth])
```

We can then transform results into a DataFrame and simply print the parameter set that got the lowest error. To do this, we will call the method idxmax() on our DataFrame.[6] Pay close attention to ensure that we are looking for the *maximum* value and not the minimum value as RandomizedSearchCV is returning the *negative* mean absolute error.

```
1  results = pd.DataFrame(data=results, columns=['Score','Best Params',↵
      ↪  'Max Depth'])
2  optimal = results['Score'].idxmax()
3  print(results.iloc[optimal])
```

Let's take a look at the results:

```
1  >> Score                                              -31.4508
2  >> Best Params      {'loss': 'exponential', 'learning_rate': 0.005}
3  >> Max Depth                                                 8
```

We can now use these parameters to run our model.

```
1  ada = AdaBoostRegressor(DecisionTreeRegressor(max_depth=8),↵
      ↪  n_estimators=100,learning_rate=0.005,loss='linear')
2  ada = ada.fit(X_train,Y_train)
3  Y_train_pred = ada.predict(X_train)
4  Y_test_pred = ada.predict(X_test)
5  kpi_ML(Y_train, Y_train_pred, Y_test, Y_test_pred, name='AdaBoost ↵
      ↪  optimized')
```

This is what we obtain:

```
1  >>                   MAE   RMSE   Bias
2  >> AdaBoost optimized
3  >> Train             10.8  24.9   0.5
4  >> Test              17.9  47.8   3.9
```

As summarized in Table 19.1, it seems that on the dataset (and with those features), AdaBoost is not able to provide any added value.

---

6 idxmax() returns the index of the highest element in a DataFrame. It is the same as the NumPy function np.argmax().

Table 19.1: Results.

Models	MAE		RMSE		Bias	
	Train	Test	Train	Test	Train	Test
Regression	17.8	17.8	43.9	**43.7**	0.0	**1.6**
Tree	17.3	18.9	42.2	46.8	0.0	2.9
Forest	14.1	17.6	35.0	44.9	−0.0	2.7
ETR	14.2	**17.5**	35.8	44.4	−0.0	2.5
AdaBoost	**10.8**	17.9	**24.9**	47.8	0.5	3.9

Is there any other way to further decrease the error? Yes, of course! We still have some more ideas and models to discuss.

But first, let's discuss AdaBoost's speed and how we can populate a forecast for multiple periods.

Speed

When we ran our forest and extra tree regressor, we could benefit from multi-processor computation (via the n_jobs parameter), as all the trees generated were independent from each other. One processor could work on the first tree as another processor would be simultaneously working on the second one. Unfortunately, this cannot happen with AdaBoost, as each new tree is built based on the results of the previous tree. This means of course that the computation time for AdaBoost is going to be much longer than for a forest or an ETR (see Figure 19.7 and Table 19.2). Computation time is one of the hurdles of AdaBoost.

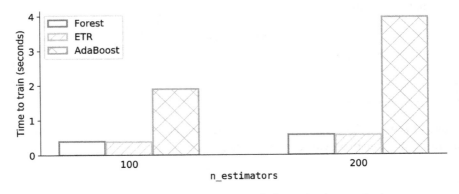

Figure 19.7: Impact of n_estimators on running time (using optimal parameters).

Table 19.2: Time to run optimal model (in seconds) based on n_estimators.

n_estimators	AdaBoost	ETR	Forest
100	1.81	0.35	0.36
200	3.75	0.49	0.49
100 -> 200	x207%	x139%	x139%

Multiple Periods

As we have discussed, AdaBoost is unfortunately slow, and it doesn't have a straight-forward way to do a randomized search. On top of that, its implementation in scikit-learn can only predict one single output at a time. This means that you can only fit your AdaBoost model to forecast one single period at a time. If you want to forecast multiple periods at once (i. e., Y_train and Y_test have multiple columns), you will have to cut these into sub-models to predict one period at a time.

Luckily, our friends from scikit-learn created a model wrapper MultiOutput Regressor, which allows us to easily fit our AdaBoost model to predict multiple periods at once.

MultiOutputRegressor behaves like any scikit-learn model and takes two inputs:

estimator This is the base estimator (i. e., our AdaBoost model) that we will use to ·predict multiple outputs.

n_jobs Just as for the forest or the ETR model, we can now use multiple cores of our machine in parallel. As for all scikit-learn, n_jobs=-1 means that you want it to use all your machine's cores. The function will dedicate one core to each period you want to predict. So, even if you can't speed up the training of one AdaBoost model, you can train multiple different models at once. Using this, we will kill two birds with one stone, as we have now sped up our training time and the ability to predict multiple periods at once.

```
1  from sklearn.multioutput import MultiOutputRegressor
2  multi = MultiOutputRegressor(ada, n_jobs=-1)
```

Finally, we can simply run our model against our dataset.

```
1  X_train, Y_train, X_test, Y_test = datasets(df, y_len=6)
2  multi.fit(X_train,Y_train)
```

20 Demand Drivers and Leading Indicators

Felix, qui potuit rerum cognoscere causas – Fortunate, who was able to know the causes of things.
Virgil (70–19 BC)

Until now, we have made our forecasts solely based on historical demand. We have discussed in Chapter 14 how to optimize our model, and we have discussed in Chapter 18 how to optimize the number of historical periods we should take into account to make a prediction. We haven't discussed the following yet: which other factors could we be looking at to predict future demand?

For many businesses, historical demand is not the only—or main—factor that drives future sales. Other internal and external factors drive the demand as well. You might sell more or less depending on the weather, the GDP growth, unemployment rate, loan rates, and so on. These **external factors** (external, as a company does not control them) are often called **leading indicators**.

The demand can also be driven by company decisions: price changes, promotions, marketing budget, or another product's sales. As these factors result from business decisions, we will call them **internal factors**.

As you can see in Figure 20.1, we will group both internal and external factors into the term **exogenous factors** (as these factors are *exogenous* to the historical demand), or, more simply, **demand drivers**.

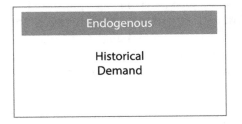
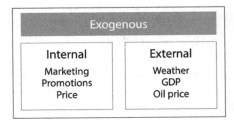

Figure 20.1: Demand drivers classification.

20.1 Linear Regressions?

As we discussed in the previous chapters, one of the limitations of the different exponential smoothing models was their inability to deal with exogenous information. Typically, in most forecasting training and classes, you will be shown linear regressions such as: "Our sales increase by 10% during weekends," or "Demand increases by 10% for every degree above 25C°." You will be shown data where this works quite well, as in Figure 20.2.

https://doi.org/10.1515/9783110671124-020

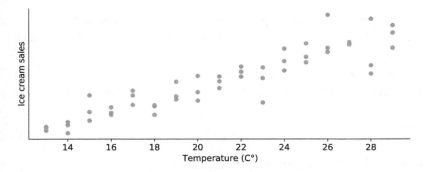

Figure 20.2: "My sales are linearly correlated to temperature!"

Unfortunately, this kind of relationship does not extend very well. Let's imagine that Figure 20.2 illustrates ice cream sales based on the daily temperature. We understand that if the temperature decreases, so will your sales. But will your sales shrink to zero if it is freezing? Will everyone stop eating ice cream? Maybe not. Will people start selling you back your ice cream if the temperature goes low enough? Most likely not.

Typically, as you can see in Figure 20.3, the sales will flatten around a certain minimum temperature.

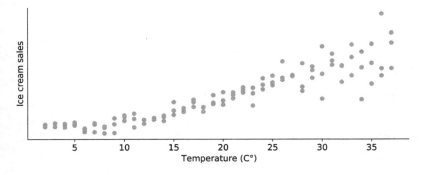

Figure 20.3: "My sales are not so linearly correlated to temperature."

We can ask ourselves many other questions:
- Is the temperature more impactful during the weekend or on Monday?
- Are the customers buying more ice cream if it has been hot for more than just one day straight?
- Do customers buy ice cream on Friday if they know that it will be a sunny weekend?
- Do sales increase during holidays, no matter what the temperature is?

Answering these questions via linear regressions would call for many different models. Yet, these models will *only* take into account temperature to predict sales, ignoring any recent historical demand level.

This is exactly where machine learning models will shine. They are very good at understanding these relationships, their limitations, and how they evolve depending on the different inputs.

20.2 Demand Drivers and Machine Learning

Should You Use Demand Drivers?

Before jumping into fine-tuning a model to external data, a good first step is to visualize any relationship between a possible demand driver and the demand. For example, as you can see in Figure 20.4, it seems that there is a correlation between GDP growth and car sales in Norway.

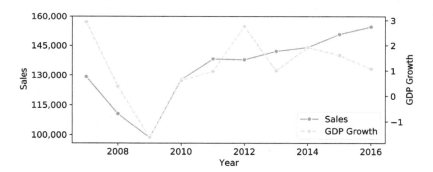

Figure 20.4: Norway's GDP and car sales.

Compared to traditional linear regressions, our machine learning models' strength is that they won't just learn the relationship between one period and a leading indicator. They will also *automatically* understand if there is a relationship between the demand during a specific period and any lagged version of that indicator. For example, we could observe an impact on car sales in Q2 if the GDP growth was high in Q1.

Does this mean that our model will be more accurate as we use leading indicators? That is not guaranteed. We will see how to include exogenous data into our machine learning data set in this chapter and will discuss the added value of using more features in Chapter 24.

Using Demand Drivers

Using the historical values of a demand driver might be useful for a machine learning model to understand historical demand ups and downs:
- *We sold less last week because the weather was bad.*
- *We sold more last month because GDP grew.*
- *We sold less last month because our marketing expenses were rather low.*

However, it might be even more interesting for the model to know the future values of the demand drivers:
- *It will be sunny next week, so we should sell more.*
- *GDP will decline next month, so we should sell less.*
- *We will increase the marketing budget next month, so we should sell more.*
- *Next month is the annual car fair, so we should sell (much) more.*

If you want to use the marketing budget as a demand driver, you could easily come up with an estimate of next quarter's spending. Unfortunately, collecting leading indicators' future values is often impossible—*Do you know the next quarter's GDP growth?*—henceforth, limiting our models to historical values.

Leading Indicators: Prediction and Actual Values

Another solution would be to use a prediction of those leading indicators. For example, when forecasting the next year's car sales in Norway, you could feed the algorithm with next year's *predicted* GDP growth (possibly along with past historical *actual* GDP growth).

This question of predicting leading indicators is very tricky. You want your model to forecast demand based on a leading indicator of historical actual values and predicted future values. To do so, you will need to include in the training set the leading indicator predictions over the future, along with its actual historical values. It means that for each historical period, you will need to keep track of the actual and predicted values of this leading indicator. This will require much data gathering and cleaning.

For example, the Norway actual GDP growth was 0.4% in 2008, but it was most likely predicted to be around 3%. So when predicting 2008, you should feed your tool with 3% as the expected GDP growth over 2008; but when predicting 2009, you should use 0.4% as the past actual GDP growth over last year.

Historical predictions of leading indicators are rather difficult to obtain (or even impossible), often resulting in the (implicit) assumption that the *forecast* of a leading indicator is as relevant as its *actual* value. Always be cautious with such assumptions.

Weather

The weather is a typical leading indicator, where the prediction accuracy of week+2 is as correct as merely taking the historical average temperature. Let's go back to our ice cream business. If you want to predict how much you will sell in the next three days, the weather forecast might be very relevant. Let's now imagine you need to order a supplier for a particular ingredient (for example, Madagascan vanilla). The lead time is one month. Can you rely on the weather forecast of day +30 to predict your sales? Most likely not.

Depending on the forecast horizon, some leading indicators can be more reliable than others. It is up to you to test different ones based on the available data and their respective prediction accuracy.

20.3 Adding New Features to the Training Set

Leading Indicators

Before discussing how we will integrate this exogenous data into our historical demand dataset, let's first recap how we formatted our initial dataset in Chapter 12. We created a training set by looping through our historical demand (see Table 20.1) using, as an input, n consecutive periods (x_len) to predict m consecutive future periods (y_len).

Table 20.1: Typical historical demand dataset.

Product	Y1				Y2				Y3			
	Q1	Q2	Q3	Q4	Q1	Q2	Q3	Q4	Q1	Q2	Q3	Q4
#1	5	15	10	7	6	13	11	5	4	11	9	4
#2	7	2	3	1	1	0	0	1	3	2	4	5
#3	18	25	32	47	56	70	64	68	72	67	65	58
#4	4	1	5	3	2	5	3	1	4	3	2	5

Table 20.2 shows you an example with $x\_len=4$ and $y\_len=1$.

Now, as shown in Table 20.3, let's add one leading indicator to this dataset—for example, the GDP growth.

How should we feed this GDP growth into our model? To answer this question, let's go one step back: *what is the relationship we want to have between GDP and our sales?* We assume that the GDP of a specific quarter will have an impact on our sales. So we will show both historical demand and historical GDP growth side by side. This will allow the tool to understand that, historically, the sales could have been high or low due to favorable or unfavorable GDP growth. To summarize, to make a forecast,

Table 20.2: Training set based on the historical dataset.

Loop	Product	Y1				Y2				Y3			
		Q1	Q2	Q3	Q4	Q1	Q2	Q3	Q4	Q1	Q2	Q3	Q4
#1	#1	5	15	10	7	6							
#1	#2	7	2	3	1	1							
#1	#3	18	25	32	47	56							
#1	#4	4	1	5	3	2							
#2	#1		15	10	7	6	13						
#2	#2		2	3	1	1	0						
#2	#3		25	32	47	56	70						
#2	#4		1	5	3	2	5						
#3	#1			10	7	6	13	11					
...	...			...	...	...	...	...					

Table 20.3: Dataset with GDP growth.

Product	Y1				Y2			
	Q1	Q2	Q3	Q4	Q1	Q2	Q3	Q4
GDP growth	1.0	0.9	1.2	1.3	2.5	2.1	2.6	2.7
#1	5	15	10	7	6	13	11	5
#2	7	2	3	1	1	0	0	1
#3	18	25	32	47	56	70	64	68
#4	4	1	5	3	2	5	3	1

our model will look at two different pieces of information: historical demand and historical GDP growth.

In practice, when creating our training dataset, we'll add the GDP growth next to the historical demand in X_train. See the implementation of X_train and Y_train in Table 20.4.

Table 20.4: X_train and Y_train creation with GDP.

Loop	Product	X_train								Y_train
		Historical demand				Historical GDP				Future demand
#1	#1	5	15	10	7	1.0	0.9	1.2	1.3	6
#1	#2	7	2	3	1	1.0	0.9	1.2	1.3	1
#1	#3	18	25	32	47	1.0	0.9	1.2	1.3	56
#1	#4	4	1	5	3	1.0	0.9	1.2	1.3	2
#2	#1	15	10	7	6	0.9	1.2	1.3	2.5	13
...	...	...	...	...	...	...	...	...	...	...

Our model will learn the relationships from Table 20.5. You can now use this training dataset directly in your favorite machine learning model.

Table 20.5: X_train and Y_train relationship.

X_train								→	Y_train
5	15	10	7	1.0	0.9	1.2	1.3	→	6
7	2	3	1	1.0	0.9	1.2	1.3	→	1
18	25	32	47	1.0	0.9	1.2	1.3	→	56
4	1	5	3	1.0	0.9	1.2	1.3	→	2
15	10	7	6	0.9	1.2	1.3	2.5	→	13
...	...	...	...	...	...	...	...	→	...

Training Set Sequence

What might be counter intuitive here is that it does not matter for our algorithm how we organize X_train. You can first put the historical demand and finish with the previous GDP, or the other way around. It won't change a thing: you could even randomly shuffle all the columns. The model does not think like a human brain. It does not project a relationship from one column to the next one, so it does not need to have any meaningful order in its inputs.

Dates and Events

Another set of information can be helpful for our model: the date! For example, let's imagine that a car exhibition is taking place at the same time every year in Norway, resulting in higher sales during this period. For the model to know this, we should show it (at least) the month number of the period it is trying to forecast.

Let's imagine that the main Norwegian car exhibition is held every year in November. By letting the algorithm know that it predicts November sales, it will surely increase its forecasts. On the other hand, it might reduce its forecast for December—it is likely that fewer sales will happen just after a major fair, despite good sales numbers in November.

As shown in Table 20.6, we don't need to pass to the training set the month for each future or historical period. Only the one value for the first period to predict is enough.

Year

Now, should we feed the tool only with the month number? What about the year? Usually, giving the year to a model might result in overfitting. Your model might learn rules

Table 20.6: X_train and Y_train creation with months.

Loop	Product	X_train				Month	Y_train
		Historical demand					Future demand
#1	#1	5	15	10	7	12	6
#1	#2	7	2	3	1	12	1
#1	#3	18	25	32	47	12	56
#1	#4	4	1	5	3	12	2
#2	#1	15	10	7	6	1	13
...	...	...	...	...	...	...	...

such as "2008 was low, 2009 was high," which won't prove any added value in making any forecasts about the future. On the other hand, using the month and/or the week number as a feature might result in extra accuracy.

Holidays and Events
Some holidays and events do not happen on the exact same period (month or week) each year. You can then include them as an extra Boolean feature.

20.4 Do It Yourself

In this section, we will include GDP data and date information in our dataset. We will analyze its added value in Chapter 24.

Extracting GDP Data

Let's imagine that we have an Excel file GDP.xlsx that contains the GDP growth of Norway per year.[1] It should look like Table 20.7.

Let's extract this data from our Excel file back into Python.

```
1  df = import_data()
2  GDP = pd.read_excel('GDP.xlsx').set_index('Year')
3  dates = pd.to_datetime(df.columns, format='%Y-%m').year
4  X_GDP = [GDP.loc[date,'GDP'] for date in dates]
```

---

[1] A simple Google search can get you such data for any country.

Table 20.7: GDP data (available on supchains.com/resources-2nd).

Year	GDP
2006	2.40
2007	2.93
2008	0.38
2009	−1.62
2010	0.60
2011	0.97
2012	2.75
2013	1.00
2014	1.92
2015	1.61
2016	1.08
2017	1.90

X_GDP is a list with the same length as our initial historical demand DataFrame df.

> **Python Mastery – pandas and datetime objects**
>
> You can easily transform a string into a datetime object in pandas by using
> pd.to_datetime(strings, format).
>
> ```
> strings = ['2020-10-31','2020-11-30','2020-12-31']
> dates = pd.to_datetime(strings,format='%Y-%m-%d')
> ```
>
> You can then access various information very simply, such as:
>
> ```
> print(dates.year)
> print(dates.month)
> print(dates.day)
> ```

Datasets

Now we can update our datasets function so that it can take an exogenous dataset as well as date information and add it to our X_train and X_test arrays. In our function, we will call the exogenous dataset X_exo to be a bit more generalistic than X_GDP.

These are the main changes we will make:

Line 4 We change our initial X_exo vector into a matrix that has the same size as our historical demand DataFrame. To do this, we will use the np.repeat() function, which simply repeats a line multiple times.

Line 5 We create an array X_months that contains the last month of each period. We extract this information from df columns, as they are encoded under the following format: '%Y-%m'.

Lines 11–14 We create the training and test sets by concatenating the corresponding exogenous data into each iteration.

Line 23 In case of a future forecast, we need to append the relevant exogenous data as well as the month to the test set.

```
1   def datasets_exo(df, X_exo, x_len=12, y_len=1, test_loops=12):
2       D = df.values
3       rows, periods = D.shape
4       X_exo = np.repeat(np.reshape(X_exo,[1,-1]),rows,axis=0)
5       X_months = np.repeat(np.reshape([int(col[-2:]) for col in df
        ↳   .columns],[1,-1]),rows,axis=0)
6
7       # Training set creation
8       loops = periods + 1 - x_len - y_len
9       train = []
10      for col in range(loops):
11          m = X_months[:,col+x_len].reshape(-1,1) #month
12          exo = X_exo[:,col:col+x_len] #exogenous data
13          d = D[:,col:col+x_len+y_len]
14          train.append(np.hstack([m, exo, d]))
15      train = np.vstack(train)
16      X_train, Y_train = np.split(train,[-y_len],axis=1)
17
18      # Test set creation
19      if test_loops > 0:
20          X_train, X_test = np.split(X_train,[-rows*test_loops],axis=0)
21          Y_train, Y_test = np.split(Y_train,[-rows*test_loops],axis=0)
22      else: # No test set: X_test is used to generate the future
        ↳   forecast
23          X_test = np.hstack([m[:,-1].reshape(-1,1),X_exo[:,-x_len:],
            ↳   D[:,-x_len:]])
24          Y_test = np.full((X_test.shape[0],y_len),np.nan) #Dummy value
25
26      # Formatting required for scikit-learn
27      if y_len == 1:
28          Y_train = Y_train.ravel()
```

```
29          Y_test = Y_test.ravel()
30
31      return X_train, Y_train, X_test, Y_test
```

From here, you can simply use this function to generate the new train and test arrays. These can then be used in the various models just as before. We will add more extra features to our dataset in Chapters 22 and 23, and we will do an in-depth analysis of all those extra features at once in Chapter 24.

21 Extreme Gradient Boosting

21.1 From Gradient Boosting to Extreme Gradient Boosting

In 2001, Jerome H. Friedman proposed a new concept to boost trees: **Gradient Boosting**.[1] The general concept of Gradient Boosting and Adaptive Boosting is essentially the same: they are both ensemble models boosting (stacking) trees on top of each other based on the model mistakes. The main difference is that in Gradient Boosting, each new weak learner is stacked directly on the model's current errors rather than on a weighted version of the initial training set.

Extreme Gradient Boosting

As is common, this first algorithm was refined by the original author over time. Later, Chen and Guestrin (from the University of Washington) proposed a new gradient boosting algorithm—called *Extreme Gradient Boosting* or *XGBoost*—and formalized it in 2016.[2] The data science community has since widely used this implementation, with excellent results. This is simply one of the most powerful machine learning algorithms currently available. In this chapter, we will focus on XGBoost rather than the *regular* Gradient Boosting. The differences between Gradient Boosting and Extreme Gradient Boosting lies in some mathematical workings of each model and their respective implementations.[3] As users, XGBoost will bring us three improvements compared to AdaBoost and regular Gradient Boosting:

- XGBoost is faster.
- XGBoost is (generally) better
- XGBoost allows for more parameters to be optimized.

21.2 Do It Yourself

Installation

Scikit-learn proposes an implementation of the original Gradient Boosting algorithm proposed by J. Friedman.[4] We will prefer the library developed around Chen's algorithm to benefit from his efficient and powerful implementation.[5]

---

1 See Friedman (2001) for the original paper, and Kashnitsky (2020) (mlcourse.ai/articles/topic10-boosting) for a detailed explanation and comparison against AdaBoost.
2 See Chen and Guestrin (2016).
3 The main mathematical difference between XGBoost and GBoost lies in the fact that in XGBoost uses a *regularized* objective function that penalizes both the number of leaves in a tree and extreme weights given to individual leaves. Even though the exact mathematics involved are beyond the scope of this book—see Chen and Guestrin (2016) for the detailed model—we will use those regularization parameters to improve our model.
4 See an example of implementation here, scikit-learn.org/stable/auto_examples/ensemble/plot_gradient_boosting_regression.html
5 See the official website xgboost.readthedocs.io

https://doi.org/10.1515/9783110671124-021

Using XGBoost will require you to install a new library. If you have a Windows machine and use Anaconda, you can install it simply by typing the following line in an Anaconda console:

```
conda install -c anaconda py-xgboost
```

Or, if you have a Mac/Linux:

```
conda install -c conda-forge xgboost
```

First Model

The xgboost library proposes different implementations in various programming languages. In order not to confuse ourselves, we will prefer the scikit-learn API. [6]
Let's start with a simple example.

```
from xgboost.sklearn import XGBRegressor
XGB = XGBRegressor(n_jobs=-1, max_depth=10, n_estimators=100,
↪    learning_rate=0.2)
XGB = XGB.fit(X_train, Y_train)
```

As you can see, xgboost.sklearn behaves exactly like the original scikit-learn.
You can plot the feature importance in one line by using the function plot_importance from xgboost.[7] You should obtain a figure similar to Figure 21.1.

```
import xgboost as xgb
XGB.get_booster().feature_names = [f'M{x-12}' for x in range(12)]
xgb.plot_importance(XGB, importance_type='total_gain',
↪    show_values=False)
```

---

6 You can find the documentation here: xgboost.readthedocs.io/en/latest/python/python_api.html# module-xgboost.sklearn
7 See xgboost.readthedocs.io/en/latest/python/python_api.html#module-xgboost.plotting for all the options. See Abu-Rmileh (2019) for a discussion about the different ways you can measure feature importance in XGBoost.

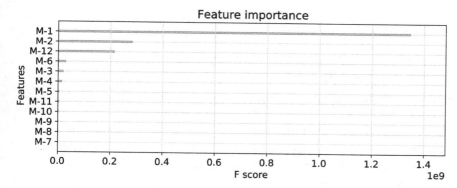

Figure 21.1: XGBoost feature importance.

Multiple Periods

Just like AdaBoost, XGBoost unfortunately cannot forecast multiple periods at once, so we will also use scikit-learn's MultiOutputRegressor. To make the model faster, you should set n_jobs=1 in XGBRegressor and n_jobs=-1 for MultiOutputRegressor. (In other words, a thread will be working independently on each of the future forecast periods, rather than multiple threads working on single forecast periods one by one.)
Here is a complete example (including future forecast):

```
from sklearn.multioutput import MultiOutputRegressor
# Training and testing
X_train, Y_train, X_test, Y_test = datasets(df, x_len=12, y_len=6, ↵
    test_loops=12)
XGB = XGBRegressor(n_jobs=1, max_depth=10, n_estimators=100, ↵
    learning_rate=0.2)
multi = MultiOutputRegressor(XGB, n_jobs=-1)
multi.fit(X_train,Y_train)
# Future Forecast
X_train, Y_train, X_test, Y_test = datasets(df, x_len=12, y_len=6, ↵
    test_loops=0)
XGB = XGBRegressor(n_jobs=1, max_depth=10, n_estimators=100, ↵
    learning_rate=0.2)
multi = MultiOutputRegressor(XGB, n_jobs=-1)
multi.fit(X_train,Y_train)
forecast = pd.DataFrame(data=multi.predict(X_test), index=df.index)
```

21.3 Early Stopping

When an XGBoost model is trained on a dataset, you can measure—after each itera-tion—its accuracy against an **evaluation set**.

> **Evaluation Set**
>
> An evaluation set is a set of data that is left aside from the training set to be used as a monitoring dataset during the training. A validation set (random subset of the training set) or a holdout set (last period of the training set) can be used as an evaluation set.

If you want to optimize your model's parameters, the best practice is of course to run a cross-validation random search. But rather than trying different models with a differ-ent number of trees, you could grow your model indefinitely, and stop it when there is no more improvement on the evaluation set (for some consecutive iterations).

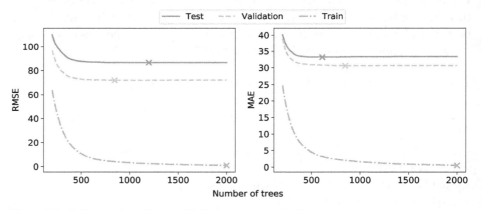

Figure 21.2: Early stopping using a validation set as an evaluation set.

As you can see in Figure 21.2, each new tree will consistently decrease the error on the training set (until it virtually reaches 0). Nevertheless, on the test and evaluation sets, the extra accuracy added by each new tree decreases over time. After a while, each new tree will slightly *increase* the error over the evaluation set rather than *decrease* it. This is when you want to stop the model from adding new trees. In practice, once the model does not see an accuracy improvement on the evaluation test for a determined number of extra trees, XGBoost will revert to the last iteration that brought extra accuracy to the evaluation set. With this technique, you get rid of the burden of number-of-trees optimization, and you are sure to grow your model up to the right level.

This early stopping technique will help us avoid overfitting our model to the training set, and at the same time, reduce training time. One stone, two birds. The early stopping technique is a very useful capability of XGBoost.

Do It Yourself

If we want to use the early stopping functionality—and we want to use it—we have to pass the parameters `early_stopping_rounds`, `eval_set`, and `eval_metric` to the `.fit()` method. There are three parameters that we need to set up for the early stopping to work properly.

eval_set The evaluation set(s) is used to evaluate the model after each iteration. Technically, `eval_set` is expecting pairs of X and Y datasets packed in a list (e. g., `eval_set=[(X1,Y1),(X2,Y2)]`). We will discuss using multiple evaluation sets later. The best practice is to pass a *validation set*[8] by extracting a random part out of the original training set. The function `train_test_split` from scikit-learn will do this for us.

early_stopping_rounds This is the maximum number of iterations (i. e., new trees) the model can perform without improving the accuracy on the `eval_set`.

eval_metric This is the metric used to evaluate the `eval_set`. You can use 'rmse' for root mean square error or 'mae' for mean absolute error.[9]

You can also set the parameter `verbose` to `True` to print out the results of each iteration. As you now set the `early_stopping_rounds`, you can set the number of estimators (`n_estimators`) to an arbitrarily high number (here, 1,000).

```
1  from sklearn.model_selection import train_test_split
2  x_train, x_val, y_train, y_val = train_test_split(X_train, Y_train,
   ↪   test_size=0.15)
3
4  XGB = XGBRegressor(n_jobs=-1, max_depth=10, n_estimators=1000,
   ↪   learning_rate=0.01)
5  XGB = XGB.fit(x_train, y_train, early_stopping_rounds=100,
   ↪   verbose=True, eval_set=[(x_eval,y_eval)], eval_metric='mae')
```

---

8 A validation set is a random subset of the training set that is kept aside to validate a model. See Section 18.2.

9 Contrary to most of the other scikit-learn models, here we need to pass 'rmse' instead of 'mse'.

Playing with Evaluation Datasets

You can pass multiple datasets to eval_set. In such a case, **only the last one** will be taken into account to trigger the early stopping round; nevertheless, the tool will print the results of each of those datasets. You can also print the evaluation metric at only specific periods by passing callbacks=[xgb.callback.print_evaluation(period=50)] as a parameter.

```
1  XGB = XGB.fit(x_train, y_train, early_stopping_rounds=100,
       ↪   verbose=False, eval_set=[(x_train, y_train), (x_val, y_val)],
       ↪   eval_metric='mae', callbacks = [xgb.callback
       ↪   .print_evaluation(period=50)])
2  print(f'Best iteration: {XGB.get_booster().best_iteration}')
3  print(f'Best score: {XGB.get_booster().best_score}')
```

See the results obtained here:

```
1   >> [0]          validation_0-mae:163.94       validation_1-mae:181.928
2   >> [50]         validation_0-mae:100.622      validation_1-mae:112.024
3   >> [100]        validation_0-mae:62.4087      validation_1-mae:70.6291
4   >> [150]        validation_0-mae:39.4113      validation_1-mae:48.5798
5   >> [200]        validation_0-mae:25.6162      validation_1-mae:38.5029
6   >> [250]        validation_0-mae:17.5486      validation_1-mae:34.1891
7   >> [300]        validation_0-mae:12.6879      validation_1-mae:32.4953
8   >> [350]        validation_0-mae:9.66251      validation_1-mae:31.7088
9   >> [400]        validation_0-mae:7.76499      validation_1-mae:31.452
10  >> [450]        validation_0-mae:6.57614      validation_1-mae:31.3125
11  >> [500]        validation_0-mae:5.75702      validation_1-mae:31.316
12  >> [550]        validation_0-mae:5.19013      validation_1-mae:31.3635
13  >> Best iteration: 463
14  >> Best score: 31.301769
```

You can also print the results on multiple metrics by passing a list of metrics to eval_metric. Again, only the **last one** will be used to trigger an early stop.

```
1  XGB = XGB.fit(x_train, y_train, early_stopping_rounds=100,
       ↪   verbose=False, eval_set=[(x_train, y_train), (x_val, y_val)],
       ↪   eval_metric=['rmse','mae'], callbacks = [xgb.callback
       ↪   .print_evaluation(period=50)])
```

> ### Going Further
>
> Instead of a validation set, you can also use a holdout dataset as the eval-
> uation dataset (as defined in Section 18.3). This can perform better on some
> datasets.
>
> ```
> 1  X_train, Y_train, X_holdout, Y_holdout, X_test, Y_test = ⌐
>    ↪ datasets_holdout(df, x_len=12, y_len=1, test_loops=12, ⌐
>    ↪ holdout_loops=12)
> 2  XGB = XGBRegressor(n_jobs=-1, max_depth=10, n_estimators=2000, ⌐
>    ↪ learning_rate=0.01)
> 3  XGB = XGB.fit(X_train, Y_train, early_stopping_rounds=100, ⌐
>    ↪ verbose=False, eval_set=[(X_holdout, Y_holdout)], ⌐
>    ↪ eval_metric='mae')
> ```

Multiple Periods and Early Stopping

You can pass fitting parameters to MultiOutputRegressor.fit() easily, as shown
here:

```
1  fit_params = {'early_stopping_rounds':25,
2                'eval_set':[(x_val, y_val)],
3                'eval_metric':'mae',
4                'verbose':False}
5  XGB = XGBRegressor(n_jobs=1, max_depth=10, n_estimators=100, ⌐
   ↪ learning_rate=0.2)
6  multi = MultiOutputRegressor(XGB, n_jobs=-1)
7  multi.fit(X_train,Y_train,**fit_params)
```

21.4 Parameter Optimization

XGBoost Parameters

XGBoost allows for more tree parameters to be set compared to the implementation of
AdaBoost or Gradient Boosting. Let's discuss some of the new and interesting parameters.

subsample This ratio is the % of training samples that each new tree is fitted on. It is
the same as the parameter max_samples for forest/ETR. As the samples are chosen
randomly, this means that each tree won't be trained on the full training dataset.
Typically, this parameter as well can vary between 50% and 90%. By reducing it,

you will make each tree more different (as they will be based on different training samples) but at the cost of them using less training data. A low value will help against overfitting, and will make the model more accurate if provided with more trees (as they are all more different). A *too* low value will result in each tree not being accurate enough to add value to the ensemble.

`colsample_bynode` This is the maximum number of features a tree can choose from when it has to split a node (exactly like `max_features` for the forest or the ETR). This means that at each node of each tree, the algorithm will only be able to choose a split on a limited random selection of features.

`colsample_bylevel` This is the subsample ratio of features selected for each level (i. e., depth) of each tree. In other words, this is similar to `colsample_bynode` but applied on a whole level/depth.

`colsample_bytree` This is just like `colsample_bynode`, and `colsample_bylevel` but applied for a whole tree.

Note that the three `colsample_by` parameters are multiplicative. So the available selection of features at a single node in a tree depends on `colsample_bytree`, `colsample_bylevel`, and `colsample_bynode`. Reducing the value of any of those parameters will help you fight overfitting (and increase the variation in the ensemble). But too many constraints might result in a lower overall accuracy.

`min_child_weight` This is the minimum sum of samples weight each leaf has to contain. This is similar to `min_samples_leaf` in forests and ETR, with the difference that now each sample is weighted. By increasing `min_child_weight`, you will prevent the model from overfitting, at the expense of some accuracy (as it won't be able to make granular predictions).

`reg_alpha, reg_lambda` Those are the *regularization* terms in the gradient boosting loss function (this is the main mathematical difference between extreme and regular gradient boosting). The exact mathematics involved are beyond the scope of this book;[10] nevertheless, the impact can be summarized easily: `reg_alpha` will penalize extreme weights given to leaves (on the contrary to AdaBoost, XGBoost allocates weights to leaves rather than to trees to make a prediction), whereas `reg_lambda` will penalize every leaf created. By using both, we will avoid overfitting, as the model will set aside useless leaves by using `reg_alpha` (as creating a new one is *costly*), and won't allocate massive weights to specific leaves, thanks to `reg_lambda`.

On top of those parameters, we also have our regular friends: `max_depth` and `learning_rate`.

Those parameters will restrain XGBoost from overfitting. `subsample` and `colsample_by` will also provide a stronger model by creating different trees. Remember that the two ensemble models (forest and ETR) were also based on the principle that many

---

10 Mathematically, we can say that `reg_alpha` is an L1 regularization and `reg_lambda` is an L2.

different predictors can create a stronger one.

```
1  params = {'max_depth': [5,6,7,8,10,11],
2            'learning_rate': [0.005,0.01,0.025,0.05,0.1,0.15],
3            'colsample_bynode': [0.5,0.6,0.7,0.8,0.9,1.0],#max_features
4            'colsample_bylevel': [0.8,0.9,1.0],
5            'colsample_bytree': [0.6,0.7,0.8,0.9,1.0],
6            'subsample': [0.1,0.2,0.3,0.4,0.5,0.6,0.7],#max_samples
7            'min_child_weight': [5,10,15,20,25],#min_samples_leaf
8            'reg_alpha': [1,5,10,20,50],
9            'reg_lambda': [0.01,0.05,0.1,0.5,1],
10           'n_estimators':[1000]}
```

> **Pro-Tip – Double Search**
>
> If you don't feel confident about setting the various parameter ranges to be tested, do not hesitate to run two optimizations one after the other—the first one with wide parameter ranges; then, a second one performed in more detail around the first optimal values found.

Optimization

Now that we have defined the parameter space we want to test, we can continue and perform a cross-validation random search. XGBoost needs some specific fitting parameters to be used. We can pack those parameters in a dictionary (fit_params) and pass it to the .fit() method of RandomizedSearchCV.[11] By doing so, we can define the proper evaluation set, metric, and the number of early stopping rounds.

```
1  fit_params = {'early_stopping_rounds':25,
2                'eval_set':[(x_val, y_val)],
3                'eval_metric':'mae',
4                'verbose':False}
5  XGB = XGBRegressor(n_jobs=1)
6  XGB_cv = RandomizedSearchCV(XGB, params, cv=5, n_jobs=-1, verbose=1,⌐
   ↵  n_iter=1000, scoring='neg_mean_absolute_error')
7  XGB_cv.fit(x_train, y_train,**fit_params)
8  print('Tuned XGBoost Parameters:',XGB_cv.best_params_)
```

---

11 See Section 15.4 for a reminder on how unpacking parameters from a dictionary works.

This is what we obtain:

```
1  >> Tuned XGBoost Parameters: {'subsample': 0.2, 'reg_lambda': 0.1, ↵
   ↵   'reg_alpha': 20, 'n_estimators': 1000, 'min_child_weight': 5, ↵
   ↵   'max_depth': 10, 'learning_rate': 0.005, 'colsample_bytree': 0.8, ↵
   ↵   'colsample_bynode': 1.0, 'colsample_bylevel': 0.9}
```

> **Pro-Tip – Faster Search**
>
> If you want to speed up your optimization process, you can try to decrease the number of trees while running your random search. Once you find a good set of parameters, you can then increase the number of trees while decreasing the learning rate, until you find a sweet spot.

We can now run a XGBoost with those optimal parameters.

```
1  best_params = XGB_cv.best_params_
2  XGB = XGBRegressor(n_jobs=-1, **best_params)
3  XGB = XGB.fit(x_train, y_train, **fit_params)
4  print(f'Best iteration: {XGB.get_booster().best_iteration}')
5  print(f'Best score: {XGB.get_booster().best_score}')
6  Y_train_pred = XGB.predict(X_train)
7  Y_test_pred = XGB.predict(X_test)
8  kpi_ML(Y_train, Y_train_pred, Y_test, Y_test_pred, name='XGBoost')
```

And these are the final results:

```
1  >> Best iteration: 820
2  >> Best score: 29.495928
3  >>            MAE  RMSE  Bias
4  >> XGBoost
5  >> Train    13.3  34.5  1.9
6  >> Test     17.3  44.2  4.1
```

By using this proper optimization, we got a better MAE than before (see Table 21.1). We do not beat the regression on RMSE: this is likely because we used MAE both as evaluation criterion when fitting XGBoost, and for the cross-validation random search. Even though we can use MAE as an evaluation criterion, the current implementation of XGBoost does not allow for a direct MAE optimization.

Table 21.1: Results.

Models	MAE		RMSE		Bias	
	Train	Test	Train	Test	Train	Test
Regression	17.8	17.8	43.9	**43.7**	0.0	1.6
Tree	17.3	18.9	42.2	46.8	0.0	2.9
Forest	14.1	17.6	35.0	44.9	−0.0	2.7
ETR	14.2	17.5	35.8	44.4	−0.0	2.5
AdaBoost	**10.8**	17.9	**24.9**	47.8	0.5	3.9
XGBoost	13.3	**17.3**	34.5	44.2	1.9	4.1

Speed

As you can see in Figure 21.3 and Table 21.2, XGBoost implementation is around 4.5 times faster than AdaBoost. XGBoost training time is more similar to the one needed to train a forest/ETR.

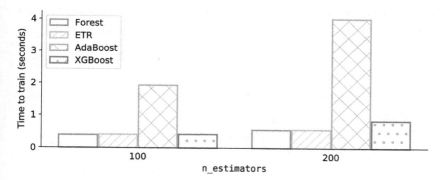

Figure 21.3: Impact of n_estimators on running time (using optimal parameters).

Table 21.2: Time to run optimal model (in seconds) based of n_estimators.

n_estimators	AdaBoost	ETR	Forest	XGBoost
100	1.81	0.35	0.36	0.39
200	3.75	0.49	0.49	0.82
100 -> 200	x207%	x139%	x139%	x209%

22 Categorical Features

As we saw in Chapter 20, we can improve our forecast by enriching our dataset—that is by adding external information to our historical demand. We saw that it might not be straightforward (nor meaningful) for all businesses to use such external macro-economic elements. On the other hand, most supply chains serve different markets (often through different channels) and have different product families. What if a machine learning model could benefit from these extra pieces of information: *Am I selling this to market A? Is this product part of family B?*

In our car sales dataset, we could imagine that instead of only having sales in Norway, we could have the sales in different markets across Europe. You could then feed the algorithm with the sales per country and indicate the market of each data sample (e. g., Sweden, Finland). We could also imagine segmenting into four categories: low cost, normal, premium, and luxury brands—or simply allowing the model to see the brand it is forecasting.

Unfortunately, most of the current machine learning libraries (including scikit-learn) cannot directly deal with categorical inputs. This means that you won't be able to fit your model based on an X_train dataset, as shown in Table 22.1.

Table 22.1: X_train with categorical data.

X_train					Y_train
Segment	Demand				Demand
Premium	5	15	10	7	6
Normal	2	3	1	1	1
Low cost	18	25	32	47	56
Luxury	4	1	5	3	2

The machine learning models that we discussed can only be trained based on numerical inputs. That means that we will have to transform our categorical inputs into numbers.

22.1 Integer Encoding

A first way to transform categories into numbers is simply to allocate a value to each category, as shown in Table 22.2.

This is a rather simple and straightforward way to transform a categorical input into a numerical one. It is meaningful if you have an **ordinal** relationship between all the categories. An ordinal relationship means that the different categories have a **nat-**

https://doi.org/10.1515/9783110671124-022

Table 22.2: Weather integer encoding.

Weather	Integer
Sunny	4
Cloudy	3
Rainy	2
Snowy	1

ural order between them—even though it might be unclear how one could measure the "distance" between two categories.

In our example of weather (in Table 22.2), it makes sense to say that Rainy is higher than Snowy, and Sunny is higher than Rainy. We acknowledge this, even though we cannot estimate the difference between Sunny and Rainy as a value. By providing numbers to our machine learning model, the algorithm will be able to *easily* ask questions such as: *Is the weather better than Rainy?*

Let's go back to our example of carmakers: we could easily imagine classifying them on a scale from 1 (low cost) to 4 (luxury), so that our algorithm would be trained on an X_train dataset that would look like Table 22.3.

Table 22.3: X_train with integer encoding.

X_train Segment	Demand				Y_train Demand
3	5	15	10	7	6
2	2	3	1	1	1
1	18	25	32	47	56
4	4	1	5	3	2

Do It Yourself

Let's segment our car brands into four segments: luxury (4), premium (3), normal (2), and low-cost (1). To make our life easy, we will by default allocate a segment of 2 (normal) to all car brands and then only update the remaining ones (low-cost, premium, and luxury).

```
1  luxury = ['Aston Martin','Bentley','Ferrari','Lamborghini','Lexus',↵
   ↪  'Lotus','Maserati','McLaren','Porsche','Tesla']
2  premium = ['Audi','BMW','Cadillac','Infiniti','Land Rover','MINI',↵
   ↪  'Mercedes-Benz','Jaguar']
3  low_cost = ['Dacia','Skoda']
```

```
4
5  df['Segment'] = 2 #By default all brands are normal
6  mask = df.index.isin(luxury) #Luxury = 4
7  df.loc[mask,'Segment'] = 4
8  mask = df.index.isin(premium) #Premium = 3
9  df.loc[mask,'Segment'] = 3
10 mask = df.index.isin(low_cost) #Low cost = 1
11 df.loc[mask,'Segment'] = 1
```

You should now have:

```
1  print(df)
2  >> Period          2007-01  2007-02  2007-03  ...  2016-12  2017-01  Segment
3  >> Make                                        ...
4  >> Alfa Romeo          16        9       21    ...        3        6        2
5  >> Aston Martin         0        0        1    ...        0        0        4
6  >> Audi               599      498      682    ...      827      565        3
7  >> BMW                352      335      365    ...      866     1540        3
8  >> Bentley              0        0        0    ...        0        0        4
9  >> ...                ...      ...      ...  ...      ...      ...      ...
10 >> Think                2        0        0    ...        0        0        2
11 >> Toyota            2884     1885     1833    ...     1238     1526        2
12 >> Volkswagen        2521     1517     1428    ...     2239     1688        2
13 >> Volvo              693      570      656    ...     1235     1158        2
14 >> Westfield           ·0        0        0    ...        0        0        2
```

Note that we can also perform integer encoding directly on the brands (i. e., each brand will be identified as an integer). We can do this very easily by using the 'category' data type from pandas.

```
1  df['Brand'] = df.index
2  df['Brand'] = df['Brand'].astype('category').cat.codes
```

Python Mastery – Pandas and the Categorical Data Type

In pandas, you can define the data type of a column (Serie) as a 'category'. Behind the curtains, pandas will then allocate a category number to each unique value in this Serie. As similar values will get the same category number, this trick will (drastically) reduce the space needed for the DataFrame, as pandas will only keep in memory for each data sample its category value rather than its full description.

See pandas.pydata.org/pandas-docs/stable/user_guide/categorical.html for more info.

Python Mastery – Pandas and Categorical Index

Pandas is a bit inconsistent with categorical data and indexes. If you directly use .astype('category') on df.index, pandas will return a 'CategoricalIndex' object. This is (unfortunately) not consistent with the use of a Serie with categorical values. You can directly access the codes of a 'CategoricalIndex' object with .codes without first using .cat. This means that in practice, we could directly use the following line of code to transform the brands into numerical values.

```
1  df['Brand'] = df.index.astype('category').codes
```

This would simplify our code a bit. Nevertheless, I prefer to use the code as given earlier (in two lines) as it is not dependent on using the index.

22.2 One-Hot Label Encoding

In many cases, the different categories you will be using are not naturally ordered (such as different markets, product families, or channels). Providing ordered numbers to the algorithm might confuse it, or make it difficult for it to focus on a couple of specific categories if they were not allocated to consecutive numbers. If you do not have naturally ordered categories, you might want to try **one-hot encoding** (otherwise known as dummification). Let's explain one-hot encoding with an example. Imagine we have a dataset with 4 different markets: Europe, USA, China, and India. To encode this categorical information into numbers, we'll create one *Boolean*[1] column per country (such as shown in Table 22.4).

This technique is called one-hot encoding, as each data sample will only have one feature different from zero, or only one hot value (as shown in Table 22.5).

One-hot encoding is rather helpful for an algorithm to quickly identify one category (or to exclude one). Indeed, our tree-based models can easily ask a question such as: *Is Europe > 0?* that is to say that the market is Europe and not the USA, China, or India. The algorithm can also easily exclude one market if needed by asking the question: *Is Europe < 1?* This wouldn't be possible with the integer-encoding technique.

---

1 A Boolean is a value that is either True or False: 1 or 0.

Table 22.4: One-hot encoding.

Market	Europe	USA	China	India
Europe	1	0	0	0
USA	0	1	0	0
China	0	0	1	0
India	0	0	0	1

Table 22.5: X_train with one-hot encoding.

X_train Segment				Demand				Y_train Demand
0	0	1	0	5	15	10	7	6
0	1	0	0	2	3	1	1	1
1	0	0	0	18	25	32	47	56
0	0	0	1	4	1	5	3	2

If markets were encoded as consecutive numbers, you would need to ask at least two questions to exclude or include only one market. This is simply less efficient than with the one-hot technique.

Drop a Column?

When using one-hot label encoding, you can always drop one column and not lose any information. For example, as shown in Table 22.6, you can have the same information as in Table 22.4, with one fewer column. You could say that the Market is Europe if Market isn't the USA, China, or India.

Table 22.6: One-hot encoding (with one less column).

Market	USA	China	India
Europe	0	0	0
USA	1	0	0
China	0	1	0
India	0	0	1

This technique is used by some to reduce the number of columns in our dataset while keeping the same amount of information. Sure. But, now, if our algorithm needs to exclude Europe, it will need to ask 3 questions (*Is USA* < 1? *Is China* < 1? and finally *Is India* < 1?). This is, of course, not efficient. Having one fewer column in our dataset might not be worth this loss of efficiency.

> **Pro-Tip**
>
> Using one-hot label encoding rather than integer encoding will allow you to remove useless features and only keep the meaningful ones, thus reducing overfitting. It is then preferred not to initially remove one random dummy column from the one-hot labels, but rather to wait for analysis only to remove the meaningless ones. We will do this in Chapter 24.

Do It Yourself

In Section 22.1, we applied integer encoding to differentiate various product segments in our dataset. Let's now use one-hot label encoding to differentiate each brand. We can retrieve the brand easily from the index, and then one-hot encode it using the pandas function pd.get_dummies().[2]

```
1  df['Brand'] = df.index
2  df = pd.get_dummies(df, columns=['Brand'], prefix_sep='_')
```

pd.get_dummies() takes a couple of parameters:

columns (default=None)

> By default, get_dummies() will transform into one-hot vectors all the columns that are defined as either categories[3] or objects (e. g., strings). You can also specify a list of columns you want to encode as one-hot vectors.

prefix (default=None)

> By default, pandas will give the initial column name as a prefix to all the new one-hot columns. You can input another prefix via this parameter.

prefix_sep (default='_')

> This separator will be used between the column name and the prefix.

drop_first (default=False)

> This Boolean will determine if get_dummies() will get rid of the first one-hot column.

By using pd.get_dummies() on the Brand column, you should obtain an extra 65 columns on the dataset:

---

2 See pandas.pydata.org/pandas-docs/stable/reference/api/pandas.get_dummies.html

3 A specific data type that pandas can use. See pandas.pydata.org/pandas-docs/stable/user_guide/categorical.html for more information.

```
1  print(df)
2  >>                   2007-01  2007-02  ...   Brand_Volvo  Brand_Westfield
3  >> Make                                 ...
4  >> Alfa Romeo             16        9   ...             0                0
5  >> Aston Martin            0        0   ...             0                0
6  >> Audi                  599      498   ...             0                0
7  >> BMW                   352      335   ...             0                0
8  >> Bentley                 0        0   ...             0                0
9  >> ...                   ...      ...   ...           ...              ...
10 >> Think                   2        0   ...             0                0
11 >> Toyota               2884     1885   ...             0                0
12 >> Volkswagen           2521     1517   ...             0                0
13 >> Volvo                 693      570   ...             1                0
14 >> Westfield              0        0   ...             0                1
```

22.3 Dataset Creation

Now that we have created the columns we want in our DataFrame df (either via integer or one-hot label encoding), we can create our datasets X_train, Y_train, X_test, and Y_test including this categorical information. To do so, we will update our datasets() function so that it can properly use a categorical input.

The idea is that we will flag the categorical columns in the historical dataset df based on their names. If you used one-hot label encoding, we can easily identify categorical columns by using the prefix_sep.

These are the new steps we will take with our function:

Line 1 Our function takes a new parameter cat_name that contains the character (or string) that will identify the categorical column(s). As any column containing cat_name will be flagged as a categorical input, you can pass the prefix separator you used in pd.get_dummies().

Line 3 Define col_cat as the categorical columns in df.

Line 4 Define D as the historical demand values by excluding the categorical columns from df.

Line 5 Define C as the categorical data.

Line 15 Stack C to X_train. We first prepare C by stacking it on top of itself multiple times to match the shape of X_train.

Line 22 In case of the future forecast, stack C to X_test.

```
1   def datasets_cat(df, x_len=12, y_len=1, test_loops=12, cat_name='_'):
2
3       col_cat = [col for col in df.columns if cat_name in col]
4       D = df.drop(columns=col_cat).values # Historical demand
5       C = df[col_cat].values # Categorical info
6       rows, periods = D.shape
7
8       # Training set creation
9       loops = periods + 1 - x_len - y_len
10      train = []
11      for col in range(loops):
12          train.append(D[:,col:col+x_len+y_len])
13      train = np.vstack(train)
14      X_train, Y_train = np.split(train,[-y_len],axis=1)
15      X_train = np.hstack((np.vstack([C]*loops),X_train))
16
17      # Test set creation
18      if test_loops > 0:
19          X_train, X_test = np.split(X_train,[-rows*test_loops],axis=0)
20          Y_train, Y_test = np.split(Y_train,[-rows*test_loops],axis=0)
21      else: # No test set: X_test is used to generate the future ⌋
        ↪   forecast
22          X_test = np.hstack((C,D[:,-x_len:]))
23          Y_test = np.full((X_test.shape[0],y_len),np.nan) #Dummy value
24
25      # Formatting required for scikit-learn
26      if y_len == 1:
27          Y_train = Y_train.ravel()
28          Y_test = Y_test.ravel()
29
30      return X_train, Y_train, X_test, Y_test
```

Let's now recap the A to Z process to create training and test sets with categorical data. For integer label encoding, we have:

```
1   df = import_data()
2   df['Segment'] = 2
3   mask = df.index.isin(luxury)
4   df.loc[mask,'Segment'] = 4
5   mask = df.index.isin(premium)
```

```
6   df.loc[mask,'Segment'] = 3
7   mask = df.index.isin(low_cost)
8   df.loc[mask,'Segment'] = 1
9   X_train, Y_train, X_test, Y_test = datasets_cat(df, x_len=12,
    ↪   y_len=1, test_loops=12, cat_name='Segment')
```

And for one-hot label encoding, we have:

```
1   df = import_data()
2   df['Brand'] = df.index
3   df = pd.get_dummies(df, columns=['Brand'], prefix_sep='_')
4   X_train, Y_train, X_test, Y_test = datasets_cat(df, x_len=12,
    ↪   y_len=1, test_loops=12, cat_name='_')
```

Now that we have proper training and test sets, we can pursue our data science process with a proper feature optimization. We will do this in Chapter 24.

23 Clustering

As discussed in Chapter 22, it can be helpful for both data scientists and machine learning models to classify the various products they have. Unfortunately, you do not always receive a pre-classified dataset. Could a machine learning model help us classify it? Yes, of course. In order to do so, we will have to use **unsupervised** machine learning models.

> **Supervised Learning**
>
> A **supervised** machine learning model is a model that is fed with both inputs and desired outputs. It is up to the algorithm to understand the relationship(s) between these inputs and outputs. It is called supervised, as you show the model what the desired output is.
>
> All the machine learning models we have seen so far are called supervised models (you cannot ask your algorithm to make a forecast if you never show it what a good forecast looks like).

> **Unsupervised Learning**
>
> An **unsupervised** machine learning model is a model that is only fed with inputs and no specific desired outputs. It is up to the machine learning algorithm to make some order of (categorize) the different data observations. You can simply see it as asking your algorithm to assign a label to each data observation. This is called unsupervised learning, as you do not label samples in any pre-given way, henceforth not requiring any specific output.

Unsupervised learning, using given meaningful features, can cluster anything from products to clients or from social behaviors to neighborhoods in a city. Usually, a product catalog is segmented based on product families (or brands). But products within the same family might not share the same demand patterns (seasonality, trends). For example, meat for barbecues will sell in a similar way as outside furniture, but not regular meat. Student notebooks will be purchased with the same seasonality as business notebooks, although they look alike.

23.1 K-means Clustering

A very famous unsupervised machine learning model is called **K-means**. This algorithm will classify each data observation into k different clusters (see Figure 23.1). Let's look in detail at how this works.

https://doi.org/10.1515/9783110671124-023

> **Algorithm – K-means**
>
> 1. Assign each **K centers** to a random coordinate (within the limits of the dataset).
> 2. Associate each data sample with its closest center.
> 3. Move each center to the middle of all the data samples associated with it.
> 4. Repeat steps 2 and 3 until the cluster centers do not move anymore.

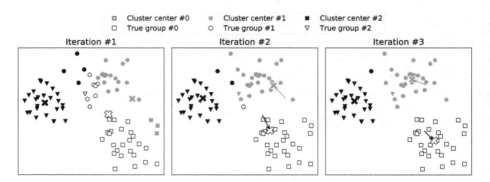

Figure 23.1: K-means with three centers.

This algorithm (as presented here and implemented in scikit-learn) dates back to 1957.[1] Note that even though this algorithm might look very linear and logical, **the results are actually random.** This is due to the initialization of the algorithm. Depending on the different initial *random* center positions, the final clusters might differ.

Distance

When you ask a K-means model to organize your dataset, you need to give it a mathematical definition of the *distance* between two data samples. You might think that there is only one definition of the distance between two points, but mathematicians came up with many different ones.

Let's keep it simple for our example and define the distance between two points as the *Euclidean*[2] distance. The Euclidean distance is basically the technical term to define the distance as we use it in our day-to-day lives: simply, the length of a straight line between two points.

---

1 It was published later in Lloyd (1982).
2 Euclid was a Greek geometrician around 300 BC.

Let's define the **inertia** of a K-means model as the sum of all the distances between each data sample and its associated cluster center. The lower the inertia, the more "accurate" the model. Reducing the inertia of such a model is very easy: just add more clusters! As you can see in Figure 23.2, the more clusters, the lower the inertia (until every data sample has its own center).

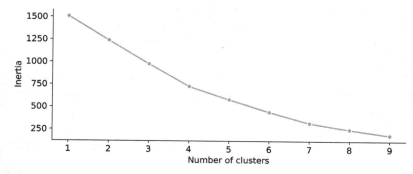

Figure 23.2: Impact of the number of clusters on inertia.

More clusters will result in lower inertia (i. e., smaller and denser clusters), but these clusters might also get less meaningful and come with a higher risk of overfitting (as we will discuss in detail in Chapter 24).

> **Going Further**
>
> Running K-means on large datasets might be time-consuming. A faster algorithm "Mini-Batch K-Means clustering" has been proposed by Sculley (2010). It is essentially the same as the traditional K-means, but the clusters update is only done on one batch of data at a time. For its implementation in scikit-learn, see scikit-learn.org/stable/modules/generated/sklearn.cluster. MiniBatchKMeans.html.
>
> K-means is one clustering technique among others. For a review of other techniques, see scikit-learn.org/stable/modules/clustering.html and Oskolkov (2019) (available here: towardsdatascience.com/how-to-cluster-in-high-dimensions-4ef693bacc6).

23.2 Looking for Meaningful Centers

We just learned a compelling and automated way to label an entire dataset, thanks to machine learning. But how can we apply this to our historical demand?

The question you should ask yourself is: *what are the features I want to categorize my products on?* Depending on each dataset, you might prefer different approaches. Here are some ideas:

Volume We can obviously start categorizing products based on their sales volume. Most likely, this categorization won't provide so much added value, as you could just do a good old *Pareto Classification*[3] to get a similar result.

Additive Seasonality If we cluster the products based on their additive seasonality factors (as defined in Chapter 11), we will cluster them based on their average volume *and* their seasonality. You might then end up with groups containing just a few products.

Multiplicative Seasonality If we take the multiplicative seasonal factors (as defined in Chapter 9), our products will then be categorized only based on their seasonal behavior—irrespective of their absolute size. This sounds much better.

As for most of our models, you will have to try different techniques (and different numbers of clusters) until you find the right one for your business.

Clustering on Seasonal Factors

An interesting way to visualize seasonal clusters is to plot a *heatmap*. This kind of visualization will help you *see* the seasonal factors of each cluster. We plotted one in Figure 23.3, where we see the cluster centers of our car brands based on their multiplicative seasonal factors (as defined in Chapter 9).

This heatmap might look strange to you. It seems that Cluster 2 contains many flat products: see how the seasonal factors are close to 1 (or 100%, if you interpret them as percentages). We also have three clusters with extreme seasonalities (clusters 0, 1, and 3) and only a few products (8 brands in total!). It seems that the products in these clusters are (more or less) only sold one month per year.

This strange behavior is because a few car brands only sold cars in a single month or nearly. If a product is only sold in March, its seasonal factors will look like: $[0, 0, 12, 0, 0, 0, 0, 0, 0, 0, 0, 0]$.[4] Our K-means algorithm deals with these extreme values by creating some very specific clusters just for them. These extreme seasonal

---

3 A Pareto classification is a rule of thumb to divide a dataset into three classes (ABC) based on volume. A class is composed of the products that account for 80% of the total demand, B for the next top 15%, and C gets the remaining small ones.

4 Remember that the sum of the multiplicative seasonal factors should be 12 (as there are 12 periods). You can observe it in Figure 23.3, where the sum of each cluster's seasonal factors is 12. See Chapter 9 for more information.

	Cluster 0	Cluster 1	Cluster 2	Cluster 3	
Jan	0.00	0.00	0.72	0.00	
Feb	0.69	12.00	0.89	0.00	
Mar	0.00	0.00	1.15	0.00	
Apr	0.00	0.00	0.97	0.00	
May	0.00	0.00	0.98	12.00	
Jun	0.00	0.00	1.13	0.00	
Jul	0.00	0.00	1.10	0.00	
Aug	8.65	0.00	0.92	0.00	
Sep	0.46	0.00	1.22	0.00	
Oct	0.46	0.00	0.97	0.00	
Nov	0.00	0.00	0.89	0.00	
Dec	1.73	0.00	1.05	0.00	
	Cluster 0 4 samples	Cluster 1 2 samples	Cluster 2 57 samples	Cluster 3 2 samples	

Figure 23.3: Cluster visualization.

factors are so extreme that they are not like any other seasonal factors and will require a cluster just for them as their (Euclidean) distance to any other seasonal factors is too long.

Due to this, the clusters we have are not meaningful.

Let's see how we can tackle this.

Scaling

The K-means algorithm is very sensitive to extreme values (that, by definition, are far away from any other values) so that we will have to normalize all the seasonal factors. It means that each product's seasonal factors will be reduced to have a mean of 0 and a *range*[5] of 1. To do so, we have to divide each set of seasonal factors by its range and then subtract its mean. This will flatten the extreme cases and should allow the K-means algorithm to give more meaningful clusters.

If we perform clustering on our new scaled seasonal factors, we obtain a meaningful result, as shown in Figure 23.4. See how samples (i. e., carmakers, in our case) are evenly distributed across clusters.

---

5 range = maximum - minimum.

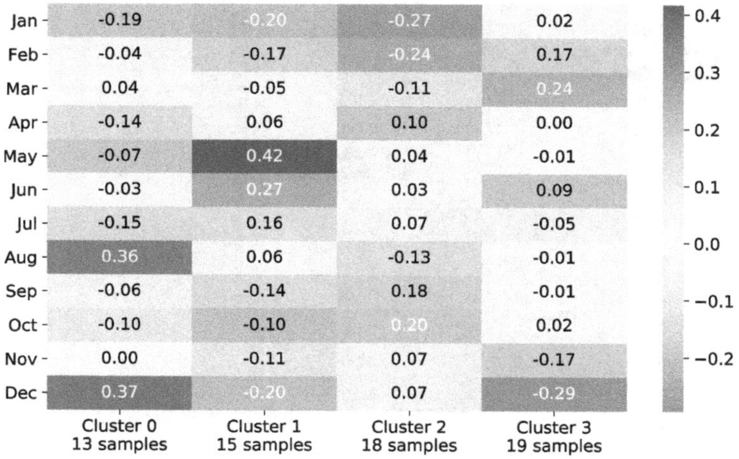

	Cluster 0	Cluster 1	Cluster 2	Cluster 3
Jan	-0.19	-0.20	-0.27	0.02
Feb	-0.04	-0.17	-0.24	0.17
Mar	0.04	-0.05	-0.11	0.24
Apr	-0.14	0.06	0.10	0.00
May	-0.07	0.42	0.04	-0.01
Jun	-0.03	0.27	0.03	0.09
Jul	-0.15	0.16	0.07	-0.05
Aug	0.36	0.06	-0.13	-0.01
Sep	-0.06	-0.14	0.18	-0.01
Oct	-0.10	-0.10	0.20	0.02
Nov	0.00	-0.11	0.07	-0.17
Dec	0.37	-0.20	0.07	-0.29
	Cluster 0 13 samples	Cluster 1 15 samples	Cluster 2 18 samples	Cluster 3 19 samples

Figure 23.4: Scaled clusters.

Recap

K-means is very sensitive to scaling; always remember to scale your dataset before applying this technique. As we did here, it is always a best practice to visualize your results to check that they are meaningful. Another good check is to count the number of products in each cluster: if you obtain some clusters with only a few items, that might be a clue that the clusters are not meaningful.

23.3 Do It Yourself

Seasonal Factors

Let's first compute the (multiplicative) seasonal factors. In order to do so, we will create a function `seasonal_factors()` that will return the seasonal factors based on a historical demand dataset (the function is very similar to the one from Chapter 9— remember that `slen` is the season length).

```
def seasonal_factors(df,slen):
    s = pd.DataFrame(index=df.index)
    for i in range(slen):
        s[i+1] = df.iloc[:,i::slen].mean(axis=1)
    s = s.divide(s.mean(axis=1),axis=0).fillna(0)
    return s
```

We will also create a scaler() function that will return the seasonality factors scaled with a range of 1 and a mean of 0.

```
1  def scaler(s):
2      mean = s.mean(axis=1)
3      maxi = s.max(axis=1)
4      mini = s.min(axis=1)
5      s = s.subtract(mean,axis=0)
6      s = s.divide(maxi-mini,axis=0).fillna(0)
7      return s
```

We can now use both our functions to populate scaled seasonal factors:

```
1  df = import_data()
2  s = seasonal_factors(df,slen=12)
3  s = scaler(s)
4  print(s.head())
5  >>                  1          2          3    ...         10         11         12
6  >> Make                                        ...
7  >> Alfa Romeo    0.415094 -0.066895  0.536878  ... -0.349914 -0.463122 -0.246141
8  >> Aston Martin -0.308333 -0.299242  0.100758  ... -0.399242 -0.199242 -0.399242
9  >> Audi         -0.454203 -0.373367 -0.080042  ...  0.000061 -0.115771 -0.020109
10 >> BMW           0.244091 -0.259060 -0.057379  ...  0.344932  0.486738 -0.107274
11 >> Bentley      -0.055556  0.308081 -0.025253  ...  0.308081 -0.358586 -0.025253
```

Cluster Definition

Let's now use the K-means algorithm implementation from scikit-learn to identify the different clusters among our products (we assume df to contain the historical demand per product).[6] We will use the function KMeans() that takes as an input the number of clusters we want (n_clusters).

```
1  from sklearn.cluster import KMeans
2  kmeans = KMeans(n_clusters=4, random_state=0).fit(s)
3  df['Group'] = kmeans.predict(s)
```

Giving a specific random_state to KMeans is rather helpful, as we can expect the same clusters each time we call the algorithm (as long as the historical values provided do

---

6 See VanderPlas (2016) for more information about K-means and its implementation in scikit-learn.

not change). This will make our analyst life much easier (you can actually give a ran-dom_state to most of the scikit-learn models).

Python Mastery – scikit-learn and random_state

Setting random_state in a scikit-learn function assures that the results are re-producible by forcing it to always use the same random values (if any).

In Python—as with all computer software—all random processes are actually *pseudo-random*. It means that the computer is *simulating* a random process, based on a **random state**. Each time we call a scikit-learn function requiring random values, it generates a new (pseudo-random) random state to generate those random numbers. If we set this seed to an arbitrary number—instead of letting scikit-learn pseudo-randomly pick one—it will consistently return the same outputs (if inputs are stable).

Experimentation

There is definitely no silver bullet when it comes to determining how many clusters you need to define. In order to do so, you can rely on three main tools:
- Plotting the inertia vs. the number of clusters (as done in Figure 23.2)
- Visualizing the seasonal factors (as done in Figures 23.3 and 23.4)
- Analyzing the number of products by cluster (as done in Figures 23.3 and 23.4)

Let's discuss these in detail.

Inertia
Let's loop through different numbers of clusters and plot the inertia obtained for each of these.

```
1  results = []
2  for n in range(1,10):
3      kmeans = KMeans(n_clusters=n, random_state=0).fit(s)
4      results.append([n, kmeans.inertia_])
5  results = pd.DataFrame(data=results,columns=['Number of clusters',⌐
   ↪ 'Intertia']).set_index('Number of clusters')
6  results.plot()
```

This code will plot a figure similar to Figure 23.2.

Cluster Visualization

```
1  import calendar
2  kmeans = KMeans(n_clusters=4, random_state=0).fit(s)
3  centers = pd.DataFrame(data=kmeans.cluster_centers_).transpose()
4  centers.index = calendar.month_abbr[1:]
5  centers.columns = [f'Cluster {x}' for x in range(centers.shape[1])]
```

Python Mastery – Calendar Library

We use the calendar library in order to get month names.

```
1  print(calendar.month_abbr[1:])
2  >> ['Jan','Feb','Mar','Apr','May','Jun','Jul','Aug','Sep','Oct','Nov',
   ↪    'Dec']
```

In order to plot a heatmap similar to Figure 23.4, we will use a new library: seaborn.

Python Mastery – Seaborn

Seaborn is a Python library that aims to create advanced statistical graphs. It was published in 2012 by Michael Waskom. As you will see, it is actually very simple to use. The official documentation is available on seaborn.pydata.org, and like the one of pandas, NumPy, and scikit-learn, it is very easy to read. Don't hesitate to look for inspiration on seaborn.pydata.org/examples. The convention is to import seaborn as sns.[a]

---

a sns was intended as a joke by the author Michael Waskom who chose these based on the initials of a TV-show character.

```
1  import seaborn as sns
2  sns.heatmap(centers, annot=True, fmt='.2f', center=0, cmap='RdBu_r')
```

heatmap() takes a few parameters:[7]

annot Boolean that will show (or not show) values in the heatmap.

fmt Format applied to the annotations (if any), '.2f' will show float numbers rounded to two digits after the period.

center Defines where the colormap will be centered.

---

7 See seaborn.pydata.org/generated/seaborn.heatmap.html

cmap Colormap used for the heatmap. In the example here, we use a colormap going from blue to red by passing cmap='RdBu_r'.

Number of Products per Cluster

We can also count the number of products inside each cluster to understand whether these are meaningful. This can be done in one line of code.

```
1  print(df['Group'].value_counts().sort_index())
```

If some clusters contain a low number of products, it means that either you have too many clusters for them to be relevant, or you should look at another set of (scaled?) features to classify your products.

Is It Helpful for Forecasting?

Now that we have created meaningful clusters for our products, we can use them by passing them to our machine learning forecasting model. We will analyze the added value of doing so in the next chapter.

24 Feature Optimization #2

In Chapters 22, 20, and 23, we discussed adding new featuress (e. g., product segments, seasonal clusters, calendar information, GDP growth) to our model in order to make more accurate predictions. As we discussed in Chapter 8, adding more features in a model can result in overfitting: the model would start recognizing patterns in the noise—as it has more opportunities to find randomly matching features—and will fail to make appropriate predictions about the future. In Section 24.1, we will create a model using all the features discussed in the previous chapters (and add some more). Then, in Section 24.2, we will see how we can select only the meaningful ones for our model.

24.1 Dataset Creation

Let's create a new dataset function datasets_full() based on the functions seen so far in Chapters 18, 22, and 20.[1]
Here are the main changes:

Line 1,3 Our function takes a parameter cat_name that contains a list with all the characters that will identify the categorical column(s). As any column containing cat_name will be flagged as a categorical input, you can pass the prefix separator you used in pd.get_dummies(). Note that we define cat_name as a list of strings, so that you can pass multiple prefix separator or category names.

Line 16–18, 20–25 We will also pass to the machine learning algorithm various information about the previous demand observations (such as the mean, max, and median). See also that on line 17 and 22 we compute the GDP growth/demand moving average over 4 periods.

Line 30–33 We create a list features that will contain the name of each feature. We will use this later when we analyze feature importance.

Line 49–59 We create the test set using the same information as for the training set.

```
1   def datasets_full(df, X_exo, x_len=12, y_len=1, test_loops=12,
     ↪   holdout_loops=0, cat_name=['_']):
2
3       col_cat = [col for col in df.columns if any(name in col for
     ↪       name in cat_name)]
4       D = df.drop(columns=col_cat).values # Historical demand
5       C = df[col_cat].values # Categorical info
```

---

1 You can download the Python code shown in this book as well as the Excel templates on supchains.com/resources-2nd (password: SupChains-2nd).

https://doi.org/10.1515/9783110671124-024

```
6    rows, periods = D.shape
7    X_exo = np.repeat(np.reshape(X_exo,[1,-1]),rows,axis=0)
8    X_months = np.repeat(np.reshape([int(col[-2:]) for col in df
     ↪  .columns if col not in col_cat],[1,-1]),rows,axis=0)
9
10   # Training set creation
11   loops = periods + 1 - x_len - y_len
12   train = []
13   for col in range(loops):
14       m = X_months[:,col+x_len].reshape(-1,1) #month
15       exo = X_exo[:,col:col+x_len+y_len] #exogenous data
16       exo = np.hstack([np.mean(exo,axis=1,keepdims=True),
17                        np.mean(exo[:,-4:],axis=1,keepdims=True),
18                        exo])
19       d = D[:,col:col+x_len+y_len]
20       d = np.hstack([np.mean(d[:,:-y_len],axis=1,keepdims=True),
21                      np.median(d[:,:-y_len],axis=1,keepdims=True),
22                      np.mean(d[:,-4-y_len:-y_len],axis=1,
                       ↪  keepdims=True),
23                      np.max(d[:,:-y_len],axis=1,keepdims=True),
24                      np.min(d[:,:-y_len],axis=1,keepdims=True),
25                      d])
26       train.append(np.hstack([m, exo, d]))
27   train = np.vstack(train)
28   X_train, Y_train = np.split(train,[-y_len],axis=1)
29   X_train = np.hstack((np.vstack([C]*loops),X_train))
30   features = (col_cat
31               +['Month']
32               +['Exo Mean','Exo MA4']+[f'Exo M{-x_len+col}' for col
                ↪  in range(x_len+y_len)]
33               +['Demand Mean','Demand Median','Demand MA4','Demand
                ↪  Max','Demand Min']+[f'Demand M-{x_len-col}' for
                ↪  col in range(x_len)])
34
35   # Holdout set creation
36   if holdout_loops > 0:
37       X_train, X_holdout = np.split(X_train,[-rows*holdout_loops],
         ↪  axis=0)
38       Y_train, Y_holdout = np.split(Y_train,[-rows*holdout_loops],
         ↪  axis=0)
39   else:
40       X_holdout, Y_holdout = np.array([]), np.array([])
```

```
41
42      # Test set creation
43      if test_loops > 0:
44          X_train, X_test = np.split(X_train,[-rows*test_loops],axis=0)
45          Y_train, Y_test = np.split(Y_train,[-rows*test_loops],axis=0)
46      else: # No test set: X_test is used to generate the future
         ↪ forecast
47          exo = X_exo[:,-x_len-y_len:]
48          d = D[:,-x_len:]
49          X_test = np.hstack((C,
50                              m[:,-1].reshape(-1,1),
51                              np.hstack([np.mean(exo,axis=1,
                              ↪ keepdims=True),
52                                         np.mean(exo[:,-4:],axis=1,
                                         ↪ keepdims=True),
53                                         exo]),
54                              np.hstack([np.mean(d,axis=1,
                              ↪ keepdims=True),
55                                         np.median(d,axis=1,
                                         ↪ keepdims=True),
56                                         np.mean(d[:,-4:],axis=1,
                                         ↪ keepdims=True),
57                                         np.max(d,axis=1,
                                         ↪ keepdims=True),
58                                         np.min(d,axis=1,
                                         ↪ keepdims=True),
59                                         d])))
60          Y_test = np.full((X_test.shape[0],y_len),np.nan) #Dummy value
61
62      # Formatting required for scikit-learn
63      if y_len == 1:
64          Y_train = Y_train.ravel()
65          Y_test = Y_test.ravel()
66          Y_holdout = Y_holdout.ravel()
67
68      return X_train, Y_train, X_holdout, Y_holdout, X_test, Y_test,
        ↪ features
```

As usual, we can use our function to create all the datasets (i. e., training, test, and holdout) we need. In this example, we won't use a holdout set—instead we will create a validation set. Note that df is assumed to have segments defined as in Chapter 22 and groups as defined in Chapter 23. Do not hesitate to download the full code on supchains.com/resources-2nd (password: SupChains-2nd).

```
1  X_train, Y_train, X_holdout, Y_holdout, X_test, Y_test, features = ⌟
   ↪   datasets_full(df, X_GDP, x_len=12, y_len=1, test_loops=12, ⌟
   ↪   holdout_loops=0, cat_name=['_','Segment','Group'])
2  x_train, x_val, y_train, y_val = train_test_split(X_train, Y_train, ⌟
   ↪   test_size=0.15)
```

Let's run an initial XGBoost with all this extra information.

```
1  XGB = XGB.fit(x_train, y_train, early_stopping_rounds=100, ⌟
   ↪   verbose=False, eval_set=[(x_val,y_val)], eval_metric='mae')
2  Y_train_pred = XGB.predict(X_train)
3  Y_test_pred = XGB.predict(X_test)
4  kpi_ML(Y_train, Y_train_pred, Y_test, Y_test_pred, name='XGBoost')
5  >>            MAE  RMSE  Bias
6  >> XGBoost
7  >> Train     12.3  31.5  0.9
8  >> Test      17.1  43.2  3.0
```

Those are already slightly better results than for our 'simple' XGBoost model from Chapter 21 (see Table 24.1 for the detailed results). Can we further optimize our model?

24.2 Feature Selection

Feature Importance

We saw that adding a lot of extra features is bringing extra value to our model. But there is a risk for (even partial) overfitting: removing some useless features might improve the overall accuracy, as the model won't be overfitting them. We should therefore identify the *useless* features that just add noise, and remove them. In order to do so, we will look at the feature importance (as discussed in Chapter 16 and in Section 21.2 for XGBoost). The following code is extracting the feature importance of an XGBoost model.[2]

---

[2] See xgboost.readthedocs.io/en/latest/python/python_api.html for more information about XGBoost and feature importance, and Abu-Rmileh (2019) for a discussion about the different ways you can measure feature importance in XGBoost.

```
1  imp = XGB.get_booster().get_score(importance_type='total_gain')
2  imp = pd.DataFrame.from_dict(imp,orient='index',columns=['Importance'])
3  imp.index = np.array(features)[imp.index.astype(str).str.replace('f', ⌐
   ⌐  '').astype(int)]
4  imp = (imp['Importance']/sum(imp.values)).sort_values(ascending=False)
5  imp.to_excel('Feature Importance.xlsx')
```

Those should be the most relevant features:

```
1  imp.head()
2  >> Demand MA4        0.284323
3  >> Demand Mean       0.119733
4  >> Demand M-1        0.118647
5  >> Demand Median     0.104672
6  >> Demand Max        0.064427
```

Going Further

In this chapter, we use XGBoost as a baseline model for which we optimize the features. But the process highlighted here can of course be applied to any other model. You can easily get the feature importance of a tree, forest, or ETR with the code shown in Chapter 16.

Backward Feature Elimination

One of the most straightforward ways to remove useless features and keep relevant ones is to remove useless features until the model reaches an optimum (this technique is called *backward elimination*). In practice, we are going to run our model multiple times by trying different feature importance thresholds: if a feature gets a feature importance below the threshold, it will be removed from the model. We will plot the MAE and RMSE obtained for each threshold (see Figure 24.1) in order to *visually* select the best threshold.

Let's first define a new model_kpi() function that returns the MAE and RMSE.

```
1  def model_kpi(model, X, Y):
2      Y_pred = model.predict(X)
3      mae = np.mean(np.abs(Y - Y_pred))/np.mean(Y)
4      rmse = np.sqrt(np.mean((Y - Y_pred)**2))/np.mean(Y)
5      return mae,rmse
```

We can then proceed with our experiments.

```
1  results = []
2  limits = [0.00005,0.0001,0.00015,0.0002,0.00025,0.0003,0.0004,0↲
   ↳ .0005,0.0006,0.0007,0.0008,0.0009,0.001,0.0011,0.002,0.004,0↲
   ↳ .008,0.01,0.02,0.04,0.06]
3  for limit in limits:
4      mask = [feature in imp[imp > limit] for feature in features]
5      XGB = XGB.fit(x_train[:,mask], y_train, ↲
       ↳ early_stopping_rounds=100, verbose=False, eval_set=[(x_val[:↲
       ↳ ,mask],y_val)], eval_metric='mae')
6      results.append(model_kpi(XGB,x_val[:,mask],y_val))
7  results = pd.DataFrame(data=results,columns=['MAE','RMSE'],↲
   ↳ index=limits)
8  results.plot(secondary_y='MAE',logx=True)
```

As you can see in Figure 24.1, it seems that we have an optimum around 0.007 (i. e., 0.7% of added value). Keep in mind that machine learning training is often random,[3] so you should be looking for a *good area* rather than for a specific spike that could be just randomly appearing. Also—as for any result shown in this book—the results shown here only apply to this specific dataset, using this specific set of features, with an XGBoost using a specific set of parameters. What is important here is not the exact threshold obtained, but the data science process that you will have to apply for any other project.

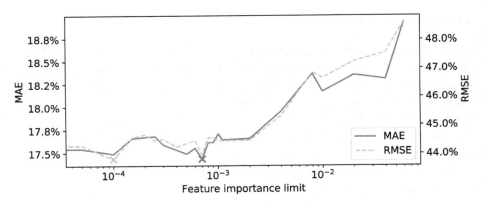

Figure 24.1: Impact of feature selection on the validation set.

---

3 This is due to the multiple subsets (features and training sets) randomly generated for each tree of the ensemble.

Let's see which features are kept if we choose a threshold of 0.0007.

```
1  limit = 0.0007
2  print(imp[imp > limit].index)
3  >> Index(['Demand MA4','Demand Mean','Demand M-1', 'Demand Median',
   ↪    'Demand Max','Demand M-12','Demand M-3','Demand M-2','Demand M-6',
   ↪    'Demand Min','Demand M-4','Demand M-5','Demand M-7','Demand M-11',
   ↪    'Demand M-8','Demand M-9','Demand M-10','Month', 'Exo Mean','Exo MA4',
   ↪    'Exo M-12','Exo M-11','Exo M0','Group','Exo M-8'], dtype='object')
```

We can now run our new model, keeping only the meaningful features.

```
1  mask = [feature in imp[imp > limit] for feature in features]
2  XGB = XGB.fit(x_train[:,mask], y_train, early_stopping_rounds=100,
   ↪    verbose=False, eval_set=[(x_val[:,mask],y_val)],
   ↪    eval_metric='mae')
3  Y_train_pred = XGB.predict(X_train[:,mask])
4  Y_test_pred = XGB.predict(X_test[:,mask])
5  kpi_ML(Y_train, Y_train_pred, Y_test, Y_test_pred, name='XGBoost')
6  >>              MAE  RMSE  Bias
7  >> XGBoost
8  >> Train      12.2  31.4   0.9
9  >> Test       17.2  43.6   3.6
```

We see that, unfortunately, in this specific dataset (with those specific features and for a specific instance of this model), we couldn't add more accuracy to our model by removing the less useful features. You might nevertheless achieve different results on different (bigger) datasets with other features.

Table 24.1: Results.

Models	MAE		RMSE		Bias	
	Train	Test	Train	Test	Train	Test
Regression	17.8	17.8	43.9	43.7	0.0	**1.6**
Tree	17.3	18.9	42.2	46.8	0.0	2.9
Forest	14.1	17.6	35.0	44.9	−0.0	2.7
ETR	14.2	17.5	35.8	44.4	−0.0	2.5
AdaBoost	**10.8**	17.9	**24.9**	47.8	0.5	3.9
XGBoost	12.2	**17.2**	31.4	**43.6**	0.9	3.6

Going Further

You could push this exercise further in multiple ways:

- Remove GDP per month and *only* include moving average 4 and yearly average.
- Include more features such as demand standard deviation, skewness, and coefficient of variation.[a]
- Include more historical periods as explained in Chapter 18.
- Run another parameter optimization (as done in Section 21.4) after you have chosen a set of features.
- Perform a *forward selection* (instead of a backward elimination). The idea is to start with a single, or a few useful features and add new features one by one—each time measuring the model results. Until adding new features does not bring added value.

a See my book *Inventory Optimization: Models and Simulations* for detailed definitions.

scikit-learn – 2010

XGBoost – 2016

pandas – 2008

NumPy – 2005

Extremely Random Trees – 2006

GBoost – 2001

AdaBoost – 1997

Python – 1991

Forest – 1995

Damped trends – 1985

**Machine
Learning**

Python

**Exponential
Smoothing**

Winters – 1960

Tree – 1963

Holt – 1957

25 Neural Networks

> **Note to the Reader**
>
> Neural networks (or *deep learning*, which usually refers to "deep" neural networks) is a vast subject. This chapter is only an introduction to the topic. It will be enough, though, to get you started in no time using some of the most recent best practices.
>
> If you are interested in learning more about neural networks, do not hesitate to apply for Andrew Ng's deep learning specialization on Coursera (www.coursera.org/specializations/deep-learning).

The 2010s saw the deep learning tsunami.

In 2012, the revolution started at the ImageNet Large Scale Visual Recognition Challenge, a data science competition to classify pictures. A team led by Alex Krizhevsky (from the University of Toronto) achieved an unprecedented error rate of 15.3%, whereas the second best model got only 26.2%. Krizhevsky used a specific type of neural networks: convolutional neural networks. Moreover, he trained his network using graphical processing units (GPU) instead of the traditional CPUs.[1] In 2012, no other participants were using neural networks in this challenge. The next year, in the 2013 edition, all participants used similar neural networks.

In 2016, AlphaGo—an AI developed by DeepMind—beat the Go world champion. Computers had ruled chess-playing since 1997, after Deep Blue beat Kasparov in a famous match.[2] But beating humans at playing Go is a much more complex challenge, with an estimated 10^{170} possible combinations against 10^{120} for chess. Many experts were surprised by this early victory that wasn't expected to happen until a decade later. DeepMind was acquired by Google in 2014 for more than $500 million.

In 2017, DeepMind released AlphaGo Zero, which beat the late 2016-AlphaGo 100 games to 0. AlphaGo Zero only required three days of training to achieve this, learning to play Go only by competing against itself. In 2017, DeepMind reported paying $243 million to its 700 employees. This amount increased twofold in 2018.[3]

In 2020, OpenAI released the third iteration of an AI specialized in producing texts: GPT-3. This AI can write poetry, tell stories, solve equations, code websites, and even write articles about itself. Earlier, in 1950, Alan Turing (1912–1946, famous En-

---

1 See Krizhevsky et al. (2012).
2 Deep Blue suffered a bug during the first game. Kasparov interpreted it as a stroke of genius from the computer. He lost confidence resulting in him losing the match, despite using a good technique in the first match: he played an unusual opening to confuse the computer. See Silver (2015) for the whole story.
3 See Shead (2019).

https://doi.org/10.1515/9783110671124-025

glish computer scientist) proposed the "Turing test" to assess if a machine could imitate human language well enough to be confused for a human. GPT-3 is now writing journal articles that are often barely recognizable from human ones. OpenAI—funded by Elon Musk—was initially a non-profit organization. It became a *capped* profit organization in 2019, capping the returns on investment at a hundred times the initial amount. Shortly after, they secured a $1 billion investment from Microsoft.[4]

25.1 How Neural Networks Work

An (artificial) neural network is a **network** of **neurons** using specific **activation functions** trained by an **optimization algorithm**. In this section and the following section, we will define and explain each of these terms.

Neuron

As shown in Figure 25.1, an (artificial) neuron is a (mathematical) unit receiving information from various **weighted inputs** (the weights are noted w_i and the inputs x_i) and a **bias** (b). The neuron will sum those weighted inputs and its bias (we note the sum z with $z = b + \sum w_i x_i$), and then apply an **activation function** ($f(z)$) to the result. This activation function determines the neuron's behavior: how it reacts to inputs. In simple words, a neuron transforms a sum of inputs by using an activation function.

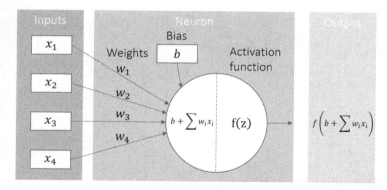

Figure 25.1: Artificial neuron with four inputs.

---

4 See Vincent (2019).

> ### A Brief History of Artificial Neurons
>
> The history of artificial neurons dates back to the 1940s, when Warren Mc-Culloch (a neuroscientist) and Walter Pitts (a logician) modeled the biological working of an organic neuron in a first artificial neuron to show how simple units could replicate logical functions.[a]
>
> ---
>
> **a** See McCulloch and Pitts (1943).

Activation Functions

Various functions are used by data scientists as activation functions.[5] As shown in Figure 25.2, the main ones are the following:

$$\text{sigmoid:} f(x) = (1 + e^{-x})^{-1}$$

$$\text{ReLu:} f(x) = \max(x, 0)$$

$$\text{tanh:} f(x) = \frac{e^x - e^{-x}}{e^x + e^{-x}}$$

As we will discuss later, using ReLu (short for *Rectified Linear Unit*) as an activation function is currently considered to be the best practice.[6] See Figure 25.3 for an example of a neuron using a ReLu activation function.

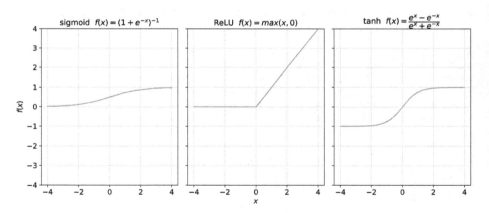

Figure 25.2: Most common activation functions.

---

5 As a technical remark, note that if we would use linear activation functions in neurons, the resulting neural network would also be a linear function. It would be nothing more than a (massive) linear regression.

6 Using ReLu results in a fast and stable training, even for deep neural networks. The exact explanation is beyond the scope of this book. See Nair and Hinton (2010) for more details.

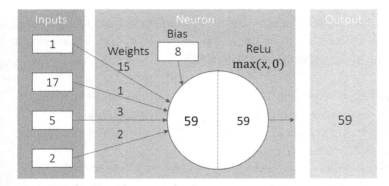

Figure 25.3: Example of a neuron using a ReLu activation function.

Neural Network

Now that we know how a neuron and an activation function work, let's take a look at a neural network's inner workings.[7] As shown in Figure 25.4, a neural network is composed of three types of layers.

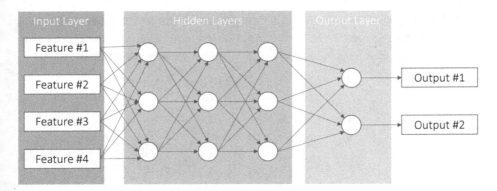

Figure 25.4: Example of neural network with four features, two outputs, and three hidden layers of 3 neurons (biases are not shown for the sake of simplicity).

Input Layer This simply passes the input features to the first hidden layer.
Hidden Layers This consists of multiple stacked layers of neurons. It is the core of the neural network.
Output Layer This is the final layer, where each neuron corresponds to the prediction of one of the outputs. Usually, this last layer uses a specific activation function,

---

7 Note that we describe here one specific type of neural network called *feed forward* neural network.

depending on the kind of outputs required (regression or classification). In a re-gression exercise (which is the case in forecasting), the output layer's activation function will often simply be the sum of its inputs.

The input layer's size depends on the number of features you want to use, whereas the output layer's size depends on the number of outputs. Setting the hidden layers' size and shape is up to you. (In Section 25.3, we will use a k-fold cross-validation random search to find a good architecture).

A neural network's inner workings are rather straightforward: the data flows from one layer to another through the various neurons (we call this **forward propagation**).

> **Forward Propagation**
>
> This is the phase when neurons propagate information through the network by applying their activation functions to their weighted inputs and biases. Dur-ing this phase, the neural network populates outputs (predictions) based on inputs.

In Figure 25.5, you can see a simple neural network with 2 layers of 2 neurons (powered by ReLu activation functions) using 2 input features (the average demand of the last 4 and 12 months—respectively, MA4 and MA12) to predict the future demand. In this example, the output neuron is simply using a sum as an activation function.

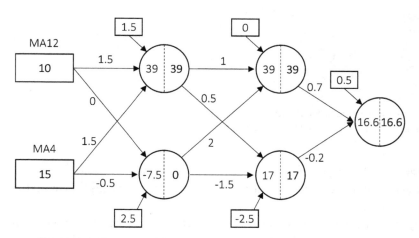

Figure 25.5: Example of forward propagation.

The type of neural networks presented here is called **feed forward** neural networks. Many other types have been developed over time. Let's mention the two most famous ones:

- Long-Short Term Memory Neural Networks (LSTM). They were introduced by Hochreiter and Schmidhuber (1997) and are mostly used for language recognition (or temporal series). See Hewamalage et al. (2020) for an analysis of their forecasting capabilities.
- Convolutional Neural Networks (CNN). The organic visual cortex inspires those neural networks initially introduced by LeCun et al. (1989). They show excellent results on image recognition.

A Brief History of the Perceptron

Inspired by Warren McCulloch's and Walter Pitts' publication, Frank Rosenblatt (a research psychologist working at Cornell Aeronautical Laboratory) worked in the 1950s on the **Perceptron**: a single layer of neurons able to classify pictures of a few hundred pixels.[a] This can be seen as the first ancestor of modern neural networks.

The genius of Rosenblatt was to implement an algorithm to train the neurons based on a dataset. Rosenblatt inspired himself from the work of the Canadian psychologist Donald Hebb, who theorized in his 1949 book *Organization of Behavior* that connections between (organic) neurons are reinforced as they are used (this would only be confirmed in the 1960s).[b] Rosenblatt's idea was to replicate this with his Perceptron.

The *New York Times* reported Rosenblatt prophesizing that Perceptrons would in the future be able to "recognize people and call out their name," "instantly translate speech in one language to speech or writing in another language," "be fired to the planets as mechanical space explorers" but also "reproduce itself" and be self-conscious.[c]

First Neural Network Winter   (1970s–mid 1980s)

Unfortunately, due to its training algorithm, the Perceptron was limited to a single layer of neurons. Despite lots of interest in those early developments, MIT professors Marvin Minsky and Seymour Papert published in 1969 a book (*Perceptrons: An introduction to computational geometry*) demonstrating that the Perceptron was limited in capabilities.[d] This resulted in the first "neural network winter" until the mid-80s.

a See Rosenblatt (1957).
b See Hebb (1949).
c See New York Times (1958).
d See Minsky and Papert (1969).

Algorithm – Perceptron Training

1. Initialize the weights and biases randomly.
2. For each data sample in the training set, compute the Perceptron's output (either 0 or 1, as it is a binary classification exercise).
3. If the output is wrong:
   - If the output should have been 0 but was 1, decrease the weights with an input of 1.
   - If the output should have been 1 but was 0, increase the weights with an input of 1.
4. Apply steps 2 and 3 until the Perceptron achieves a perfect accuracy (or until another criterion is reached).

25.2 Training a Neural Network

Once you have determined an architecture for your neural network and gathered a training set, the big question is: *how do we set all those inner weights (and biases)?* This is done by using **gradient descent**—a general optimization technique—together with **backpropagation**.

Gradient Descent

In 1847, Augustin-Louis Cauchy—a French mathematician—proposed a method to find the minimum (or maximum) of an unknown function: the gradient descent.[8] His idea can be explained simply. Imagine you are somewhere on a mountain and you would like to walk down to the sea. You just have to do the following:
1. Assess the slope of your immediate environment.
2. Walk in the direction of the steepest downward slope. Walk faster if the slope is steeper.
3. Repeat steps 1 and 2 until you reach the sea.

---

8 See Cauchy (1847).

In short, act as a ball rolling along a slope.

Algorithm – Gradient Descent

If we formalize this mathematically, here is how to find the minimum of an unknown function:

1. Start at a random point x.
2. Compute the gradient (slope) around x: $\frac{\partial f(x)}{\partial x}$
3. Update your position (x) as $x - \eta \frac{\partial f(x)}{\partial x}$ where η (eta) is a learning rate (or a step-size).
4. Repeat steps 2 and 3 until $\frac{\partial f(x)}{\partial x}$ is lower than a threshold.

See Figure 25.6 for an illustration.

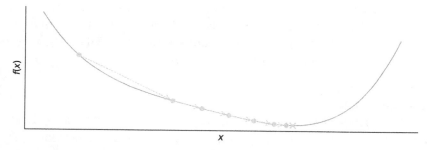

Figure 25.6: Example of gradient descent (first six steps).

Gradient descent is one of the most common techniques to minimize a **cost function**, as long as it is locally differentiable (in simple words, as long as you can estimate its slope locally).

Cost Function

This is the function that an algorithm is set to minimize. In the case of our machine learning algorithms, the cost function is often the (R)MSE or the MAE.

Pitfall #1: Local Minimum

The main limitation of using gradient descent to optimize a function is the risk of falling in a **local minimum**. In our mountain analogy: what if there is a lake along your way to the sea? You might get stuck in a local minimum where the (local) slope is zero, as shown in Figure 25.7.

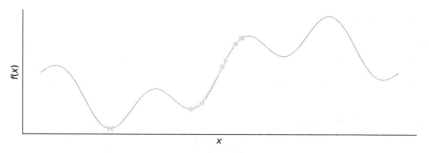

Figure 25.7: Gradient descent trapped in a local minimum.

Hopefully, if you are optimizing a function in a high-dimensional space (which is the case with neural networks—think about all the weights and biases to be optimized), there is a low risk of ending up in a local minimum—there will most likely be at least one dimension allowing further improvement. In our mountain example, you could use the *fourth dimension* to escape the lake and continue your way to the sea.

On top of this high-dimensional effect, a machine learning algorithm's cost function is very noisy (due to all the outliers and variation in our demand dataset), allowing the gradient descent to jump out of a local minimum.

Pitfall #2: Learning Rate

Another pitfall of gradient descent is determining its optimal learning rate η. If set too high (fast), you risk never converging to a minimum, as the gradient descent won't stabilize and will face the risk of ending up oscillating around the minimum (as shown in Figure 25.8). If set too low, you risk a slow optimization.

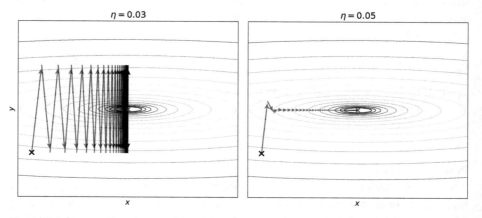

Figure 25.8: Impact of learning rate (η) on gradient descent (the second gradient descent never converges).

Backpropagation

Gradient descent is a good technique to minimize a (cost) function. But if you cannot *analytically* compute the function local derivatives, you will instead have to compute the slope *manually* by evaluating the function around a neighborhood. Translated to the example of descending a mountain, it is like either walking with your eyes wide open (analytical way) or being blindfolded and having to walk a few steps in each direction, each time you want to assess the slope around you (manual way). This manual option is very time-consuming, especially if you have many parameters—which is the case with neural networks.

Hopefully, a technique was found to analytically compute the local derivatives in a neural network: backpropagation. The idea is that a neural network can be used in two directions:

1. **Forward propagation,** where neurons propagate information through the network by applying their activation functions to their weighted inputs and biases. In this phase, the neural network is populating predictions based on inputs (features). This is the flow of information we have been discussing so far (as shown in Figure 25.5).

2. **Backpropagation,** where neurons propagate their local derivatives (that is the impact of changing weights, input values, and biases). In other words, each neuron will propagate how much a change in one of its inputs (weights, input values, and biases) will impact its own output.

During the training phase of a neural network, forward propagation and backpropagation will be performed in turns. Forward propagation will be used to generate predictions (as data flow through the network). Backpropagation will be used to tune the weights based on the latest prediction errors. The exact math involved is beyond the scope of this book.[9]

A Brief History of Backpropagation

Paul Werbos, in his 1974 PhD thesis, was the first to propose using backpropagation to optimize neural networks.[a] As we were in the first neural network winter, his work went unnoticed by the research community. It is only later, with the work of Rumelhart et al. (1986), that backpropagation was popularized as a training technique for neural networks. Armed with backpropagation, researchers could now use neural networks in many use cases. Notably,

---

9 If you are interested in the matter, the YouTube channel 3Blue1Brown made a series of excellent videos on how backpropagation works. They are available here: www.youtube.com/playlist?list=PLZHQObOWTQDNU6R1_67000Dx_ZCJB-3pi. See Sanderson (2017).

neural networks were used to recognize handwritten digits based on a technique proposed in 1989 by Yann LeCun.[b] His model was successfully implemented, ending up reading digits written by hand in around 10 to 20% of all checks processed in the US.

Nevertheless, a new issue soon appeared, causing training to become slow and unstable.

Second Winter (mid 1990s–mid 2000s)

As neural networks became deeper (with more stacked layers), backpropagation became slower, due to the *vanishing gradients problem*. Simply put, the backpropagation algorithm requires using the activation functions' derivatives (slopes). And, back then, the activation functions in use were mostly sigmoid and tanh. Their derivatives are, unfortunately, close to zero, except in $x \in [-1, 1]$ (as shown in Figure 25.2). When you stack multiple layers, the gradient descent becomes henceforth slower and slower for the deeper layers, resulting in an exponentially slow optimization.[c]

a See Werbos (1974).
b See LeCun et al. (1989).
c See Nielsen (2015) for a detailed mathematical analysis of the vanishing gradient problem, available here: neuralnetworksanddeeplearning.com/chap5.html

Better Gradient Descent Algorithms

Mini-Batch Gradient Descent

The gradient descent technique had been widely used to optimize neural networks' weights until a new idea came forward: mini-batch gradient descent. With the original gradient descent algorithm, the neural networks' weights are updated each time the full training dataset is processed. With mini-batch gradient descent, weights are updated each time a few data samples are processed (usually around 100 to 300 samples). In other words, instead of showing the whole training dataset to the neural network and then updating its weights, we will only show a few hundred samples before doing a weight update. This technique usually makes training much faster.

Let's take another look at our analogy of walking down a mountain to the beach. With mini-batch, the hiker will not perform a full analysis of her immediate surroundings before taking a step toward the steeper slope. Instead, she will quickly look around before moving on. From time to time, this will result in a few steps in the wrong direction. But, overall, she will get to the beach faster.

Adam

Mini-batch gradient descent was further improved with smarter optimizers. The most famous one being Adam (for *Adaptive Moment Estimation*), making the gradient descent smoother and faster.[10] Adam is relying on two main ideas: keeping track of the gradient *momentum* (*m*) and keeping track of its *variance* (*v*). Both are estimated after each mini-batch by using an exponential smoothing technique:

$$m_t = \beta_1 m_{t-1} + (1 - \beta_1)g_t$$
$$v_t = \beta_2 v_{t-1} + (1 - \beta_2)g_t^2 \tag{25.1}$$

where β_1 and β_2 are learning rates (just as for exponential smoothing models discussed in Part I), and g_t is the gradient computed based on the current mini-batch. Keep in mind that this estimation is made in a high-dimensional space, as neural networks have tens of thousands of parameters (all the weights and biases). You have to picture this as estimating the gradient of every single parameter.

The new value of each parameter x is computed as:[11]

$$x_{t+1} = x_t - \frac{\eta}{\sqrt{v_t}}m_t \tag{25.2}$$

The intuition here is that the step-size for each parameter (in each direction) is reduced if the gradient has a high variance. We do not want to take big steps if we aren't sure of the direction. In other words, the difference between x_{t+1} and x is small if $\sqrt{v_t}$ is big. The step-size is also done in the direction of an (exponentially smoothed) estimation of the gradient (m_t) that is more resistant to local variations which are common in noisy cost functions (such as those that neural networks face).

By keeping track of previous gradient estimations and being more cautious when the gradient fluctuates more, Adam is usually more stable and allows for better optimization through valleys (as shown in Figure 25.9).

A Brief History of Deep Learning

In the mid-2000s, multiple new algorithms were tried. They resulted in faster, more stable optimization, allowing neural networks to grow much deeper. Let's mention a few aspects.

---

10 See Kingma and Ba (2015) for the initial paper on Adam.

11 Note that this is a **simplified** expression of how Adam is evaluating the gradient. The exact math is beyond the scope of this book. See Ruder (2016) for a review of various optimizers (arxiv.org/pdf/1609.04747.pdf). You can find an implementation (as well as visualization) of most optimizers here: github.com/ilguyi/optimizers.numpy

- Better gradient descent optimizers were developed (such as Adam, released in 2014).
- Multiple analyses (Nair and Hinton (2010) being one of the most recognized) recommended using ReLu as an activation function instead of sigmoid or tanh, to avoid vanishing gradients.
- Better weight initializations were used (the exact mathematics are out of scope).
- More data was available to train bigger neural networks.
- Computation power rose. Moreover, on some tasks, GPU shined compared to CPU.

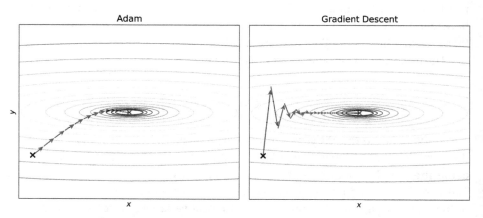

Figure 25.9: Comparison of Adam and gradient descent going through a valley (Adam in 32 steps, gradient descent in 89).

Going Further

For more information about the history of neural networks, see the book *Quand la machine apprend: La révolution des neurones artificiels et de l'apprentissage profond* by Yann LeCun,[a] or the series of blog articles *A 'Brief' History of Neural Nets and Deep Learning* by Andrey Kurenkov.[b]

_____

a LeCun (2019), not translated.
b Kurenkov (2015), available here: www.andreykurenkov.com/writing/ai/a-brief-history-of-neural-nets-and-deep-learning/

25.3 Do It Yourself

We will use the MLPRegressor class from scikit-learn to build our neural networks (MLPRegressor stands for Multi-Layer Perceptron Regressor).[12]

```
1  from sklearn.neural_network import MLPRegressor
2  NN = MLPRegressor().fit(X_train, Y_train)
```

Parameters

We will divide our discussion about parameters into three different parts: the parameters that define the architecture of the neural network, those related to the solver Adam, and those related to early stopping.[13] For the sake of simplicity, we will only discuss the parameters that apply to Adam, as it is considered the best practice for optimizing neural networks.[14]

Neural Network Parameters

`hidden_layer_sizes` These set the size of our neural network by defining the number of hidden layers and the number of neurons in each. Note that in the scikit-learn implementation, the number of neurons in the input layer is set as the number of features, and the number of neurons in the output layer is set as the number of outputs. Usually, more layers and neurons allow the neural network to learn more complex relationships, but this is done at the expense of a higher risk of overfitting.

> **Pro-Tip**
>
> It seems that around four layers with twenty neurons each is a good start for most monthly demand forecasting models.

`alpha` A regularization parameter,[15] this will prevent your neural network from overfitting by penalizing high weights in the neural network. The higher the alpha, the bigger the penalty.

---

12 See scikit-learn.org/stable/modules/neural_networks_supervised.html for detailed explanations on how neural networks work in scikit-learn.

13 See scikit-learn.org/stable/modules/generated/sklearn.neural_network.MLPRegressor.html for more information about the various parameters.

14 This is only the beginning of the 21st century, so it is very likely those best practices will evolve in the future.

15 Mathematically, `alpha` is an L2 regularization.

Adam Parameters

`learning_rate_init` This is the initial learning rate used by Adam (η in eq. 25.2). The higher the initial learning rate, the faster the neural network will update its weights, facing the risk of too many fluctuations and not being able to settle in an optimal spot.

`beta_1` This is an exponential smoothing parameter used by Adam to smooth out variations from one mini-batch to another (β_1 in eq. 25.1). Specifically, `beta_1` is used to estimate the gradient mean. `beta_1` is generally close to 0.9—a higher value means that the estimation of the gradient mean will be smoother, but less reactive. This is similar to alpha in exponential smoothing (as discussed in Chapter 3). Pay attention to the fact that beta is the inverse of alpha: a higher beta value means a smoother estimation.

`beta_2` This is the same as `beta_1` but is used to estimate the gradient variation (β_2 in eq. 25.1). It is generally close to 0.999.

Let's define a first set of potential values for our parameters. We will use these later, once we run a random search.

```
1 hidden_layer_sizes = [[neuron]*hidden_layer for neuron in range(10,
  ↪  60,10) for hidden_layer in range(2,7)]
2 alpha = [5,1,0.5,0.1,0.05,0.01,0.001]
3 learning_rate_init = [0.05,0.01,0.005,0.001,0.0005]
4 beta_1 = [0.85,0.875,0.9,0.95,0.975,0.99,0.995]
5 beta_2 = [0.99,0.995,0.999,0.9995,0.9999]
6 param_dist = {'hidden_layer_sizes':hidden_layer_sizes, 'alpha':alpha,
  ↪  'learning_rate_init':learning_rate_init, 'beta_1':beta_1, 'beta_2':
  ↪  beta_2}
```

Training Parameters

Similar to XGBoost in Chapter 21, we can benefit from an early stopping (`early_stopping`) when training our neural network. This early stopping works as follows: after each **epoch**, it checks that the error achieved on a validation set (`validation_fraction`) is still progressing by a tolerance (`tol`). If it does not progress after a fixed number of iterations (`n_iter_no_change`), the training will stop and returns the model as in the best iteration.

> **Epoch**
>
> One epoch consists, for the neural network learning algorithm, to run through all the training samples. The number of epochs is the number of times the learning algorithm will run through the entire training dataset.

For the sake of simplicity, let's put all those parameters into a dictionary (param_fixed). We will also include the activation function (ReLu) and the solver (Adam) as we stick to the best practices.

Note that we use here a high value of n_iter_no_change, as the dataset is particularly small. On bigger datasets, to reduce training time, you might want to decrease this value.

```
1  activation = 'relu'
2  solver = 'adam'
3  early_stopping = True
4  n_iter_no_change = 50
5  validation_fraction = 0.1
6  tol = 0.0001
7  param_fixed = {'activation':activation, 'solver':solver,
     ↪   'early_stopping':early_stopping, 'n_iter_no_change':
     ↪   n_iter_no_change, 'validation_fraction':validation_fraction,
     ↪   'tol':tol}
```

Early Stopping

Let's run a neural network with those early stopping parameters, and set verbose to True to observe the results.

```
1  NN = MLPRegressor(hidden_layer_sizes=(20,20), **param_fixed,
     ↪   verbose=True).fit(X_train, Y_train)
```

You should obtain something similar to the code extract below. Unfortunately, both the validation score and the loss displayed by scikit-learn are not always very meaningful—the loss is the neural network loss function (the lower, the better); whereas the validation score is a measure of its accuracy against the validation set (the higher, the better).

```
1  >> Iteration 1, loss = 18961.13660344
2  >> Validation score: 0.931895
3  >> Iteration 2, loss = 3634.50283117
4  >> Validation score: 0.943246
5  >> Iteration 3, loss = 3082.95275344
6  >> Validation score: 0.944469
7  >> Iteration 4, loss = 2939.45889834
8  >> Validation score: 0.943030
9  >> Iteration 5, loss = 2853.50089399
```

```
10  >> Validation score: 0.942133
11  >> Iteration 6, loss = 2780.68751554
12  >> Validation score: 0.942229
13  >> Iteration 7, loss = 2785.38001387
14  >> Validation score: 0.942783
15  >> Iteration 8, loss = 2749.35945397
16  >> Validation score: 0.943580
17  >> Iteration 9, loss = 2750.36122337
18  >> Validation score: 0.942395
19  >> Validation score did not improve more than tol=0.000100 for 5 ⏎
        ↪ consecutive epochs. Stopping.
```

Optimization

Now that we have set up our early stopping process, we can run a k-fold cross-validation random search to optimize Adam and the neural network parameters.

```
1  NN = MLPRegressor(**param_fixed)
2  NN_cv = RandomizedSearchCV(NN, param_dist, cv=10, verbose=2, ⏎
       ↪ n_jobs=-1, n_iter=200, scoring='neg_mean_absolute_error')
3  NN_cv.fit(X_train,Y_train)
4  print('Tuned NN Parameters:', NN_cv.best_params_)
5  print()
6  Y_train_pred = NN_cv.predict(X_train)
7  Y_test_pred = NN_cv.predict(X_test)
8  kpi_ML(Y_train, Y_train_pred, Y_test, Y_test_pred, name='NN ⏎
       ↪ optimized')
```

This is what we get for this specific dataset and on a specific iteration. (Keep in mind that training a neural network is a very stochastic process, so you can expect different results on another run.) See Table 25.1 for a comparison with other models.

```
1  Tuned NN Parameters: {'learning_rate_init': 0.05, ⏎
       ↪ 'hidden_layer_sizes': [50, 50, 50, 50], 'beta_2': 0.9999, 'beta_1':⏎
       ↪ 0.95, 'alpha': 0.5}
2
3                   MAE   RMSE   Bias
4  NN optimized
5  Train          17.7   44.2    2.1
6  Test           17.5   44.2    3.7
```

Table 25.1: Results.

Models	MAE		RMSE		Bias	
	Train	Test	Train	Test	Train	Test
Regression	17.8	17.8	43.9	43.7	0.0	**1.6**
Tree	17.3	18.9	42.2	46.8	0.0	2.9
Forest	14.1	17.6	35.0	44.9	−0.0	2.7
ETR	14.2	17.5	35.8	44.4	−0.0	2.5
AdaBoost	**10.8**	17.9	**24.9**	47.8	0.5	3.9
XGBoost	12.2	**17.2**	31.4	**43.6**	0.9	3.6
NN	17.7	17.5	44.2	44.2	2.1	3.7

> **Going Further**
>
> Of their own confession, scikit-learn is not specialized in deep learning. If you want to build more complex neural networks, you should check other libraries such as Keras (keras.io), TensorFlow (www.tensorflow.org), or PyTorch (py-torch.org).

AlphaGo – 2016

Adam – 2014

ReLu – 2010

Backpropagation – 1986

Perceptron – 1957

Artificial Neuron – 1943

Neural Networks

Part III: **Data-Driven Forecasting Process Management**

26 Judgmental Forecasts

The desire to be right and the desire to have been right are two desires, and the sooner we separate them, the better off we are. The desire to be right is the thirst for truth. On all counts, both practical and theoretical, there is nothing but good to be said for it. The desire to have been right, on the other hand, is the pride that goes before a fall. It stands in the way of our seeing we were wrong, and thus blocks the progress of our knowledge.

Willard Van Orman Quine

In Parts I and II, we discussed how to make a statistical or ML-driven forecast engine. This engine will populate a forecast baseline for you. Is forecast baseline the end of the forecasting process in a supply chain? No, it can still be enriched by humans by using various sources of insights and information. A human-created forecast is called a **judgmental forecast**, as it relies on human judgment. Using judgmental forecasts comes with a lot of risks, as we will discuss in this chapter. Nevertheless, if done properly, it will add value to your baseline forecast (as we will discuss in Chapter 27).

Judgmental forecasts are also appropriate to forecast products when you lack historical data to use a model, or when significant changes are ongoing (due to changing client behavior, new competition, changing legislation, the COVID-19 pandemic, etc.).

Before discussing judgmental forecasts further, keep in mind that a demand forecast should be the best *unbiased* estimate of a supply chain's future demand. This is nothing like a *budget*, a *sales target* to incentivize sale representatives, or a *production plan*.

26.1 Judgmental Forecasts and Their Blind Spots

As shown in Figure 26.1, Oliva and Watson (2009) proposed a framework to classify sources of bias in judgmental forecasts into two categories: intentional and unintentional sources. Let's review those in detail.

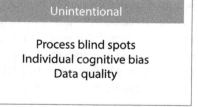

Intentional	Unintentional
Misalignment of incentives Power and influence	Process blind spots Individual cognitive bias Data quality

Figure 26.1: Sources of bias in judgmental forecasts.

https://doi.org/10.1515/9783110671124-026

Misalignment of Incentives

Different supply chain stakeholders have different objectives and goals based on their respective incentives. For example, a sales representative might get a bonus if she oversells compared to the forecast, so she has an interest in reducing the forecast. Another department, such as customer service, might want to secure enough inventory to be sure to satisfy all client orders, therefore overforecasting.[1] Some teams might want to push some specific products forward, resulting in overforecasts. Think about a project manager advocating for her new product. In some other cases, let's imagine a company that is underselling compared to the initial yearly sales budget—political pressure might push the forecast to go back to the yearly budget, henceforth using the forecast as a goal for the company.

Power and Influence

Suppose that a stakeholder (or group of stakeholders) in the supply chain (e. g., a specific channel manager, production planner, or sales team) has more power or influence than others. In that case, they can influence the forecast to suit their needs, multiplying the impact of *misalignment of incentives*. If the loudest team member in the room heavily influences the forecast, you might be facing this issue. Note that power and influence are also driven by who has access to the appropriate information, and, in the end, by the last person who decides on the forecast. This issue is often faced when executives do not want to sign off a forecast showing declining sales or that they are not meeting previous sales targets. This influence can also be indirect—if senior management pressures forecasters for detailed justifications of downward forecasts, this pressure can lead to upward adjustments, resulting in an overforecast.

Process Blind Spots and Data Quality

A forecast might result in an over- or under-pessimistic estimation of future demand because it relies on partial, biased, or incomplete information. For example, the forecasting process might put more emphasis on looking at the number of shop closures rather than openings; on product launches rather than product discontinuations; on marketing efforts rather than competitor pricing, and so on. By only looking at some reports or only including in the process stakeholders that bring a certain type of information to the table, you might create blind spots in the forecasting process.

---

1 If you are afraid of not having enough inventory, overforecasting is not the appropriate tool; keeping the appropriate amount of safety stock is. See Vandeput (2020) to assess the right amount of safety stock needed.

> **Attention Point**
>
> The most common case of informational blind spot is to look at historical sales rather than demand. Most supply chains do not track the *real* demand, but only the sales. Only looking at sales data without including the number of lost sales will invariably result in biased information. Collecting lost sales in a B2C environment can be particularly tricky, if not impossible. Yet, any progress toward collecting data about lost sales will help you to get an unbiased demand forecast. In a B2B environment, you can start collecting lost orders from your clients. In any case, you can also track the percentage of each time the stock keeping unit (SKU) is out of stock. This should give a first indication if any sales were lost due to a lack of inventory.

> **SKU**
>
> A stock keeping unit (SKU) refers to a specific material kept in a specific location. Two different pieces of the same SKU are indistinguishable.

Individual Cognitive Bias

Next to process blind spots, everyone tends to have their own blind spots and erroneous mental images. Let's discuss two types of cognitive bias.

Confirmation Bias As humans, we are all prone to *confirmation bias*: we will tend to look for (and see) information supporting our current beliefs.[2] We will also need more supporting evidence to accept any theory that would contradict our current beliefs. Let's apply this to forecasting. For example, if you are currently thinking that next month is going to be a good month, then when you're be looking for information about next month's sales, you will (subconsciously) prefer information supporting the idea that your company is going to do great. Confirmation bias is often reinforced by the fact that we tend to look for information that supports what we want or have an interest in believing.

Anchoring Bias We are also prone to *anchoring bias*: when making a prediction, the first number we think of—even if unrelated—will impact the final guess. This was observed by Tversky and Kahneman (1974). In an experiment, they asked participants to guess the number of African countries in the UN. They showed that participants were influenced by a number given by spinning a wheel of fortune. If a

---

2 See Wason (1960) for one of the first analyses of confirmation bias. See the online article by Cunff (2019) if you wish to learn more about cognitive bias.

prediction can be influenced so easily by something as uncorrelated to the task as a wheel of fortune, imagine the impact when a team member starts a meeting by saying, "I believe we will sell 20% more than last quarter."

26.2 Solutions

As we just saw, a forecasting process that is not properly defined or supervised will face many pitfalls. Fortunately, solutions exist.[3]

Accountability and Accuracy Tracking

As data scientists, we should keep track of the results of our models. As process owners, we should keep track of how well each step of our process is performing. To reduce the intentionally biased, judgmental forecast, we should separately track the extra accuracy (or error) created by *each* team member that tweaks the forecast. We will discuss those ideas in detail in Chapter 27. As each stakeholder's added value (or each step of the forecasting process) will be measured, they will naturally become *accountable* for their predictions. Judgmental bias will appear as you track forecast KPIs over the long-term.

Group Forecast

Instead of relying on one person to make a prediction—we just saw that we all suffer from cognitive bias and limited information—you can ask the opinion of multiple team members. By involving multiple people in making a prediction, you implicitly hope that their cognitive bias and sources of information will be different and complementary. This is another application of the wisdom of the crowd: the average opinion of a group of people is going to be more precise on average than the opinion of a single member of the group. Of course, to benefit the most from group forecasting, it should be done with an open mindset: listening and valuing different opinions and relying on different sources of information.

There is an obvious parallel between a group forecast and the ensemble models that we discussed in Part II. Instead of gathering predictions from different trees into a forest (see Section 15.1), we gather the predictions of different team members into a single common number.

---

3 See Oliva and Watson (2009), Tetlock and Gardner (2016); and Gilliland (2010) for more detailed discussions, ideas, and best practices.

Independence and Anonymity

Coming up with a prediction that is independent of any political pressure is important. As discussed earlier, due to the anchoring bias, any noisy information can potentially alter a prediction. Therefore it is critical to keep each stakeholder of the forecasting process as independent as possible to the opinion of other team members and political pressure. By empowering independence, you will get the most out of group forecasting. In practice, one straightforward way to achieve independence is to make anonymous predictions. For example, you could start an important S&OP meeting by asking each participant to note down the number of sales they expect for the next quarter. Revealing the numbers noted down should get the discussion started in the right direction.

Discuss Assumptions

Discussing expected raw sales numbers will often leave too much room for bias and influence. A discussion about final numbers will often be sterile. Instead, it is advised to discuss the assumptions and leading indicators that drive this number (market share, global market growth rate, macro economics, pricing, new product launches, and so on).

> **Going Further**
>
> In their excellent book *Superforecasting: The Art and Science of Prediction*, Philip E. Tetlock and Dan Gardner describe the best practices used by competing teams to make (probabilistic) predictions about anything from elections to the gold price. They recommend that forecasters be accountable for their predictions (and track their accuracy), leave their ego aside, embrace divergence of opinions, and various sources of information. Those best practices should be a source of inspiration for any forecaster.
>
> If you are interested in best practices on forecasting process management, do not hesitate to read *The Business Forecasting Deal: Exposing Myths, Eliminating Bad Practices, Providing Practical Stouolutions* by Michael Gilliland.

27 Forecast Value Added

In this chapter, we will identify how to improve a forecast baseline using the best practices of judgmental forecast (as seen in Chapter 26). We will first discuss, in Section 27.1, how to use smart KPIs to manage a portfolio of products and focus on products that matter the most. Then, in Section 27.2, we will see how to track the value added by each team in the forecasting process.

27.1 Portfolio KPI

When we discussed forecast KPIs in Chapter 2, we considered each item separately: we wanted our forecast engine to find the best model for each product, independently of the others. On the other end, demand planners do not have the time to inspect every single product (on every single location) one by one. As a demand planner, you need to scale up from analyzing in detail one single item to working on a portfolio with thousands of SKUs. To do so, you will have to prioritize your work by focusing on products that matter the most. In short: your time is constrained, so you should prioritize it. The forecast engine's time isn't, so you can let it do its best on each item.

Smart Weighting

As a demand planner, you have the opportunity to review *some* of your product forecasts during each forecast exercise. But on which items should you spend your time? The first idea would be to look at the products with the most significant forecast error. Let's imagine an example where you are responsible for nails and hammers. As shown in Table 27.1, the absolute forecast error is more significant on the nails (500 pieces) than on the hammers (50 pieces). Should you, therefore, focus your time and efforts on nails?

Table 27.1: Forecast KPI.

Product	Forecast	Demand	Error	|Error|
Hammer	150	100	50	50
Nail	1000	1500	−500	500
Total	1150	1600	−450	550
			−28.1%	34.4%

Obviously, not every SKU is created equal: some bring more profits, some are costly, some use constrainted resources (e. g., space), some are of strategic importance...

https://doi.org/10.1515/9783110671124-027

while others are just not critical. In short, the impact of each SKU on the supply chain is different, and you want to focus your work on those that matter.

Let's imagine you want to focus your time on products that drive the most profits (assuming that the unit profit is a good proxy for their impact on your supply chain).[1] In order to do so, you have to use a *weighted* forecast error KPI that will allocate more importance to profitable items. Let's compute the **weighted forecast error** (e_w) as

$$e_w = w(f - d)$$

where w is the weight (i. e., importance) of this particular product (in our example, that would be its unitary profit).[2] We can then compute the usual forecast KPI, as shown in Table 27.2.

Table 27.2: Weighted forecast KPIs (where d_w is the weighted demand).

KPI	Absolute	Weighted
Bias	$\frac{1}{n}\sum e_w$	$\frac{\sum e_w}{\sum d_w}$
MAE	$\frac{1}{n}\sum \lvert e_w \rvert$	$\frac{\sum e_w}{\sum d_w}$
RMSE	$\sqrt{\frac{1}{n}\sum e_w^2}$	$\frac{\sqrt{\frac{1}{n}\sum e_w^2}}{\frac{1}{n}\sum d_w}$

As we can see in Table 27.3, the product that should get your attention is the hammer, with a weighted absolute error of 250 (compared to the nails' weighted absolute error of 5).

Table 27.3: Weighted forecast KPIs.

Product	Forecast	Demand	Profits (per piece)	Weighted Error	Weighted |Error|
Hammer	150	100	5.00	250	250
Nail	1000	1500	0.01	−5	5
Total	1150	1600		245	255
				47.6%	49.5%

---

1 For the sake of simplicity, we use here an example relying on different products with various profits. In practice, you might need to do this exercise per SKU (i. e., product-location combination).
2 Feel free to weigh the products based on their unit costs or prices rather than their profits.

> **Attention Point**
>
> With a tool such as weighted errors, there is a temptation to penalize (or weigh) positive and negative forecast errors differently. Obviously, in supply chains, the cost of having one product too many (extra holding costs) or one product too few (unhappy clients, lost sales) is not the same. Nevertheless, by giving more importance to overforecast or underforecasts, you will get biased forecasts. This will, in turn, result in a lack of trust for the rest of your organization, with various planners using their own forecast estimates. It is always better to balance the risk of overforecasting and underforecasting each product independently by setting the proper service level targets and allocating the right amount of safety stocks. For more information, see my book *Inventory Optimizations: Models and Simulations*.

Forecast Horizon and Granularity

When reviewing forecasts, you should also focus your attention on the forecast granularity (e. g., forecast at daily, weekly, or monthly levels) and horizons (e. g., forecast for the next days, weeks, or months) that matter the most to your supply chain. Forecasts are only helpful for a supply chain if they empower its stakeholders to take action. This means that you have to choose the granularity of your model and which lags to focus on, based on the rhythm of your supply chain and the decisions you can make in response to the forecast.

When determining the most relevant lags and granularity, keep in mind that supply chains are broad and complex. Forecasts can be used for capacity planning, supply planning, budgeting, S&OP, and so on. All those planning processes have their own granularity and relevant horizons.

For example, imagine that you work on a forecast to help a supply planner process his or her orders for a supplier. The inventory policy follows a monthly periodic review (the order is placed during the very last days of the month), and the supplier quotes a lead time of one month. This means that when you create your forecast (early in the month), you should focus on next month's numbers to optimize the order that will be made later this month.

Note that if you have a supply chain with different supply lead times, you could look at different forecast KPIs, depending on the product. For products with short lead times, you might look at the accuracy for next month (M+1). Whereas with products with long lead times (maybe sourced overseas?), you could look at the accuracy over multiple months ahead.

> **Attention Point**
>
> Sometimes, supply chain managers get confused with insights such as: "As we need to order our products from our supplier three months in advance, only the forecast for month +3 is relevant to us." This is not true. Obviously, even if you update your short-term forecast, you cannot change the orders you already made. But, changing forecasts within the supply lead time will result in updated inventory projections, which will, in turn, lead to changes for the next order.

27.2 What Is a Good Forecast Error?

Throughout this book, we created forecasting models. Initially, we focused on statistical models, and later, we focused on machine learning models. Usually, you will try these models against your own demand dataset, first trying a simple model and then moving on to more complex ones. As soon as you get the first results from your model, you will ask yourself this very question: *Are these results good?* How do you know if an MAE of 20% is good? What about an MAE of 70%?

The accuracy of any model depends on the demand's inner complexity and random nature. Forecasting car sales in Norway per month is much easier than predicting the sales of a specific smartphone, in a particular shop, during one specific day. It is exceedingly difficult to estimate what is a good forecast error for a particular dataset without using a benchmark.

Benchmarking

To know if a certain level of accuracy is good or bad, you must compare it against a benchmark. As a forecast benchmark, we will use a naïve model.[3] We will then compare any forecast against this naïve forecast, and see by how much extra accuracy (or error reduction) our forecasting model will beat it. In Table 27.4, you can see an example of results where the ML model could beat the benchmark by 7 points of MAE.

Table 27.4: Forecast benchmarking.

Method	RMSE	MAE	Bias
Benchmark (naïve)	88%	52%	−1%
ML model	72%	45%	−3%

---

3 A naïve forecast is simply the latest observed demand projected in the future (see Chapter 1). If your demand is seasonal, you might want to use a seasonal naïve forecast by using the last-year-same-period value as a forecast rather than the last period.

> ### Pro-Tip – Choosing the Right Benchmark
>
> As a benchmark, you could also use a moving average. This method often provides (much) better results than a naïve forecast, while being just as straightforward.
>
> If you face a seasonal demand, you can use a **seasonal naïve forecast**. Instead of using the previous period to forecast the next one, you have to use the demand during the same period last year (or last season) to forecast each new period. You also use a seasonal moving average by using the average over previous seasonal cycles of the period you want to forecast.

Forecast Value Added

Gilliland (2002) introduced the concept of **forecast value added** (FVA).[4] His brilliant idea was to measure the value added by a model—and each consecutive step in the forecasting process, as we will discuss later—compared to a reference benchmark. The forecast value added is expressed as a percentage point reduction (or as a percentage reduction) compared to a benchmark.

Let's show how it works with an example. Imagine that you trained an ML model to predict your demand. In order to know if this new model is helpful, you compare it against a benchmark. As shown in Table 27.5, a naïve model achieved 52% MAE when predicting your demand against a test set, while the machine learning model achieved an error of 45% on the same dataset. The forecast value added of the machine learning model is 7 points.

Table 27.5: Example of forecast value added (a positive value denotes an improvement).

Method	RMSE	FVA	MAE	FVA	Bias	FVA
Benchmark (naïve)	88%		52%		−1%	
ML model	72%	16	45%	7	−3%	−2

---

4 See his book *The Business Forecasting Deal* for a more detailed discussion. As he wrote to me: "While most people were focused on modeling, from my fifteen years as a forecaster in industry, I observed that the real problem was the forecasting process, and all the wasted efforts that either weren't adding value or were just making the forecast worse. So I've spent my career talking and writing about this issue. It is nice to see now, in 2020, there is quite a bit of attention paid to FVA and forecasting process issues. My most valuable contribution has probably been in "marketing" the ideas—inventing the term 'FVA,' and writing and speaking about the topic to spread the adoption of FVA approaches."

> **Attention Point**
>
> If you measure the FVA in relative terms, the difference in bias can be signifi-cant (it would be –200% in Table 27.5), as it is usually a small, absolute num-ber. It might, therefore, be more relevant to measure it in absolute terms.

> **Pro-Tip – Naïve Forecasts and Bias**
>
> Naïve forecasts, if analyzed over a full season cycle, tend not to be too biased. Their bias should be equal to your sales growth rate—or decline rate, if you are unlucky. Henceforth, they usually result in a low bias. On the other hand, most supply chain forecast models (if done at product level) will suffer from small negative bias. This is normal: forecasting the declining trend of old products is easy for a forecast model, whereas predicting the future apparition of brand-new products that do not exist today is impossible.

Process and Forecast Value Added

Forecast value added is not only meant to measure the added value of a model com-pared to a (naïve) benchmark, but also to track the *efficiency* of each step in the fore-casting process. By performing an FVA analysis of the whole forecasting process, you will be able to highlight steps that are efficient (i. e., reducing the forecast error while not consuming too much time) and those that both consume resources and do not bring any extra accuracy. FVA is the key to process excellence. For each team (or stake-holder) working on the forecasting process, you will need to track two aspects:
- their FVA compared to the previous team in the forecasting process flow
- the time spent working on the forecast

Those teams can be the demand planners, the sales team, senior management, and so on. (You can even track the FVA of each individual separately.) As you will track the FVA and time spent by each step of the forecasting process, you will have the right tools to reduce most judgmental bias, either intentional or unintentional (as discussed in Chapter 26).

Best Practices
Let's review the best practices when using the forecast value added framework.
- FVA process analysis should be performed over multiple forecast cycles—anyone can be (un)lucky from time to time.

–   If you want to push FVA further and focus on the most critical items, you should use it together with weighted KPIs (as discussed earlier in Section 27.1). Demand planners should then focus on the SKUs for which the forecast model got the highest weighted error over the last periods, or on the items for which they think the model will lack insights (as we will discuss in the following section).
–   If you are in a supply chain with different sales channels (or business units) implying different information, teams, and buying behavior, it is advised to track FVA separately for each business unit.

As a final piece of advice, we can review the conclusion drawn by Fildes and Goodwin (2007) who looked at the forecast adjusting process of four British companies. They saw that planners were making many small adjustments to the forecasts, bringing nearly no added value and consuming time. They also noted that larger adjustments were more likely to improve accuracy. This is due to the fact that they require more explanations from senior management, as well as a higher (personal) risk if they are wrong. Finally, they saw that planners tend to be overly optimistic (a usual cognitive bias), resulting in too many positive adjustments. This is so much of an issue that in order to improve forecast added value, the authors provocatively suggest banning positive adjustments.

Process Efficiency

With the help of FVA, you will quickly realize that the marginal improvement of each new team working on the forecast is decreasing. It might be easy to improve the most significant shortcomings of a forecast model. But it is much more challenging to improve a forecast that has already been reviewed by a few professional teams relying on multiple sources of information. This is fine, as FVA is here to help businesses allocate the appropriate resources to forecast edition. Past a certain point, working more on the forecast will not be worth it.

Example

Let's imagine a three-step forecasting process, as shown in Table 27.6.

Table 27.6: Example of a forecasting process analyzed with FVA.

Method	Person-hour	RMSE	FVA	MAE	FVA	Bias	FVA
Benchmark		88%		52%		−1%	
ML model		72%	+16	45%	+7	−3%	−2
Demand planners	72	68%	+4	43%	+2	1%	+2
Sales team	20	68%	+0	45%	−2	5%	−4
Management	8	69%	−1	45%	+0	4%	+1

1. The demand planners are the first to update the ML baseline. They managed to remove 4 points of MAE while working 72 hours on the forecast.
2. The sales team comes into action next. Unfortunately, despite 20 hours spent on the forecast, they worsen the forecast by increasing the MAE by 2 points and the bias by 4.

    Problem The sales team might be prone to *intentional* judgmental bias (as discussed in Chapter 26): they are inputting a high forecast to secure inventory.

    Solutions Work together with supply chain planners to find ways to secure inventory without biasing the forecast. As the sales team couldn't improve the forecast accuracy, they should spend *less* time on updating the forecast and focus on the few products they are the most sure about.
3. The last step of the process is senior management final validation. Their work resulted in a worsened forecast error (RMSE -1) but better bias.

    Problem Senior management seems less biased than the sales team, but is still prone to overforecasting. Their detailed review resulted in more forecast error (RMSE increased).

    Solutions Senior management may be updating the forecast with what they *hope* to sell and not what they *expect* to sell. They should separate the forecast (*how much we think the demand will be*) and the plan (*how much should we produce/source*). Similar to the sales team, as their modification did not bring extra accuracy, they should spend less time tweaking the forecast and focus on the overall amounts.

    It is worth noting that without a data-driven FVA analysis, it would be very difficult to convince senior management to act on those problems (or even identify those problems in the first place).

Pro-Tip – RMSE vs. MAE Reduction

Explaining a different FVA in RMSE and MAE—or even an increase in one and a decrease in the other—can be difficult. A possible interpretation is to read a decrease of MAE as a reduction of the *overall* forecast error, and a decrease of RMSE as a reduction of the *biggest* errors.

Going Further

Forecast value added can also be used together with customer segmentation and collaboration. If you collaborate with your customers on their demand forecasts, you can easily track your customer FVA to improve your collaboration.

Teaming Up with the AI

In many fields and situations (such as chess-playing or medical decisions), teams of humans working together with AI have shown better results than AI alone or humans alone.[5] The idea is that current AIs are not all-knowing and still lack some capabilities and information—even AIs have cognitive bias! As humans, we can see patterns and use insights that are not accessible to our models. It means that even if AI alone is better at some cognitive tasks than humans alone, by working *together*, we can achieve even better results. Those human-machine teams (sometimes called *cyborgs*) are considered by many to be the future of the workplace. Somehow, this is just another example of the wisdom of the crowd magic: by bringing different points of view to the table and smartly mixing them, you get more accurate results.

If we apply this to demand planning, you can easily imagine an ML-driven baseline forecast that you can enrich by using insights that are not available to the model. For example, you could call your main clients to ask if they are about to make specific big orders or if they already have enough inventory of some critical items. The information gathered is then available for you to update the forecast baseline. The ability of demand planners to add information on top of ML-generated forecasts will depend on their understanding of those models. In other words, a good understanding of your model's short-sights will enable you to add more value. If you know that your model doesn't have access to pricing and that a price change will occur next month, you know that you should update the baseline forecast. On the other hand, if the method used to populate the forecast is a black-box, you will lose many opportunities to add value to the ML-generated forecast baseline. This means that training demand planners on forecasting models will allow them to be more efficient.

I often hear practitioners complaining that models are not perfect and lack some insights. I think this is an opportunity for demand planners to shine by bringing added value. As a demand planner, you should work *together* with ML as an efficient duo by letting the ML do the heavy lifting while you focus on bringing new insights by using your network and communication skills.

---

5 See Baraniuk (2015) for chess-playing; MIT Insights (2019) for medical decisions.

Now It's Your Turn!

Your task is not to foresee the future, but to enable it.

Antoine de Saint-Exupéry

The real purpose of this book was not *just* to explain different models but, more importantly, to **give you the appetite to use them**. This book is a toolbox that gives you the tools and models to create your **own forecast models**. Hopefully, it has ignited ideas for you to create *unique* models and has taught you the methodology to test them.

You have learned in Part I how to create a robust statistical baseline forecast by using the different exponential smoothing models. Moreover, we have discussed different ideas (especially the different initialization methods) to tweak them to any dataset. We also have created a robust model to detect—and correct—outliers in an automated fashion. We have discussed various forecast KPIs, ensuring that you will be able to assess your models properly.

In Part II, you have discovered how machine learning could create advanced forecast models that could learn relationships across a whole dataset. Machine learning will allow you to classify your products and uncover potential *complex* relationships with any demand driver.

Finally, in Part III, we discussed the best practices required for judgmental forecasting and how to use the forecast value added framework to create—and sustain—an efficient forecasting process.

Now, it is your turn to work on creating your own models. The most important message is: **You can do it**. Start your journey by collecting historical demand data. Once you have gathered enough data (aim for five years), build your first model using simple machine learning models (such as random forests). You can then refine your model by either including new features (pricing, promotions, historical stock-outs, etc.) or using more advanced ML techniques. Remember that to succeed, you will have to test many ideas; avoid overfitting, and avoid the temptation to add too much complexity at once. Openly discuss your ideas, models, and results with others.

You will achieve astonishing results.

The future of demand planning is human-machine teams working hand-in-hand. You have learned here the keys to creating your own machine-learning driven models and how to best interact with them to create even more value.

This is the future of supply chain forecasting.

https://doi.org/10.1515/9783110671124-028

A Python

If this is your first time using Python, let's take some time to quickly introduce and discuss the different libraries and data types we are going to use. Of course, the goal of this book is not to give you full training in Python; if you wish to have an in-depth introduction (or if you are not yet convinced to use Python), please refer to the recommended courses in the Introduction.

How to Install Python

There are multiple ways to install Python on your computer. An easy way to do this is to install the Anaconda distribution on www.anaconda.com/download. Anaconda is a well-known platform used by data scientists all over the world. It works on Windows, Mac, and Linux. Anaconda will take care of installing all the Python libraries you need to run the different models that we are going to discuss. It will also install Spyder and Jupyter Notebook, two Python-code editors that you can use to type and run your scripts. Feel free to check both and use your favorite.

Lists

The most basic object we will use in Python is a list. In Python, a list is simply an ordered sequence of any number of objects (e. g., strings, numbers, other lists, more complex objects, etc.). You can create a list by encoding these objects between []. Typically, we can define our first time series ts as:

```
1  ts = [1,2,3,4,5,6]
```

These lists are very efficient at storing and manipulating objects, but are not meant for number computation. For example, if we want to add two different time series, we can't simply ask ts + ts2, as this is what we would get:

```
1  ts = [1,2,3,4,5,6]
2  ts2 = [10,20,30,40,50,60]
3  ts + ts2
4  Out: [1, 2, 3, 4, 5, 6, 10, 20, 30, 40, 50, 60]
```

Python is returning a new, *longer* list. That's not exactly what we wanted.

https://doi.org/10.1515/9783110671124-029

NumPy Arrays

This is where the famous **NumPy**[1] library comes to help. Since its initial release in 2006, NumPy has offered us a new data type: a NumPy array. This is similar to a list, as it contains a sequence of different numeric values, but differs in the way that we can easily call any mathematical function up on them. You can create one directly from a list like this:

```
1  import numpy as np
2  ts = np.array([1,2,3,4,5,6])
```

As you will see, NumPy is most often imported as np.

We can now simply add our array ts to any other array.

```
1  ts2 = np.array([10,20,30,40,50,60])
2  ts + ts2
3  Out: array([11, 22, 33, 44, 55, 66])
```

Note that the result is another NumPy array (and not a simple list).

NumPy most often works very well directly with regular lists, because we can use most of the NumPy functions directly on them. Here is an example:

```
1  alist = [1,2,3]
2  np.mean(alist)
3  Out: 2.0
```

You can always look for help on the NumPy official website.[2] As you will see yourself, most of your Google searches about NumPy functions will actually end up directly in their documentation.

Slicing Arrays

To select a particular value in a list (or an array), you simply have to indicate between [] the index of its location inside the list (array). The catch—as with many coding languages—is that the index starts at 0 and not at 1; so the first element in your list will have the index 0, the second element will have the index 1, and so on.

---

1 NumPy is short for **Numeric Python**.
2 docs.scipy.org/doc/numpy/reference/

```
1  alist = ['cat','dog','mouse']
2  alist[1]
3  Out: 'dog'
4  anarray = np.array([1,2,3])
5  anarray[0]
6  Out:  1
```

If you want to select multiple items at once, you can simply indicate a range of index with this format: [start:end]. Note the following:
–   If you do not give a start value, Python will assume it is 0.
–   If you do not give an end, it will assume it is the end of the list.

Note that the result will **include** the start element but will **exclude** the end element.

```
1  alist = ['cat','dog','mouse']
2  alist[1:]
3  Out: ['dog','mouse']
4  anarray = np.array([1,2,3])
5  anarray[:1]
6  Out: np.array([1])
```

If you give a negative value as the end, Python will start by counting backward from the last element of your list/array (–1 being the last element of your array).

```
1  alist = ['cat','dog','mouse']
2  alist[-1]
3  Out: ['mouse']
4  alist[:-1]
5  Out: ['cat','dog']
```

You can slice a multi-dimensional array by separating each dimension with a comma.

```
1  anarray = np.array([[1,2],[3,4]])
2  anarray[0,0]
3  Out:  1
4  anarray[:,-1]
5  Out: array([2, 4])
```

Pandas DataFrames

Pandas is one of the most used libraries in Python (it was created by Wes McKinney in 2008). The name comes from **pan**el **da**ta, because it helps to order data into tables. Think Excel-meets-databases in Python. This library introduces a new data type: a **DataFrame**. If you're a database person, just think of a DataFrame as an SQL table. If you're an Excel person, just imagine a DataFrame as an Excel table. Actually, a DataFrame is a sort of data table in which each column would be a NumPy array with a specific name. That will come in pretty handy, because we can select each column of our DataFrame by its name.

There are many ways to create a DataFrame. Let's create our first one by using a list of our two time series.

```
1  import pandas as pd
2  pd.DataFrame([ts,ts2])
```

```
1  Out:
2       0    1    2    3    4    5
3  0    1    2    3    4    5    6
4  1   10   20   30   40   50   60
```

The convention is to import pandas as pd and to call our main DataFrame df. The output we get is a DataFrame where we have 6 columns (named '0','1','2','3','4' and '5') and 2 rows (actually, they also have a name—or index—'0' and '1').

We can easily edit the column names:

```
1  df = pd.DataFrame([ts,ts2])
2  df.columns = ['Day1','Day2','Day3','Day4','Day5','Day6']
3  print(df)
```

```
1  Out:
2      Day1  Day2  Day3  Day4  Day5  Day6
3  0      1     2     3     4     5     6
4  1     10    20    30    40    50    60
```

Pandas comes with very simple and helpful official documentation.[3] When in doubt, do not hesitate to look into it. As with NumPy, most of your Google searches will end up there.

---

3 pandas.pydata.org/pandas-docs/stable/

Creating a DataFrame from a Dictionary

Another way to create a DataFrame is to construct it based on a dictionary of lists or arrays. A **dictionary** is a collection of elements that links (unique) keys to values. You can create one by including between {} a key and a value (both can be any Python object).

```
1  dic = {'Small product':ts,'Big product':ts2}
2  dic
3  Out:
4  {'Small product': array([1, 2, 3, 4, 5, 6]),
5   'Big product': array([10, 20, 30, 40, 50, 60])}
```

Here, the key 'Small product' will give you the value ts, whereas the key 'Big product' will give you ts2.

```
1  dic['Small product']
2  Out: array([1, 2, 3, 4, 5, 6])
3  dic['Small product'] + dic['Big product']
4  Out: array([11, 22, 33, 44, 55, 66])
```

We can now create a DataFrame directly from this dictionary.

```
1  df = pd.DataFrame.from_dict(dic)
2  Out:
3      Small product  Big product
4  0              1           10
5  1              2           20
6  2              3           30
7  3              4           40
8  4              5           50
9  5              6           60
```

We now have a DataFrame where each product has its own column and where each row is a separate period.

Slicing DataFrames

There are many different techniques to slice a DataFrame to get the element or the part you want. This might be confusing for beginners, but you'll soon understand that each of these has its uses and advantages. Do not worry if you get confused or overwhelmed: you won't need to apply all of these right now.

- You can select a specific column by passing the name of this column directly to the DataFrame—either with df['myColumn'], or even more directly with df.myColumn.
- You can select a row based on its index value by simply typing df[myIndexValue].
- If you want to select an element based on both its row and column, you can call the method .loc on the DataFrame and give it the index value and the column name you want. You can, for example, type df.loc[myIndexValue, 'myColumn'].
- You can also use the same slicing method as for lists and arrays based on the position of the element you want to select. You then need to call the method .iloc to the DataFrame. Typically, to select the first element (top left corner), you can type df.iloc[0,0].

As a recap, here are all the techniques you can use to select a column or a row:

```
1  df['myColumn']
2  df.myColumn
3  df[myIndexValue]
4  df.loc[myIndexValue,'myColumn']
5  df.iloc[0,0]
```

Exporting DataFrames
A DataFrame can easily be exported as either an Excel file or a CSV file.

```
1  df.to_excel('FileName.xlsx',index=False)
2  df.to_csv('FileName.csv',index=False)
```

The parameter index will indicate if you want to print the DataFrame index in the output file.

Other Libraries

We will also use other very well-known Python libraries. We used the usual import conventions for these libraries throughout the book. For the sake of clarity, we did not show the import lines over and over in each code extract.

   SciPy is a library used for all kinds of scientific computation, optimization, as well as statistical computation (SciPy stands for **Sci**entific **Py**thon). The documentation is available on docs.scipy.org/doc/scipy/reference but it is unfortunately not always as clear as we would wish it to be. We mainly focus on the statistical tools and only import them as stats.

```
1  import scipy.stats as stats
```

To make our code shorter, we will import some functions directly from `scipy.stats` in our examples. We can import these as such:

```
1  from scipy.stats import normal
```

Matplotlib is the library used for plotting graphs. Unfortunately, matplotlib is not the most user-friendly library, and its documentation is only rarely helpful. If we want to make simple graphs, we will prefer using the `.plot()` method from pandas.

```
1  import matplotlib.pyplot as plt
```

Seaborn is another plotting library built on top of matplotlib. It is actually more user-friendly and provides some refreshing visualization compared to matplotlib. You can check the official website seaborn.pydata.org, as it provides clear and inspiring examples.

```
1  import seaborn as sns
```

Bibliography

Abu-Rmileh, A. (2019). The multiple faces of 'feature importance' in XGBoost. https://towardsdatascience.com/be-careful-when-interpreting-your-features-importance-in-xgboost-6e16132588e7. Online; accessed 06 July 2020.

Baraniuk, C. (2015). The cyborg chess players that can't be beaten. *BBC*. https://www.bbc.com/future/article/20151201-the-cyborg-chess-players-that-cant-be-beaten. Online; accessed 21 July 2020.

Bourret Sicotte, X. (2018). AdaBoost: Implementation and intuition. https://xavierbourretsicotte.github.io/AdaBoost.html. Online; accessed 26 May 2020.

Breiman, L. (2001). Random forests. *Machine Learning*, 45(1):5–32.

Breiman, L. et al. (1998). Arcing classifier (with discussion and a rejoinder by the author). *The Annals of Statistics*, 26(3):801–849. Online; accessed 22 May 2020.

Brown, R. (1956). Exponential smoothing for predicting demand. *Management Science*.

Cauchy, A. (1847). Méthode générale pour la résolution des systemes d'équations simultanées. *Comptes Rendus Sci. Paris*, 25(1847):536–538.

Chen, T. and Guestrin, C. (2016). XGBoost: A scalable tree boosting system. In *Proceedings of the 22nd ACM SIGKDD International Conference on Knowledge Discovery and Data Mining*, KDD '16, pages 785–794, New York, NY, USA. ACM.

Cunff, A.-L. L. (2019). Confirmation bias: believing what you see, seeing what you believe. https://nesslabs.com/confirmation-bias. Online; accessed 23 July 2020.

Drucker, H. (1997). Improving regressors using boosting techniques. In *Proceedings of the Fourteenth International Conference on Machine Learning*, ICML '97, pages 107–115, San Francisco, CA, USA. Morgan Kaufmann Publishers Inc.

Fildes, R. and Goodwin, P. (2007). Good and bad judgement in forecasting: Lessons from four companies. *Foresight*, 8:5–10.

Freund, Y. and Schapire, R. E. (1997). A decision-theoretic generalization of on-line learning and an application to boosting. *Journal of Computer and System Sciences*, 55(1):119–139.

Friedman, J. H. (2001). Greedy function approximation: A gradient boosting machine. *The Annals of Statistics*, 29(5):1189–1232.

Gardner, E. S. and Mckenzie, E. (1985). Forecasting trends in time series. *Management Science*, 31(10):1237–1246.

Geurts, P., Ernst, D., and Wehenkel, L. (2006). Extremely randomized trees. *Machine Learning*, 63(1):3–42.

Gilliland, M. (2002). Is forecasting a waste of time? *Supply Chain Management Review*, 6(4):16–23.

Gilliland, M. (2010). *The Business Forecasting Deal: Exposing Myths, Eliminating Bad Practices, Providing Practical Solutions*. John Wiley & Sons, Hoboken, N.J.

Hebb, D. O. (1949). *The Organization of Behavior: A Neuropsychological Theory*. J. Wiley; Chapman & Hall.

Hewamalage, H., Bergmeir, C., and Bandara, K. (2020). Recurrent neural networks for time series forecasting: Current status and future directions. *International Journal of Forecasting*.

Ho, T. K. (1995). Random decision forests. In *Proceedings of 3rd International Conference on Document Analysis and Recognition*, volume 1, pages 278–282. IEEE.

Hochreiter, S. and Schmidhuber, J. (1997). Long short-term memory. *Neural Computation*, 9(8):1735–1780.

Holt, C. C. (2004). Forecasting seasonals and trends by exponentially weighted moving averages. *International Journal of Forecasting*, 20(1):5–10.

Hunter, J. D. (2007). Matplotlib: A 2D graphics environment. *Computing in Science & Engineering*, 9(3):90–95.

https://doi.org/10.1515/9783110671124-030

Hyndman, R. J. and Athanasopoulos, G. (2018). Forecasting: principles and practice. https://otexts.com/fpp2/. Online; accessed 22 May 2020.

Insights, M. T. R. (2019). The AI effect: How artificial intelligence is making health care more human. *MIT Technology Review Insights*. https://www.technologyreview.com/hub/ai-effect/. Online; accessed 21 July 2020.

Kashnitsky, Y. (2020). mlcourse.ai – open machine learning course. https://mlcourse.ai/articles/topic10-boosting/. Online; accessed 13 August 2020.

Kearns, M. (1988). Thoughts on hypothesis boosting. https://www.cis.upenn.edu/mkearns/papers/boostnote.pdf. Online; accessed 26 May 2020.

Kearns, M. and Valiant, L. G. (1989). Cryptographic limitations on learning boolean formulae and finite automata. In *Proceedings of the Twenty-First Annual ACM Symposium on Theory of Computing*, STOC '89, pages 433–444, New York, NY, USA. Association for Computing Machinery.

Kingma, D. P. and Ba, J. (2015). Adam: a method for stochastic optimization. *International Conference on Learning Representations*, pages 1–13.

Kissinger, H. A., Schmidt, E., and Huttenlocher, D. (2019). The Metamorphosis. *The Atlantic*. https://www.theatlantic.com/magazine/archive/2019/08/henry-kissinger-the-metamorphosis-ai/592771/. Online; accessed 28 May 2020.

Krizhevsky, A., Sutskever, I., and Hinton, G. E. (2012). Imagenet classification with deep convolutional neural networks. In *Advances in Neural Information Processing Systems*, pages 1097–1105.

Kurenkov, A. (2015). A 'brief' history of neural nets and deep learning. http://www.andreykurenkov.com/writing/ai/a-brief-history-of-neural-nets-and-deep-learning/. Online; accessed 16 August 2020.

LeCun, Y. (2019). *Quand la machine apprend: la révolution des neurones artificiels et de l'apprentissage profond*. Odile Jacob, Paris.

LeCun, Y., Boser, B., Denker, J. S., Henderson, D., Howard, R. E., Hubbard, W., and Jackel, L. D. (1989). Backpropagation applied to handwritten zip code recognition. *Neural Computation*, 1(4):541–551.

Levenson, R. M., Krupinski, E. A., Navarro, V. M., and Wasserman, E. A. (2015). Pigeons (columba livia) as trainable observers of pathology and radiology breast cancer images. *PLoS ONE*, 10(11):1–21.

Lloyd, S. P. (1982). Least squares quantization in pcm. *IEEE Transactions on Information Theory*, 28:129–137.

McCulloch, W. S. and Pitts, W. (1943). A logical calculus of the ideas immanent in nervous activity. *The Bulletin of Mathematical Biophysics*, 5(4):115–133.

McKinney, W. (2010). Data structures for statistical computing in Python. In Stéfan van der Walt and Jarrod Millman, editors, *Proceedings of the 9th Python in Science Conference*, pages 56–61.

Minsky, M. and Papert, S. (1969). Perceptrons: An Introduction to Computational Geometry. *Cambridge tiass., HIT.*

MITx (2019). Introduction to computer science and programming using python.

Morgan, J. N. and Sonquist, J. A. (1963). Problems in the analysis of survey data, and a proposal. *Journal of the American Statistical Association*, 58(302):415–434.

Nair, V. and Hinton, G. E. (2010). Rectified linear units improve restricted boltzmann machines. In *ICML*, pages 807–814.

Nielsen, M. A. (2015). *Neural Networks and Deep Learning*. Determination Press. http://neuralnetworksanddeeplearning.com/chap5.html. Online; accessed 16 August 2020.

Oliphant, T. E. (2006). *A Guide to NumPy*, volume 1. Trelgol Publishing USA.

Oliva, R. and Watson, N. (2009). Managing functional biases in organizational forecasts: A case study of consensus forecasting in supply chain planning. *Production and Operations Management*, 18(2):138–151.

Oskolkov, N. (2019). How to cluster in high dimensions. https://towardsdatascience.com/how-to-cluster-in-high-dimensions-4ef693bacc6. Online; accessed 10 September 2020.

Pedregosa, F., Varoquaux, G., Gramfort, A., Michel, V., Thirion, B., Grisel, O., Blondel, M., Prettenhofer, P., Weiss, R., Dubourg, V., VanderPlas, J., Passos, A., Cournapeau, D., Brucher, M., Perrot, M., and Duchesnay, E. (2011). Scikit-learn: Machine learning in Python. *Journal of Machine Learning Research*, 12:2825–2830.

Rosenblatt, F. (1957). *The perceptron, a perceiving and recognizing automaton Project Para*. Cornell Aeronautical Laboratory.

Ruder, S. (2016). An overview of gradient descent optimization algorithms. *arXiv preprint*.

Rumelhart, D. E., Hinton, G. E., and Williams, R. J. (1986). Learning representations by back-propagating errors. *Nature*, 323(6088):533–536.

Sanderson, G. (2017). Neural networks. https://www.youtube.com/playlist?list=PLZHQObOWTQDNU6R1_67000Dx_ZCJB-3pi. Online; accessed 16 August 2020.

Schapire, R. E. (1990). The strength of weak learnability. *Machine Learning*, 5(2):197–227.

Sculley, D. (2010). Web-scale k-means clustering. In *Proceedings of the 19th International Conference on World Wide Web*, pages 1177–1178.

Shead, S. (2019). Alphabet's deepmind losses soared to $570 million in 2018. *Forbes*. https://www.forbes.com/sites/samshead/2019/08/07/deepmind-losses-soared-to-570-million-in-2018/#4358b1633504. Online; accessed 18 August 2020.

Silver, N. (2015). *The Signal and the Noise: Why So Many Predictions Fail—but Some Don't*. Penguin Books.

Stetka, B. (2015). Using pigeons to diagnose cancer. *Scientific American*. https://www.scientificamerican.com/article/using-pigeons-to-diagnose-cancer/. Online; accessed 26 May 2020.

Tetlock, P. E. and Gardner, D. (2016). *Superforecasting: The Art and Science of Prediction*. Broadway Books.

Times, T. N. Y. (1958). New navy device learns by doing. *The New York Times*. https://www.nytimes.com/1958/07/08/archives/new-navy-device-learns-by-doing-psychologist-shows-embryo-of.html. Online; accessed 16 August 2020.

Tversky, A. and Kahneman, D. (1974). Judgment under uncertainty: Heuristics and biases. *Science*, 185(4157):1124–1131.

Vandeput, N. (2020). *Inventory Optimization: Models and Simulation*. De Gruyter.

VanderPlas, J. (2016). In-depth: Kernel density estimation. https://jakevdp.github.io/PythonDataScienceHandbook/05.11-k-means.html. Online; accessed 09 June 2020.

Vincent, J. (2019). Microsoft invests $1 billion in OpenAI to pursue holy grail of artificial intelligence. *The Verge*. https://www.theverge.com/2019/7/22/20703578/microsoft-openai-investment-partnership-1-billion-azure-artificial-general-intelligence-agi. Online; accessed 18 August 2020.

Virtanen, P., Gommers, R., Oliphant, T. E., Haberland, M., Reddy, T., Cournapeau, D., Burovski, E., Peterson, P., Weckesser, W., Bright, J., van der Walt, S. J., Brett, M., Wilson, J., Jarrod Millman, K., Mayorov, N., Nelson, A. R. J., Jones, E., Kern, R., Larson, E., Carey, C., Polat, İ., Feng, Y., Moore, E. W., VanderPlas, J., Laxalde, D., Perktold, J., Cimrman, R., Henriksen, I., Quintero, E. A., Harris, C. R., Archibald, A. M., Ribeiro, A. H., Pedregosa, F., van Mulbregt, P., and Contributors (2020). SciPy 1.0: Fundamental Algorithms for Scientific Computing in Python. *Nature Methods*, 17:261–272.

Wallis, K. F. (2014). Revisiting francis galton's forecasting competition. *Statistical Science*, pages 420–424.

Wason, P. C. (1960). On the failure to eliminate hypotheses in a conceptual task. *Quarterly Journal of Experimental Psychology*, 12(3):129–140.

Werbos, P. (1974). Beyond regression: New tools for prediction and analysis in the behavioral sciences. *PhD dissertation, Harvard University*.

Winters, P. R. (1960). Forecasting sales by exponentially weighted moving averages. *Management Science*, 6(3):324–342.

Glossary

accuracy The accuracy of your forecast measures how much spread you had between your forecasts and the actual values. The accuracy of a forecast gives an idea of the magnitude of the errors but not their overall direction. *See page* 10

alpha A smoothing factor applied to the demand level in the various exponential smoothing models. In theory: $0 < \alpha \leq 1$; in practice: $0 < \alpha \leq 0.6$. *See page* 28

array A data structure defined in NumPy. It is a list or a matrix of numeric values. *See page* 266

bagging Bagging (short word for *Bootstrap Aggregation*) is a method for aggregating multiple sub-models into an *ensemble* model by averaging their predictions with equal weighting. *See page* 139

beta A smoothing factor applied to the trend in the various exponential smoothing models. In theory: $0 < \beta \leq 1$; in practice: $0 < \beta \leq 0.6$. *See page* 41

bias The bias represents the overall direction of the historical average error. It measures if your forecasts were on average too high (i. e., you *overshot* the demand) or too low (i. e., you *undershot* the demand). *See page* 10

Boolean A Boolean is a value that is either `True` or `False`: 1 or 0. *See page* 203

boosting Boosting is a class of *ensemble* algorithms in which models are added *sequentially*, so that later models in the sequence will correct the predictions made by earlier models in the sequence. *See page* 168

bullwhip effect The bullwhip effect is observed in supply chains when small variations in the downstream demand result in massive fluctuations in the upstream supply chain. *See page* 45

classification Classification problems require you to classify data samples in different categories. *See page* 122

data leakage In the case of forecast models, a data leakage describes a situation where a model is given pieces of information about future demand. *See page* 30

DataFrame A DataFrame is a table of data as defined by the pandas library. It is similar to a table in Excel or an SQL database. *See page* 268

demand observation This is the demand for a product during one period. For example, a demand observation could be the demand for a product in January last year. *See page* 4

ensemble An ensemble model is a (meta-)model constituted of many sub-models. *See page* 139

epoch One epoch consists, for the neural network learning algorithm, to run through all the training samples. The number of epochs is the number of times the learning algorithm will run through the entire training dataset. *See page* 242

Euclidean distance The Euclidean distance between two points is the length of a straight line between these two points. *See page* 210

https://doi.org/10.1515/9783110671124-031

evaluation set An evaluation set is a set of data that is left aside from the training set to be used as a monitoring dataset during the training. A validation set or a holdout set can be used as an evaluation set. *See page 192*

feature A feature is a type of information that a model has at its disposal to make a prediction. *See page 122*

gamma A smoothing factor applied to the seasonality (either additive or multiplicative) in the triple exponential smoothing models. In theory: $0 < \gamma \leq 1$; in practice: $0.05 < \gamma \leq 0.3$. *See page 70*

holdout set Subset of the training set that is kept aside during the training to validate a model against unseen data. The holdout set is made of the last periods of the training set to replicate a test set. *See page 162*

inertia In a K-means model, the inertia is the sum of the distances between each data sample and its associated cluster center. *See page 211*

instance An (object) instance is a technical term for an occurrence of a class. You can see a class as a blueprint and an instance of a specific realization of this blueprint. The class (blueprint) will define what each instance will look like (which variables will constitute it) and what it can do (what methods or functions it will be able to perform). *See page 126*

level The level is the average value around which the demand varies over time. *See page 27*

Mean Absolute Error MAE $= \frac{1}{n} \sum |e_t|$ *See page 16*

Mean Absolute Percentage Error MAPE $= \frac{1}{n} \sum \frac{|e_t|}{d_t}$ *See page 14*

Mean Square Error MSE $= \frac{1}{n} \sum e_t^2$ *See page 17*

naïve forecast The simplest forecast model: it always predicts the last available observation. *See page 5*

noise In statistics, the noise is an unexplained variation in the data. It is often due to the randomness of the different processes at hand. *See page 5*

NumPy One of the most famous Python libraries. It is focused on numeric computation. The basic data structure in NumPy is an array. *See page 266*

pandas Pandas is a Python library specializing in data formatting and manipulation. It allows the use of DataFrames to store data in tables. *See page 268*

phi A damping factor applied to the trend in the exponential smoothing models. This reduces the trend after each period. In theory: $0 < \phi \leq 1$; in practice: $0.7 \leq \phi \leq 1$. *See page 60*

regression Regression problems require an estimate of a numerical output based on various inputs. *See page 122*

Root Mean Square Error RMSE $= \sqrt{\frac{1}{n} \sum e_t^2}$ *See page 17*

S&OP The sales and operations planning (S&OP) process focuses on aligning mid- and long-term demand and supply. *See page XXI*

SKU A stock keeping unit refers to a specific material kept in a specific location. Two different pieces of the same SKU are indistinguishable. *See page 251*

supervised learning A supervised machine learning model is a model that is fed with both inputs and desired outputs. It is up to the algorithm to understand the relationship(s) between these inputs and outputs. *See page* 209

test set A test set is a dataset kept aside to test our model against unseen data after its fitting (training). *See page* 37

training set A training set is a dataset used to fit (train) our model. *See page* 37

trend The trend is the average variation of the time series level between two consecutive periods. *See page* 41

unsupervised learning An unsupervised machine learning model is a model that is only fed with inputs and no specific desired outputs. It is up to the machine learning algorithm to order (categorize) the different data observations. You can simply see it as asking your algorithm to give a label to each data observation. *See page* 209

validation dataset A validation set is a random subset of the training set that is kept aside during the training to validate a model against unseen data. *See page* 131

weak model A weak model is a model that is slightly more accurate than luck. *See page* 167

Index

CPSIA information can be obtained
at www.ICGtesting.com
Printed in the USA
JSHW010302221221
21418JS00004B/18